FINDING GRAMMIE'S SECRETS:

A Black Genealogist Detective
Discovers the Untold Story
Behind a Family Legacy

Kathy Lynne Marshall

Copyright © 2025 Kathy Lynne Marshall

All rights reserved. No portion of this book may be used or reproduced in any manner whatsoever without written permission from the publisher or author, except in the case of brief quotations embodied in articles or reviews. While the author has used her best efforts in preparing this book, she makes no representations or warranties with respect to the accuracy or completeness of the contents of this book. The advice and strategies contained herein may not be suitable for your situation.

ISBN: 978-1-7375733-7-1

FIRST EDITION

Cover artwork by Karen Phillips.

Cover image provided by Kenora Davis.

Editor: Jean L. Cooper

Publisher: Kathy Lynne Marshall Art and Books
PO Box 1202, Elk Grove, CA, 95759-0001

Available on Amazon Kindle, African American Literature Book Club, and other online booksellers:

Printed in the United States of America

Dedicated to my mother,
Mary Ellen Carter Marshall,
who had a passion to bring our
Roy & Carter ancestors' stories to life.

I choose to be a genealogist
not because it is easy
but because it is hard.
Commemorating our
ancestors' lives in writing is a challenge
we genealogists are willing to accept,
one we are unwilling to postpone,
and one which we intend to win.

Kathy Lynne Marshall

INTRODUCTION	1
PROLOGUE	5
CHAPTER 1: The Black Ancestor Detective's First Clue	9
CHAPTER 2: Decoding the Maternal Legacy	13
CHAPTER 3: Unsealing Grammie's Truths	35
CHAPTER 4: Life on a Sheep Ranch	47
CHAPTER 5: Charting Ella's Lineage	59
CHAPTER 6: Alexandria, A Mother's Shadow	69
CHAPTER 7: Solving the Washington DC Roy Puzzle	77
CHAPTER 8: Tidewater Trio of Spotsylvania, Caroline & Stafford	93
CHAPTER 9: Albert Roy's Enduring Legacy	101
CHAPTER 10: Return To Ol' Virginny	117
CHAPTER 11: Identifying the Roys' Enslavers	125
CHAPTER 12: The Identity of Ella Roy's Father	137
CHAPTER 13: Echoes of a Woman's Tale	151
CHAPTER 14: The Search for Robert Carter's Roots	161
CHAPTER 15: The Carter Family's Bondage	175
CHAPTER 16: The Journey to Springfield	179
CHAPTER 17: The Trials of Widowhood	189
CHAPTER 18: Mom, We Have Problem …	193
CHAPTER 19: Grammie's Children	201
EPILOGUE	211
ABOUT THE AUTHOR	217
ACKNOWLEDGMENTS	219
APPENDIX A: Guide to Research Your Ancestry	223
APPENDIX B: Can DNA Find Ella's Dad?	229
APPENDIX C: Neighborhood Analyses	233
APPENDIX D: Roy Deeds in Mount Vernon, OH	241
BIBLIOGRAPHY	245
END NOTES	248

ILLUSTRATIONS

Figure 1: Photograph of Ella Roy "Grammie Carter," ca. 1884. 4
Figure 2: Kathy Marshall, ca. 1976. 9
Figure 3: Mary Carter & Carrie Marshall at Grammie Carter's, 2003. 13
Figure 4: Otho and Myrtle Williams at 16 Sandusky St. 2009 14
Figure 5: Mary Carter Marshall's "Memoir Journal, 1996-2006" 16
Figure 6: Map 1: Downtown Mount Vernon, OH. 17
Figure 7: Kathy Marshall Meets Cousins in Mount Vernon, OH, 2023 20
Figure 8: Grammie with Bessie Carter's Descendants 22
Figure 9: 1880 US Federal Census for Albert Roy, Knox, OH 26
Figure 10: Mary Marshall's Letter to OH Division of Vital Records. 28
Figure 11: Ella Roy Carter's Death Certificate, Knox, OH, 1962. 30
Figure 12: Myrtle Booker, Pearl Williams, Mary Carter & Kathy, 1958. 36
Figure 13: 2003 Family Reunion in Columbus, OH 37
Figure 14: Kathy Holds 2xGGF Joseph Booker's Masonic Sword. 40
Figure 15: Where Aunt Norma & Mother Mary Worked in the 1950s 41
Figure 16: Paul Lynde's Thunderbird at Knox Historical Museum 42
Figure 17: Cooper's Foundry Machinery Knox Museum, OH, 2023. 43
Figure 18: Grammie Carter's Obituary, Mount Vernon, OH, 1962. 44
Figure 19: Ella & Robert Carter's Children's Births. 46
Figure 20: Columbus Delano's LakeHome Manor, Martinsburg Rd. 47
Figure 21: Kathy Marshall in the Delano's Parlor, 2023. 51
Figure 22: Delano's LakeHome Mills Flyer from 1880. 53
Figure 23: Typical Exquisite Woodwork at LakeHome. 55
Figure 24: Ella Roy, 31 Dec 1866 Freedmen's Bureau Hospital Record. 61
Figure 25: Agnes and Ella Roy were received March to April 1867. 65
Figure 26: Transportation for Agnes & Child to Boston, 22 Apr 1867 66
Figure 27: Labor Contract: Walker Millan and Agnes Roy. 67
Figure 28: Alexandria African American 1865 Census Districts. 72
Figure 29: Map-District Boundaries in Alexandria, 1865. 72
Figure 30: Former Slave Pen 74
Figure 31: Present-Day Freedom Center Museum 74
Figure 32: Complaint Letter Against Agnes Roy, 3 Nov 1866. 76
Figure 33: Roys in DC in 1870 Census. 79
Figure 34: Roys in DC City Directories in 1865, 1869, 1870 & 1871. 81
Figure 35: 1871 Lucy Roy's Bank Record with Peter & Aga Roy. 82
Figure 36: DC Directory for Columbus Delano in 1871 84
Figure 37: Map-Proximity of Roys to Columbus Delano in DC: 1871 85
Figure 38: 1874 Manassas Death Register for Agnes Roy 89
Figure 39: Map of Pertinent Virginia Counties. 92
Figure 40: Mary Hampton (m. Waller) Will Mentions Roys, 1857. 95
Figure 41: Enslaved People "Migrating" from Fredericksburg to DC. 96
Figure 42: Runaways from Nancy Rowe's Estate, Spotsylvania, VA 97
Figure 43: Albert Roy (1838-1931) & Wife Alice Burrows (1847-1913) 101
Figure 44: Site of Albert's Restaurant on Main Street in MV, OH, 1900. 108
Figure 45: Is Albert Roy Guilty As Charged for Bastardy? 109
Figure 46: Map-of Downtown Mount Vernon, ca. 1900. 110
Figure 47: Albert Roy's Death Certificate, 1931. 112
Figure 48: Alice Roy's Death Notice. 113
Figure 49: Wayman Chapel AME Church. Mary Carter Peers Into Window 116

Figure 50: 1870 Manassas, VA, Census 117
Figure 51: Albert Witnessed a Loyalty Oath 122
Figure 52: Was Albert Enslaved by the Weirs at Liberia Plantation? 124
Figure 53: Agnes & Albert in Some Slaves in PWC Wills, 1723-1872. 126
Figure 54: Was Redmon Foster Our Enslaver? 127
Figure 55: Sleuthing Owners & Owned in PWC. 130
Figure 56: Richard Atkinson Sells Gerard's slaves 132
Figure 57: Walker Millan's 1860 Slave Schedule: Agnes & Her Mom? 135
Figure 58: Was Ella Roy's Daddy at Freedmen's Village? 136
Figure 59: DNA Matches to the Millan Family 140
Figure 60: Millan Family Tree & George Washington Millan. 141
Figure 61: Does "Thru-Lines" Cinch a Jackson Fatherhood? 143
Figure 62: December 1865 Work Contract with William Jackson. 145
Figure 63: 1870 Agricultural Census in Manassas: William Jackson 146
Figure 64: Deed with Henry Jackson in Alexandria in 1865. 148
Figure 65: U.S. Civil War Draft Registration Records. 149
Figure 66: USCT Service Record for Henry Jackson. 150
Figure 67: Artificial intelligence image of Grandpa Arthur Carter Sr. 162
Figure 68: Robert & Ella's Marriage License, 4 Dec 1884 163
Figure 69: Robert Carter's Death Certificate, Bangs, OH, 1909. 164
Figure 70: 1876-77 Mount Vernon (OH) City Directory for Carters. 165
Figure 71: 1880 Knox, OH, Census for Carters 165
Figure 72: 1884-85 Mount Vernon City Directory for Carters. 166
Figure 73: Where Robert Carter worked/lived in 1884/85. 166
Figure 74: Carters and Jacksons Lived Near Delanos. 167
Figure 75: Searching for Robert Carter in 1870 and 1880 DC Census. 169
Figure 76: Looking for Relatives with Jetts. 170
Figure 77: Looking for Traces of Robert Carter in DC. 172
Figure 78: Robert Carter in Ward 7, DC, 1870 173
Figure 79: Freedmen's Bureau Access Portal. 175
Figure 80: Enslaver John Carter Marries Hannah Chew 177
Figure 81: Springfield, Clark County, Ohio, 1900. 178
Figure 82: Industries Near Where Robert & Ella Live in Springfield 183
Figure 83: Carters in Springfield, OH, in 1889. 185
Figure 84: Robert and Richard Carter, 1942. 187
Figure 85: Robert Carter's last years in Bangs Asylum, OH. 189
Figure 86: Pearl Williams, 1926. 193
Figure 87: Pearl Carter (left) & her stair-step kids, c. 1940. 197
Figure 88: Arthur Carter's WWII Draft Registration, 1940. 198
Figure 89: Arthur Carter's SSN Card. 199
Figure 90: Arthur Carter Divorce Decree, Columbus, OH, 1971 200
Figure 91: Records of Arthur Carter's life after MV, 1908-1995. 200
Figure 92: Carter home at 101 W. Walnut St., MV, OH, 1949-1988. 206
Figure 93: Wayman AME Church, MV, OH. Is Grammie Sitting Here? 209
Figure 94: Different Phases of Grammie Ella Roy Carter. 210
Figure 95: Author Kathy Lynne (& Kanika) Marshall. 217
Figure 96: Sample of Kathy Lynne Marshall's Books on Amazon 218
Figure 97: Examples of Kathy's genealogy-based photo books 226
Figure 98: Different Methods for Leaving a Written Legacy 227
Figure 99: Exploring DNA cM matches with Jacksons in Their Trees. 230
Figure 100: Blaine Bettinger's Shared cM Project Chart. 231
Figure 101: DNAPainter.com Table with DNA Matches. 232

Figure 102: Map--Albert Roy's Properties in Mount Vernon, OH............243

TABLES

Table 1: Hospital Records for Residents Treated on 14 Dec 1866............64
Table 2: "R" Surnamed Blacks in Alexandria Census, 1865.............71
Table 3: Freedmen's Bureau Name Index to Tenement Book.............78
Table 4: Peter Roys in 1870 and 1880 in DC and Spotsylvania, VA.............87
Table 5: Peter Roys in 1870 and 1880 in Spotsylvania, VA.............88
Table 6: "FAN Club" Data in the 1870 Spotsylvania, VA, Census.............94
Table 7: 1900 Census for Roys in Mount Vernon.............107
Table 8: 1850 and 1860 Census for John and Elizabeth Reid Millan.............134
Table 9: DNA Matches to Super-testers with Millan Descendants.............140
Table 10: Carters, Roys & Jacksons Travel from Caroline Co., 1867.............176
Table 11: Robert & Ella Carter's Residences 1889-1906: City Directories.............182
Table 12: 1870 Manassas, VA, 1870 Census Community Analysis.............234
Table 13: 1880 Knox County, OH, Blacks and Mulattos Analysis, page 1.............237
Table 14: Albert Roy's Properties in Mount Vernon, OH.............242

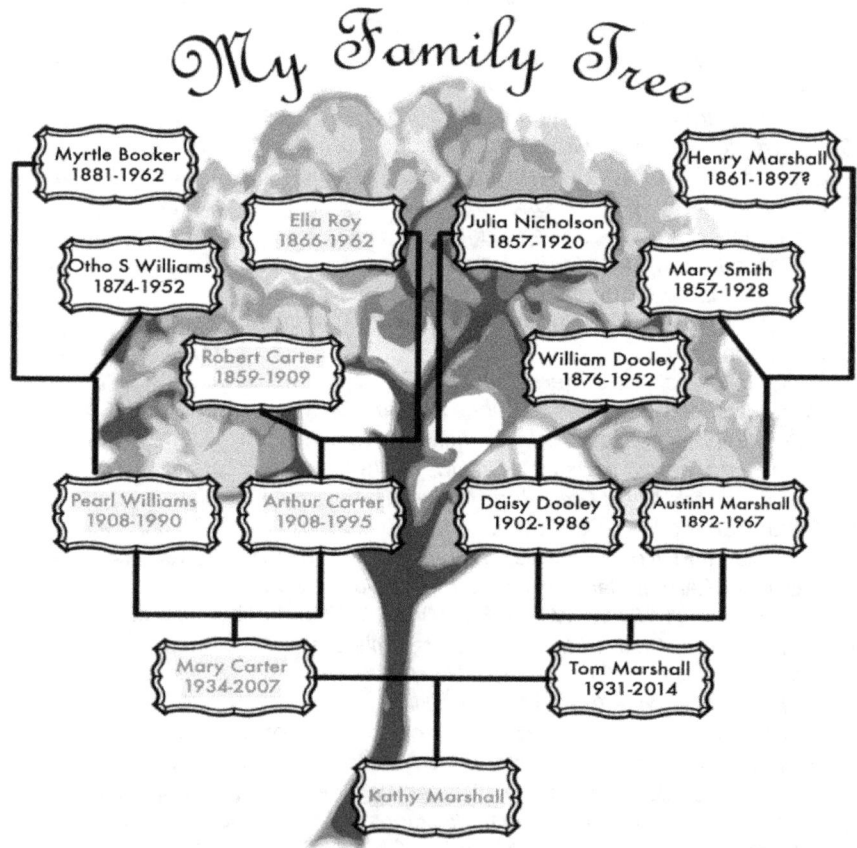

INTRODUCTION

How did "Grammie" Ella Roy Carter do it? Some say she never seemed to lift a finger for a paycheck, yet she owned a lovely, mortgage-free house on Cherry and West Vine Street in Mount Vernon, Ohio (OH). She adorned her house with Tiffany lamps, beautiful carpets, lovely furnishings, and interesting antiques. We always wondered if the source of her wealth and leisure lay with her father, who was whispered to be one of the richest White men in Mount Vernon. But which guy?

This wasn't just a fun family anecdote. It was an unsolved mystery—a decades-old puzzle waiting for a "Black Ancestor Detective" to complete the picture. When my mother retired from her distinguished career as an elementary school principal, she had a clear mission: to turn 80, to crack the code of Grammie's effortless elegance, and to track down the truth about her own absentee father, Arthur Carter.

Then, in 2006, a devastating medical diagnosis introduced a desperate urgency to Mom's quest. Suddenly, our deep dive into the Roy and Carter lineages wasn't just a hobby—it became a race against time. This book is a tribute to my mother and a record of our thrilling, twenty-year journey. It's a deeply personal odyssey of love, perseverance, and the desperate search for the keys to Grammie's Secrets.

I launch every book project with two burning questions that spark my curiosity: 1) What pieces of the puzzle do I already possess about the ancestor I'm chasing? and 2) Can modern DNA testing provide more clues to relatives who have key documents that confirm our shared bloodlines?

In this case, I knew that Grammie was born in Alexandria, Virginia, in 1866—a city rich with Civil War echoes and untold secrets. Among our living relatives, not a single one can recall Grammie's parents' names. Nobody can shed light on her childhood or explain the circumstances of her migration to Ohio.

She later married Robert Carter in Mount Vernon in 1884. But how did she journey from the bustling streets of postbellum Virginia to the quiet neighborhoods of Mount Vernon? That remained a tantalizing mystery.

Grammie's youngest son, Arthur Taft Carter—my grandfather—seemed to vanish after 1942, leaving nothing but whispers and unanswered questions in his wake. Even the story of Grammie's husband, Robert Carter, is shrouded in shadows.

And the greatest enigma of all: how did Grammie, with her quiet yet firm air and elegant possessions, manage to live in such perceived comfort for several decades? The answers are out there, and with each clue, the story becomes more fascinating—and more urgent—to uncover.

My major research goals for this book were to:

1) Discover Ella Roy's parents and their enslaver(s);
2) Uncover Robert Carter's parents and their enslaver(s);
3) Investigate what happened to my Grandpa Arthur Carter; and
4) Determine how Grammie Carter afforded her luxuries.

This book bursts with captivating photographs and revealing genealogy records because I want you to walk alongside me on this adventure of discovery.

Appendix A contains a guide to help the reader plan their own research project and assemble the data to commit their findings to writing. The specific goal is to uncover the family ties of women, minorities, and poor people whose stories didn't make it into the public school history books. Appendix B has a short DNA primer to explain the basics of DNA testing and how to use online tools to determine your family ties. For die-hard researchers, Appendix C contains a barebones Community Analysis for the Manassas, Virginia (VA), 1870 Census. Appendix D summarizes some deed transactions involving an important character in this book.

I love a riveting story, so I let the ancestors tell their tales in parts of the Prologue and Chapters 2, 4, 13, 18, and 19. For the research-forward chapters, I—Kathy Lynne Marshall, Grammie's great-granddaughter— am generally the main speaker.

Tip: Appendix A contains a guide to help YOU uncover your family lineage: how to start researching, how to define research goals, and how to structure a book template. It has links to genealogy references, and ideas on how to write and print your ancestor stories. My goal is to encourage you to enhance the American historical record for future generations.

I hope this book serves as a tool to help you to research and analyze your own family history. I am purposely divulging the steps I took to prove or disprove my theories in the hope that the strategies book will help you to find your family secrets. The 19 *TIPS* and four appendices will illustrate my process and, hopefully, encourage you to trace your family lineage.

WE CAN LEAVE A WRITTEN LEGACY OF FAMILY HISTORY!

Warning: this is not a story about sugar-plum fairies in the Land of Oz. The girl doesn't always get the mate she desires. And there's no magic genie who grants wishes.

No, this is the story about a people forced to work for free for centuries. But in 1865, they found themselves with the agency of independent human beings. **Hallelujah!**

Some free people of color blossomed into property owners, others took advantage of new educational opportunities, and some collected precious objects ... like expensive Tiffany lamps.

This is a joyful and exciting story, yet chilling at the same time. Maybe that's why so many of our elders don't like to talk about the past.

The only thing we present-day genealogist detectives can do is interview our relatives, scrutinize documents that clarify our lineage, and DNA test our families to gain a glimpse at our genetic ancestral past.

This important work celebrates the phenomenal resilience of African American people. It gives successive generations hope for a better life.

Some say an old African proverb states, "Speak their names and they will live on forever."

So buckle up. It's going to be a thrilling roller-coaster ride to reveal the complicated story of Finding Grammie's Secrets.

Figure 1: Photograph of Ella Roy "Grammie Carter," ca. 1884. Photo courtesy of Kenora Davis.

PROLOGUE

What's Wrong, Grammie?

My heart pounds a desperate beat as I run through the dark space, my eyes streaming. **"Where are you, Mama?"** I scream. The silence is a familiar villain, and the fear feels physical, pricking my skin like tiny needles. I wake with a sudden, sharp gasp, feeling as small and lost as I did all those decades ago. The same horrible dream, a fresh terror, every single night.

I am ninety-plus years old. I have lived long enough to know the value of a good lie. Though the scent of sadness sometimes invades my nostrils, I faithfully paint on a bright smile and create light for everyone I meet. My life is one of aromatic flowers, a drop of elegant perfume, and the solid comfort of family and faith. But none of those blessings can truly banish the darkness of that nightly dream. The past isn't over when you're this old—it's just better hidden. And I have a secret that's about to break free.

"Grammie?" The sweet voice of my teenaged great-granddaughter, Kenora, startles me from my reverie. She looks so cute in her short-sleeved white blouse and striped pedal pushers. Her favorite cousin, Patricia—the kids call her PattyAnn—dresses identically, with white anklets and brown saddle shoes. The girls dust my furniture every Saturday morning as they chatter about this and that. Such a whirlwind of dust cloth and youthful energy—a stark contrast to the stillness of the eerie photograph hanging above the sofa in my front room.

"Who is that beautiful lady?" Kenora points at a picture on the wall in my front room, her voice low.

"A movie star?" PattyAnn guesses, as her brown doe eyes stare at the mysterious woman holding a strange object against her thighs.

I turn around to study the statuesque lady in the faded portrait (Figure 1). Her grey-green eyes match the grey-green colors in her form-fitting, high-necked silk dress. Her Mona Lisa smile hints at private thoughts unshared.

"That's me, child. Ella Roy from about eighty years ago." I turn my gaze toward the two girl-women standing before me, then glance back at the static picture. *Where has the time gone?*

Kenora's eyes widen in disbelief. "But Grammie, that can't be *you*! She looks so ..." Her voice trails off, searching for the right word.

PattyAnn yells out, "So strong, like a warrior princess holding a sword to protect herself and her family." The girls pretend to slash at some invisible beast, whipping their dusters around with fury.

A hollow laugh escapes my throat. "Warriors and princesses are for fairy tales, my dears. No, the woman in that photograph was someone far more ordinary, just a servant girl who worked for rich people a decade after the Civil War."

The grin vanishes from PattyAnn's face, replaced with a frown. "But why are you wearing that unusual dress?" She pouts.

I trace the outline of the woman in the photograph with my finger. A coldness seeps into my bones. "Unusual is one way to describe it, child. Distressing is another."

Kenora tilts her head and scrunches her brows, not understanding. "Distressing? How could a dress make you feel like that?"

I fall silent, the weight of the past pressing down on me. Some memories are best left undisturbed. Truth be told, I rarely share anything about my past. But maybe I should, now that I'm inching toward the big 100. *How do I explain the difficult circumstances of our Negro history?*

"Girls, let me share a short story with you." I draw my two great-granddaughters close. "Back in the day, it was a different world for girls and women, especially Negro women. We learned to blend into the background rather than attract too much male attention to ourselves."

I pause, recalling unshared memories. Gesturing to the faded photograph on the wall, "I had to wear that magnificent dress while accompanying my boss, the Honorable Columbus Delano, to the Town Square right here in Mount Vernon.[1] He was quite the local legend, always spinning tales of his adventures as a big-time politician in Washington, District of Columbia (DC), when he was the United States Secretary of the Interior. He spoke about his ventures in banking, his railroad dealings, and his grand sheep ranch, which is now owned by the Mount Vernon Nazarene University. I used to live in his mansion on a big sheep farm when I was your age." The girls glance at each other, perhaps wondering what a life amongst the rich and famous would be like.

"But amidst his stories of progress, there was always a hint of darkness. Mr. D—that's what I called him—would complain about the obstacles to westward expansion. He cursed the 'darn Indians' who stood in the way of progress. Truthfully, I never understood why he insisted on having me by his side in that flowy silk dress. But it made me feel like a Virginia slave from the stories my Uncle Albert and Aunt Alice used to tell. You know, those poor souls who were auctioned off like cattle?" Kenora frowns. "They teach you about slavery in school, don't they?"

Both girls gaze at their youthful hands and shake their heads.

"No? Well, before 1865, cruelty marked our country's history for most people like us, then called Negroes or colored or other less respectable names. Most of us were just property, like a cow or a plow." The girls' mouths drop open. "Our enslaved ancestors stood naked, on display to be inspected, sold, forced to work for nothing, and often subjected to harsh treatment. And, those slave masters often tore our families apart."

The girls, trying to imagine such loss, look anxiously at me. "I was fortunate to be born in 1866, one year *after* slavery ended, and I am delighted to be safe here with you two now." I reach over and give each girl a heartfelt hug.

Kenora changes the subject. "So, how did you get such lovely things in your house, like those expensive Tiffany lamps? I love being in this room during late afternoon when the sunlight bursts through the stained glass, causing brilliant colors to dance on the walls." Kenora twirls around the room like she's dancing with the colored lights.

PattyAnn says, "Well, I love hearing your fancy Victrola play music, but I wish you had more modern records to play, like Sarah Vaughan, Billie Holiday And I always feel like a Queen when we eat dinner on those gold-rimmed china plates. Grammie, I'd expect to see those things in rich people's houses."

I nod. "Yes, they are treasures to people like us, but hand-me-downs to others. You probably never noticed the slight cracks in both lamps." The girls scamper to where Ella points at a faint imperfection in the glass. "I forget where Uncle Albert said he got those lamps, but I feel lucky to have what I have … compared to my mother's struggles living in Virginia during slavery days." I turn away from the girls to hide my tears. "It's sad, but I can't even remember what my mother's face looked like. It was so long ago when I was very young." I reach into my apron pocket for a tissue to dab my eyes.

"Grammie," Kenora asks in a soft voice. "Who was your Daddy? The kids at school sometimes ask why some of us are so pale."

My shoulders shrug. "I never knew my father, but judging by my easy-to-sunburn skin, I'm guessing that Daddy was most likely a White man. But as you know, our family looks like a rainbow, from the lightest to the darkest of skin tones.[2] Truthfully, I can't remember much of my childhood at all." *Hmm, could my recurring nightmares have anything to do with those blank years?*

I force a cheerful smile and put some pep in my voice. "That's why I tell you girls all the time that thinking about the past is a waste of time. Just enjoy the present and plan for your future. All I know is that Uncle Albert and Auntie Alice Roy raised me like their own precious daughter, and I thank the Lord for them every day. They gave me a home, brought me to Mount Vernon, taught me how to be a good person, and helped me raise my children in a safe space." I close my eyes, basking in the endearing memories of family members who treated me like their own.

"Uh, Grammie?" PattyAnn waves her wave in front of me. "Did you hear me?"

The trance interrupted, my eyes focus on her voice. Patty Ann holds the dust rag in one hand and furniture oil in the other, waiting for my answer. Her face scrunches up, looking concerned.

"Wha-what did you say, child?" I stammer, trying to wake up my brain.

"Is anything wrong, Grammie? Your face looks a little green. Do you feel sick? Can I get you some water, or should I get MomBessie to come and help you?" The girls look helpless.

Melancholy presses in on my thoughts as I feel the void of my long-dead guardian parents, but I muster a smile and wave my hand in the air. "No, child. I'm fine. I just need a nap. See you both next week?" They nod and I walk toward the stairs, grasp the handrail, then, pull myself up past the flowered wallpaper in the stairwell, step-by-step up to my small bedroom. I fall into the arms of sleep as soon as my head hits the pillow, reunited in dreams with my husband, Robert Carter, who died fifty years ago.

A thunderous rapping jolts me from my drowsy stupor. I hear the front door creak open, then a rhythmic tap-tap-tap against the worn wooden floor. The sound is coming up the stairs, heading straight for my room! Is it that awful man who frequents my nightmares? My heart quickens as the steps grow louder, coming closer. The door flings open and I cover my eyes with my hands, ready for that bad man.

"Mother! Mother!" My only living daughter, Bessie Carter Payne—the kids call her MomBessie—hurries into my sunny bedroom. She's wearing a pale-pink, calf-length shift, with her signature pearls around her honey-colored neck. Her hot-comb pressed brown hair curls behind her ears, and a wide smile stretches her apple-round cheeks.

Groggy, I sit up from my afternoon nap as quickly as my old bones will allow. "What's wrong, Bessie dear?" I ask, concerned.

"Twins, Mother! My Beatrice gave birth to two beautiful girls this morning. She named them JoAnn and Jeannette," Bessie announced, her voice as bright as a full moon.

"Well, bless my soul! 1956 will be a busy year. Beatrice and Gene will have their hands full with two-year-old Michael and now twin girls? That's two more great-grandbabies for me to love on. Bessie, help me out of this bed, would you? I have some new babies to meet!"

CHAPTER 1: The Black Ancestor Detective's First Clue

Figure 2: Kathy Marshall, ca. 1976.

"Grammie Carter was always old." That's what my mother, Mary Ellen Carter Marshall told me when I asked about my maternal great-grandmother, Ella Roy Carter. Mom's words still echo in my mind decades later, a tiny puzzle piece in a family history shrouded in mystery.

Back in 1976, America's Bicentennial[3] birthday, I was nineteen, had just earned a degree from Sacramento City College and started a full-time job with the California Highway Patrol.[4] I was tired of people always asking, "What are you?" and "Is yo' daddy White?" as they poked my olive skin and touched my frizzy hair (Figure 2). I decided to stop being passive. That summer, I took control of the narrative, sending urgent letters to my grandmothers in Ohio. I was no longer asking for stories. I was demanding the identity I was owed.

My paternal grandmother, Daisy Dooley Marshall, spun tales of our Marshall and Dooley heritage with a strange gleam in her eye. She insisted that we carried the proud blood of Blackfoot Indians and hardy Negroes. Meanwhile, my maternal grandmother, Pearl Williams Carter, openly admitted her confusion about our roots. She passed my letter to Granduncle George Booker and his savvy wife Geraldine. Their lengthy reply arrived in the mailbox with a jolt of intrigue. They said our forebears hailed from Germany and Africa. My heart leapt. Could I stumble upon my own Kunta Kinte[5] moment so effortlessly? The possibility sent a thrill through my veins. But names and stories still eluded us, like shadows just out of reach, leaving us with a maze of questions and precious few answers.

From 2000 to 2006, my mother and I launched ourselves into a cross-country adventure, tracing our family's tangled roots with the persistence of detectives on a fresh case. In those days, genealogy wasn't a simple computer mouse click away.

Back in the day, it demanded road trips to courthouses cloaked in the dust of distant counties. We snail-mailed handwritten letters requesting birth certificates and clues. Each envelope opened was like cracking a code from the past. But the towering wall of slavery's legacy loomed before us, a formidable barrier for African Americans bold enough to chase down our ancestors who lived before 1865. Legal documents recording the names of the enslaved were rare treasures, virtually impossible to unearth.

Despite her illness, my mother's determination burned bright. She was obsessed with the mystery of her elusive father, Arthur Taft Carter—the man who vanished like mist after pressing a nickel into her tiny palm on her fifth birthday. That brief memory, all she had of her "Daddy Dearest," both haunted and motivated her. Our quest was no longer just about names on a chart—it was about reclaiming voices lost to history. With courage, curiosity, and unyielding hope, we yearned to stitch together the epic, unfinished story of our family.

We both wanted to learn why Arthur's mother, Ella Roy Carter, migrated from her birthplace in Alexandria[6] in Virginia, to Mount Vernon, four hundred miles to the northwest.[7] What was Ella's life like in Virginia and where, exactly, did she live? Who were her parents, and if someone had enslaved them, who were their enslavers? When did she meet her husband, Robert Carter, and who were his kin and their enslavers? How did Ella purchase what looked like expensive Tiffany lamps in a mortgage-free home, in a small town where only one percent of the population was Black?

Mom and I chattered like schoolgirls trying to dig up the truth of our Roy and Carter ancestors. Our (then) cutting-edge dial-up modems[8] buzzed and burbled to connect our home computers to a Bulletin Board[9] predecessor of FamilySearch.org,[10] a free genealogy website run by the Church of Jesus Christ of Latter Day Saints. We thought we were so tech-savvy reviewing the 1880 Virginia Census from our home computers! Sadly, we could not answer most of our lineage questions before breast cancer took my mother on 27th of January in 2007.[11]

For the next decade, I dabbled in family history research an hour or two every few months. I unintentionally gathered the same genealogy documents time and time again, throwing them into a box in the closet or on my computer, never really understanding what the data meant.

When I turned sixty, my *spirited* ancestors ordered me to get my genealogy act together. They enticed our family historian, M. "Lavata" Williams, to visit me in June 2016. Horrors! I could NOT let her see my messy box of genealogy papers. Oh, how disgusted she would be learning I hadn't done much with the oral history she and her 107-year-old-mother, Reba Williams, had given me over four decades of questions.

Lickety split, two weeks before Lavata's arrival, I retrieved every bit of printed family data I had collected since 1976. I laid them out on my family room floor, then sorted the reams of legacy documents by family line, then person within each family group, then in chronological order by date. I purchased a dozen three-ring binders, labeled them by family line, then stuffed the sorted papers inside. Finally!

The day before my esteemed Cousin Lavata came to visit, I slid the brand-spanking-new binders onto bookshelves in my "research room" which doubled as a guest bedroom. The morning after she arrived, I proudly set the Williams history binder in front of her, eager that we would spend the next two weeks talking *genealogy shop*. Guess what? She could have cared less about that binder. Since her mother passed away in 2014, Lavata had been living life as she wished. She was not interested in discussing family history with me. So, it was on my broad shoulders to carry on Lavata's exemplary legacy. I had to get busy, but how to start after 40 years of failing to piece together our maternal and paternal puzzles?

> ***TIP:** Organize the genealogy documents you've already collected by family line, and then by person within the family to make it easier to analyze the data. An organized approach will help you find lineage documents to write your family stories.*

On October 1, 2016, I grew into my size 11 genealogist shoes by developing a QuickStart Guide for Solving Your Family Mystery (Appendix A). It was based on a standardized how-to-complete-written-assignments process I developed and taught to 600 analysts during my 36-year career with the California Highway Patrol. This methodology helped me respond to the ancestors' mandate to publish one book per year.

The Ancestors Are Smiling! was my first family heritage book, published in 2017. It contained one chapter per descendant of the main character in my first success at finding enslaved ancestors.

The Ancestors Are Smiling! was part of the *Finding Otho: The Search for Our Enslaved Williams Ancestors* book project released in 2018, about my enslaved Williamses in Maryland and Ohio.

Seven more lineage books followed, one in each successive year, as shown in the *About the Author* section of this book. I documented as much source information and wrote relatable stories about most of my paternal lines (Marshalls, Dooleys, Borders, Cunninghams, Marshalls, and Smiths). My maternal family lines included Bookers and Williamses, leaving me to complete the Roys and Carters in 2025. The Myers and Madagascar families are planned for 2026. *Yes, I said Madagascar, Africa, where DNA says my matrilineal line is from.* How exciting is that?

The ancestors appreciate these efforts. They want their stories recorded for their descendants and the wider American historical record, thus highlighting the contributions of ALL people who shaped America, no matter their race or gender.

But also to inspire others to take the plunge and document their family histories, I am including helpful "***Tips***" throughout the book and a *Guide to Solving Your Family Mystery* (Appendix A).

Researching this Roy/Carter story has *not* been a straightforward walk in the park. Black ancestors do not reveal their stories easily. So, I consulted with Virginia and Ohio genealogy experts and cousins, who shared helpful documents and insights about our family history.

Genealogical discoveries rarely happen in order, but I've organized the findings logically, combining facts with narrative to make the history engaging. Visual aids like photos, family trees, charts, and data screenshots are included throughout to support this genealogical journey.

Get ready to explore the lineage, legacy, and secrets of Ella Roy "Grammie" Carter.

CHAPTER 2: Decoding the Maternal Legacy

The Fairytale Corner

Figure 3: Mary Carter & Carrie Marshall at Grammie Carter's, 2003.

Grammie's house, perched on the corner of Cherry and West Vine Streets, was only a couple of blocks from the lively bustle of Riverside Park—a place of scraped knees, baseball games, and laughter that soared on the tallest swings in town. Yet, her home wasn't part of that rough-and-tumble world; it was a sanctuary. To my mother, it was a "fairy tale sprung to life."

The home itself was wrapped in a gentle magic: shimmering white paint, horizontal slats, and whimsical wooden spindles that seemed to greet the sun. (Figure 3) The wide porch, draped in a cascade of lush pink bougainvillea, didn't just invite you in—it beckoned you to step into a world of warmth and wonder. Inside, my cousins swore Grammie owned actual Tiffany lamps, expensive rugs, an ornate dining table, and the fanciest of dishware. It was immaculate, elegant, and quiet. In stark, emotional contrast, the house ten blocks away—Mom's childhood home, sitting beside the gritty Cooper-Bessemer Ironworks—was always bursting, overflowing with "too much life."

Figure 4: Otho and Myrtle Williams at 16 Sandusky St.

Sixteen of Mom's family members crowded into a two-story, white clapboard row house at 217 North Norton Street in Mount Vernon. It was a worker's "row house" on the premises of the noisy Cooper-Bessemer engine manufacturing plant. (Figure 4)

Mom often recalled her discomfort at having to share one bed with her Sister Norma at one end and Brothers Arthur (Sonny) and George at the other. Her youngest siblings, Dale and Elizabeth (Betty), nestled in a crib. Sister Sara claimed a pallet on the floor because she often wet the bed.[12] The three girls shared a three-foot-wide closet for their clothes. What tight quarters!

Their mother, Pearl Williams Carter, found a sleeping space in the tiny kitchenette that her father, Otho Sherman Williams, built onto the rented house. Meanwhile, the rest of the house contained eight extended family members who shared more spacious rooms than Mom's family of eight. This disparity fueled a quiet longing in young Mary to one day have a house of her own.[13]

"Escaping to Grammie's was an adventure," Mom often said, but their mother forbade her and her siblings to visit Grammie Carter by themselves. Mom did not know what secrets clouded the relationship between her beloved mother and equally treasured Grammie Carter. Kids being kids, though, they would sneak away from the nearby park for a quick howdy-do to their beloved grandmother. Their laughter and funny antics echoed through the streets as they made their way toward their grandmother's perfectly pruned hedges and vibrant flower beds. Grammie Carter always welcomed her grandchildren with open arms, hugging each one, then treating them to a plateful of freshly baked cookies. Stories unfolded, laughter exploded, and cookies-and-milk moustaches belied their secret visits.

The pinkie-peach camellias in the front yard became a symbol of Grammie's enduring love, a legacy Mom carried with her, planting camellia bushes wherever life took her. Even decades later, after Grammie died in 1962, the mere mention of her beautiful house softened my mother's eyes. It reminded her of a simpler time, a testament to the enduring power of magic. Indeed, Grammie's place was a stark contrast to Mom's otherwise mundane childhood memories of crowded spaces, babysitting the neighborhood White kids, and helping her mother clean the local dentist's office at night.

Kathy Unravels the Enigma of Ella Roy Carter

Make no mistake, Grammie Carter was a quiet woman shrouded in mystery. Her family had long been curious about her past, her ancestral lineage, and how she gained her lovely home and furnishings. Mom and our cousins who lived near Grammie said she kept her secrets close to the vest. Nobody knew who her parents were or how she had come to live in Mount Vernon. My lineage questions went unanswered for decades, but after my mother's death in 2007, I caught a glimpse into Grammie's world. Sorting through Mom's *Reflections of a Mother's Heart* Memoir Journal (Figure 5), I unearthed a treasure trove of family stories, including two reflections involving Grammie Carter. One memory was regarding her fear of animals, and the other was how nice it was to visit our "little Dutch lady" grandmother.[14]

Figure 5: Mary Carter Marshall's "Memoir Journal, 1996-2006"

Through letters and phone calls during the worst years of the COVID epidemic, when people had to shelter in their homes from 2020 through April 2021, Kenora and my Uncle Dale Carter unveiled further tales about Grammie. I soaked up their stories like gravy on a fluffy biscuit.

Fast-forward to November 2023. During a ten-day genealogy trip to Mount Vernon, several generous relatives filled some gaps in my research. For example, my second cousin (2C) Kenora told me charming stories about the summers she spent with her grandmother Bessie Carter Payne. She also shared a pile of precious family documents with me. She said, "MomBessie (Grammie's daughter) lived next door to Grammie Carter on West Vine Street and took care of Grammie during her last five years of her life." Then, my 2C JoAnn Fields filled in more blanks with plenty of pictures and stories that she remembered.

I studied the history of Mount Vernon. It was founded in 1805 and nestled among the picturesque rolling hills and verdant valleys of central Ohio. As the Knox County seat, it boasts some of the state's most historic areas, making it a delightful destination for history enthusiasts and curious travelers alike. The pretty Downtown District encircles the Public Square (Figure 6) and extends along South Main Street with architectural styles that span centuries: Italianate influences stand alongside Art Déco, Greek Revival, and Colonial designs.

The Public Square has always been a bustling commercial hub. In the 1950s, it included Ringwalt Department store where my mother worked after school, from age 15 to 21. She dressed the store windows with paint and dressed mannequins with fashionable clothing. The upscale Rudin's Department store employed my elegant Aunt Norma Carter. The classy Alcove restaurant was for White patrons only, and Black folk could only enjoy the movie theatre on Fridays.

I remember visiting Mount Vernon in 1967. One morning, Mom led us children on a walk "downtown" where we could buy two shiny gumballs or Tootsie Roll pops for a penny from the candy store. At the Bakery, we tasted the heaven that is a chocolate eclair.

The Downtown District now serves as an anchor for three more residential areas enshrined on the National Registry of Historic Places. Each district features meticulously preserved buildings that date as far back as 1829, offering a glimpse into a past which included where Grammie and her relatives worked or lived from the 1880s to 1960s.

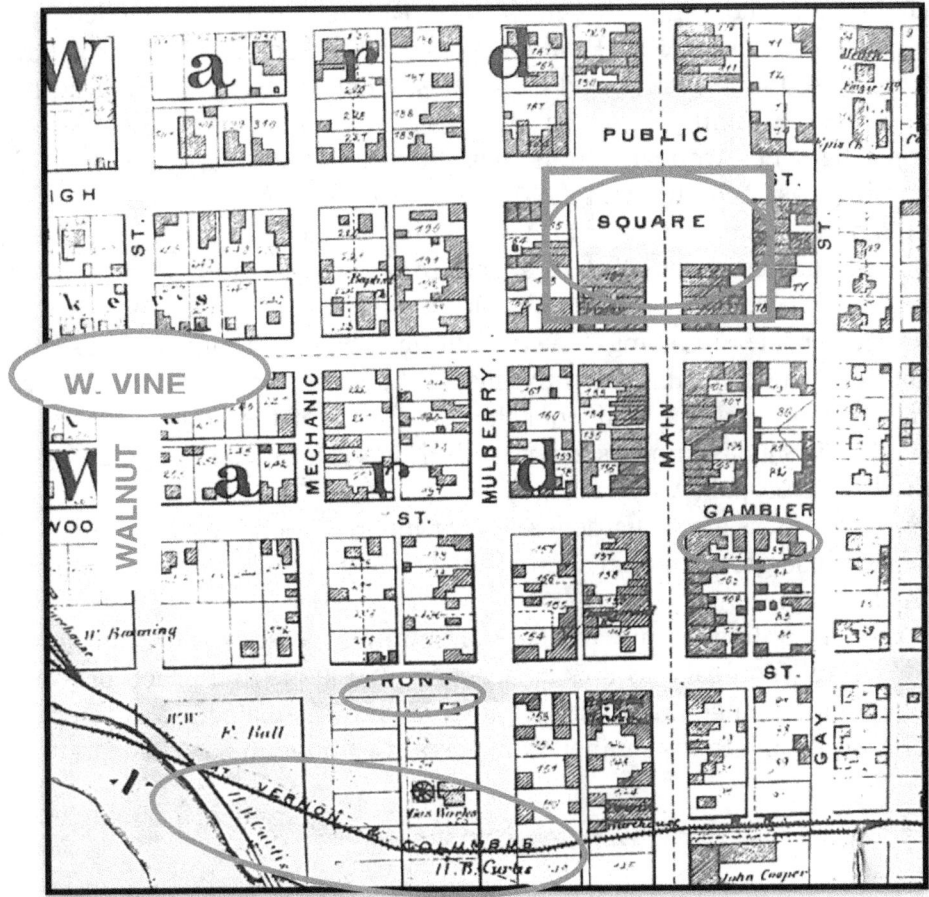

Figure 6: Map 1: Downtown Mount Vernon, OH.

Ornamental trees and vibrant flower beds still line the downtown streets, splashing bold colors and fragrant blooms across the city, transforming every stroll into a visual feast.

By night, decorative streetlamps—evoking the old-world charm of gaslights—cast a golden glow, making the town's historic heart shimmer and inviting locals and visitors alike to lose themselves in its magic at any hour. Quaint shops bustled with energy, the clink of dishes and laughter spilled from lively restaurants. A striking Civil War-era monument stood proudly in the public square, anchoring Mount Vernon's legacy with a dramatic flair. Together, these touches made exploring Mount Vernon's historical district not only memorable, but enchanting—an experience that lingered long after we left.

Only four blocks south of downtown, history pulsed through the neighborhood. The mighty Mount Vernon Bridge Company, founded by real estate visionary John Sellers Braddock, once thrived here, while railroad tracks converged—Mount Vernon and Columbus, Cleveland, and Delaware lines—right where my family lived on High, Vine, Walnut and Norton Streets. I couldn't help but wonder: could these railroads have carried secrets from Grammie's past, echoing with the rhythm of her footsteps?

Grammie's house was a world unto itself, a place where elegance reigned despite her modest means. Like a scene from a vintage film, she draped fresh white sheets over tables and sofas during the week, a ritualistic veil that preserved her fine furnishings. Every Saturday, the house came alive as Kenora and her cousin Patty Ann dutifully dusted the gleaming surfaces—the tables, China cabinet, Victrola, and bookshelves. That set the stage for the grand spectacle of Sunday dinners after soulful services at the Wayman African Methodist Episcopal (AME) Chapel.

Grammie was also a gardener extraordinaire. Her sprawling garden burst with life—lush greens, sweet snap peas, ruby tomatoes, and juicy fruits ready for the picking.

And, according to my mother, Grammie's desserts were the stuff of legend: angel food cake as airy as a dream, and apple and peach pies whose tangy sweetness lingered on the tongue long after the last crumb disappeared. No one, according to my mother, could rival Grammie in the kitchen.

In 2023, on a sun-drenched, brisk November afternoon in 2023 near Dayton, OH, I finally met my second cousins Kenora and JoAnn face-to-face. What started as a simple meeting swiftly morphed into a rollicking pajama party—an impromptu celebration of family.

Surrounded by genealogy documents and precious old photographs, we laughed, and swapped stories and memories as if we'd known each other forever. My phone camera worked overtime, the click-click-click was a soundtrack to our reunion, as I tried to capture each kernel of truth for future sleuthing at home. Navigating around their oxygen tanks and tubes, we giggled and reminisced like teenagers at a slumber party—a fantastic, freewheeling night with women who made me feel at home.

For someone who grew up in California, far from extended family, their stories and warmth were a healing salve, soothing my soul and connecting me at last to the legacy of the remarkable Ella Roy Carter.

Cousin Kenora said, "Grammie was always so closemouthed when we asked questions. We were told many years ago that Grammie was born in 1863, that she was the product of her slave owner, that her mother died, and she was adopted by the Roys. Also, as a young woman, someone said she taught others how to read and write. As far as employment, I think Grammie did ironing for people. I remember ironing dinner napkins and handkerchiefs with an iron that you put on the stove to heat up. I know nothing about the house except that as the oldest great-granddaughter, I wanted to have a house like hers when I grew up. I loved the formal living room and the elaborate dining room furnishings and lamps that my cousin Pat and I dusted every week. Grammie's house had a stairway with a landing and lots of steps. The outhouse was in the backyard, *utilized* regularly."

A few days later during my 2023 trip, I visited another new-to-me cousin named Joyce Myers. Her Myers, Crewett and Chandler ancestors will be subjects for my tenth (and last) ancestor detective book which my ancestors compelled me to schedule back in 2016. After we warmed to each other, Joyce allowed me to photograph a table *full* of Myers and Booker obituaries, church programs, photographs, and other treasure trove documents from Maryland to Barnesville to Mount Vernon. I took pictures of over 1,000 precious documents on that trip, intending to share them with all my cousins, siblings, and others on Ancestry.com. I plan to leave a written legacy for future descendants to enjoy.

The doorbell rang at Joyce's house. I was delighted to see cousin Joseph Booker and his childhood friend, Susan Walker. Susan and I had been emailing information for months (Figure 7).

I relished listening to Joe and Joyce talk about the old days in Mount Vernon. My favorite story was them talking about how fun Monday Negro Night was at the skating rink. Yes, Black people could only skate on Monday nights and visit the cinema on Friday nights. Segregation was alive and well in the northern states too.

I relished listening to Joe and Joyce talk about the old days in Mount Vernon. My favorite story was them talking about how fun Monday Negro Night was at the skating rink. Yes, Black people could only skate on Monday nights and visit the cinema on Friday nights. Segregation was alive and well in the northern states too.

Figure 7: Kathy Marshall Meets Cousins in Mount Vernon, OH, 2023
Top: JoAnn Fields, Kenora Hogan, Joyce Myers.
Bottom: Susan Walker, Joseph G. Booker.

Sadly, cousin Joe died the following year, but I'll always remember his infectious smile and the three times we met during that trip—at Joyce's, at the Knox County Museum, and at a historic bar one night in the downtown Main Square. Joe's parents were the Booker pen pals who piqued my interest in 1976 to sleuth our mixed-race ancestral roots.

Those friendly relatives helped paint a full picture of Black life in Mount Vernon, where my great-grandmother Ella Roy "Grammie" Carter lived off and on until her last breath in 1962. However, none of us knew anything about the first fourteen years of Grammie's life, when she lived and worked in the uber famous Columbus Delano's mansion.

TIP: Don't wait to interview and videotape your elders. Access their family knowledge, NOW! Time waits for no one ...

TIP: Bring DNA test kits when you visit family. Genetic DNA from the elders is priceless, for they are closest to family born during the era of slavery. Interview relatives who have already collected ancestral information and stories that will enhance your family tree and research.

Kathy Marshall and Her Mother Talk Shop

"Mom," I began, curiosity pinging my eager brain in 2006, "Why do you think your mother—Grandma Pearl Williams—forbade you kids from visiting Grammie Carter by yourselves?" A flicker of something I couldn't quite decipher crossed Mom's once pretty face. Steroids—part of her cancer-fighting regime—made her swell up like a balloon.

"Maybe ..." Mom mused, her dominant left index finger stroking her chin, "it was because my father, Arthur Taft Carter—Grammie's youngest child—had seven children he didn't support. My father didn't live with us. But every time he visited, he created another baby that my grandparents had to help support. His negligence forced my mother to work as a maid during the day and a janitor at night. She barely made enough money to put bread on the table for us seven kids. I'm assuming Mom thought Grammie Carter should have forced her son to be a responsible family man, instead of letting him lounge around her house."

"That makes perfect sense to me," I said, imagining how difficult my Grandma Pearl's life must have been with all those kids to raise.

My mother continued, her voice a bit strained. "I heard that my parents and their first baby—my oldest sister, Norma—lived with Grammie Carter in 1929 after Norma was born. My Dad's grown brothers, Roy and Richard Carter, also lived at Grammie's house. None of the brothers seemed to have regular jobs, according to the 1930 Census. However, my cousins believed they worked part-time jobs in an auto body shop, or as gardeners.

She continued. "Something must have happened between Mom and Dad because after 1930, only my mother and Norma were living in my Williams grandparents' house. Eight other Williams family members were already there, so it was a tight squeeze after the rest of my siblings were born. Just imagine, sixteen adults and children living under one roof.

"I think my mother and Grammie had a falling out of some sort, but it didn't matter to us kids. We still visited Grammie at every opportunity, with or without permission."

I shifted gears in my questioning. "So, Mom, what did Grammie Carter look like?"

Mom's eyes crinkled as her full lips parted. "As I remember, Grammie wore her silky white hair milkmaid style, crisscrossing two braids over the top of her head. And she often wore a white apron over a light-colored house dress. She looked ghostly pale, like a Dutch lady." Mom paused, then added in a whisper, "We kids always wondered if one of Grammie's parents was White."

The first time I saw Grammie, standing at the left side of the black-and-white picture (Figure 8), I immediately understood why Mom felt that way. We all suspected that Grammie's father or grandfather had to be a White man.

Figure 8: Grammie with Bessie Carter's Descendants

Left: Ella Roy Carter, Bessie Carter, Ruth Payne, daughter Kenora Hogan and son Greg. Back row: Patricia Payne Ingram, Mount Vernon, c. 1960. Courtesy of Kenora Davis.

Mom, "What was your favorite memory about your grandmother Ella?"

Her beautiful smile lit up her face. "Kathy, we knew down to our very soul that Grammie enjoyed seeing us, even though we were a noisy bunch of hooligans. She'd hug us like we were sunshine itself. Her warm reaction made each of us feel special. And she treated my Cousin Lavata—the only child of Reba Williams [who lived to be 107]—in the same friendly way." Mom's expression turned dreamy, her head lolling back and forth like she was drunk. "And those oatmeal-raisin cookies were … umm, umm, umm." Then she smacked her lips at the memory.

"They were the best in the world!" I finished for her. I had heard that proclamation many times before. "Yours are pretty darn good too, Mom. In fact, let's bake some chocolate oatmeal cookies after we're done talking shop, okay?"

Mom's eyebrows wriggled up and down playfully. "You're on!" But then, a shadow fell over her face, and she stopped smiling, perhaps seeing something disturbing from her past.

"What is it?" I asked, intrigued, and a little worried. Was she experiencing a painful jab somewhere in her body?

Mom murmured, "I just remembered the unease I sometimes felt at Grammie's."

"What do you mean? Unease? Was it haunted or something?" I teased.

"No, silly," Mom scoffed. "We didn't dare ask our elders any questions."

"What do you mean?"

Mom continued, almost whispering, "How could an old Black woman, who didn't seem to work a day in her life, have a paid-off house, rich man's Tiffany lamps, fine china, and mahogany furniture, during a time when …"

I put my hand up to interrupt my mother. I knew what she was going to say next. I had heard it so many times before, I could recount the phrase in my sleep. "Sorry, Mom. Were you about to say '*During a time when most Black women were relegated to blue-collar labor jobs as cooks, laundresses, or maids*?'"

Mom grinned, but a hint of defiance overtook her gaze. "I guess I've said that once or twice because it's the gosh-awful truth. My mother wanted to become a secretary after she graduated from the integrated Mount Vernon High School in 1926.[15] But there was no way in Sam Hill the townsfolk would let a Black woman named Pearl Williams have a respectable office job instead of cleaning all day long. Society expected White women to stay home, raise children, and let the man bring home the bacon.

She continued, "Now, it *is* true that many of our Black men obtained decent jobs in the glass factory and Cooper's engine manufacturing shop. But our Black female caste? Menial jobs only. They called it *days work,* cleaning White folk's houses and taking care of their rambunctious children. Or, we could be a janitor or street cleaner, in addition to performing our own tasks when we got home from work. My mother never intended to have a bunch of kids and a non-supportive husband. But she made the best of a difficult situation and I admire her for never giving up on us kids."

"Kathy, my mother gave her all every day for our sake in the 1930s through the 1950s. She reared us well. Even though she made little money, we always had tasty food to eat. Mom cooked the same thing each day of the week––like SPAM on Mondays, baked beans and hot dogs on Thursdays, and chicken with dandelion greens on Sundays. My favorite was meatloaf, mashed potatoes, green beans and dessert on Wednesdays. *She* served our plates from a pot on the stove. There were no seconds or leftovers. We ate it all. Waste not, want not.[16]

"Mom always made sure our small housing space was clean. We did not live in a negative environment[17] either, like others who call each other hurtful names, yell, or fight inside the house. That did not happen in our home."

"Even though my mother did her best, I vowed early on that my life would be different. I'd get out of that small town and buy a pretty house with at least three bedrooms. It would be in a friendly neighborhood where people treated us like human beings, instead of lowly day workers. I'd have a car so my family wouldn't have to walk everywhere in the rain and snow. And I would get a college degree to help me get whatever job I wanted."[18]

Mom exhaled. "The limited opportunities for growth in my hometown prompted me to set myself on a different course. A blind date at the skating rink in Zanesville Ohio in 1952 would change my life forever."

"I cannot wait to hear that story!" I interjected, ready to her next words.

Mom sat back in her chair and her eyes became unfocused, and dreamy. "It was springtime in 1952. I was a senior in highschool, serving as the creative editor for the Mount Vernon Highschool Yearbook. My older sister, Sarah, was dating a college fellow from Cleveland. Late one spring afternoon, on a Monday, Sarah's boyfriend drove two hours down to Mount Vernon to pick her up to go roller-skating in Zanesville. He brought along a friend of his. They asked if I wanted to go skating with them on Negro Night. My eyes looked at the tall, handsome, Thomas Richard Marshall.[19] I said yes to skating that night, and three years later, I said yes to his marriage proposal."

"That sounds romantic, Mom."

"It was," she agreed. "We married in 1955 after I turned 21. Tom was still attending the Ohio State College of Medicine in Columbus, OH. He graduated in 1958[20] after you were born, Kathy. You and I lived with Tom's mother, while he finished school. Then, we moved to Seattle, Washington, where Tom performed Medical Corps duties as a Lieutenant in the Navy.[21] After your sister, Carrie, was born in Seattle, Tom transferred to the Navy Medical Corps at Camp Pendleton in San Diego, CA. Then, he finished his medical residency in Stockton, CA, where your brother Greg was born.

"In 1964, our family moved to Sacramento, CA, where your father opened his Obstetrics/Gynecology medical practice. The following year, he somehow skirted redlining prohibitions[22] that most cities in America foisted on Black people who sought home ownership. In 1965, he purchased a brand-new house for $16,000. He moved us into the nearly all-White Larchmont Riviera neighborhood, at the eastern outskirts of Sacramento, far away from our Black friends.

"I had already seen the writing on the wall in the early 1960s."

"What do you mean, Mom?"

"I saw the looks women gave your father. A tall, smart, athletic, good-looking Black obstetrician would face many temptations. So, I obtained an Associate degree at Sacramento City College before he flew the coop. The next two years were tough, but I earned a Bachelor of Arts in early childhood education. Then, I became an elementary school teacher. I started working at 35, late in life. So I went to next school to obtain a Masters degree in School Administration to spend 15 more years as a principal.

"Kathy, all of that success was made possible by me meeting your father that night in 1952, marrying him, and the availability of birth control after your brother was born in the mid-1960s. That helped ensure I had fewer children to manage than my mother. So, when Tom divorced me in 1966 to marry our attractive dancing instructor, we four survived and thrived. I could retire at 55 to follow my lifelong dream of becoming a professional watercolorist, a competitive tennis and golf player. And, I could compete in bridge competitions, before and during my 17-year retirement. I love my life and wanted to be a beacon for change, breaking free from the normal constraints that bound women who were bred to *only* be housewives and mothers. As a result, you children are freer to pursue your goals and lead fulfilling lives."

Tears glistening in my eyes, I reached over to hug my Shero of a mother. "Mom, I thank you so much for giving us that exemplary tutelage on how to live an authentic life. Our ancestors are so proud of you, Mom, as are your children, your coworkers, your Alpha Kappa Alpha sorority, and your friends!"

Who Planted Ella's Seed?

From 2000 to 2006, I helped Mom fill out her *Reflections of a Mother's Heart* memoir journal. It consisted of about two hundred questions that she had to answer, like "Describe your childhood bedroom," and "Describe a typical day in school," and "What were your childhood chores?" She filled out one third of the questions over a ten-year period. I helped her fill out another third after cancer cells raced from her breast to her brain.

Mom lived in a cozy two-bedroom house in an active adult community in South Sacramento. She had built an enclosed sunroom where her three grandchildren could play and sleep on some weekends. My siblings and I played board games or tennis with Mom, chatted about the educational system, and enjoyed Sunday dinners together at her cozy house.

On rare occasions, Mom told a few stories about her tough-love maternal grandmother, Myrtle Booker Williams. Mom, her mother, and six siblings lived her first fifteen years in her grandparents' cramped house on North Norton Street. Sixteen total people in that two-story row house owned by great-grandpa Otho Williams's employer, "Cooper-Bessemer." I only had to share a small bedroom with one sister. I could not imagine seven kids in one small bedroom. What a tight squeeze!

Mom's eyes glistened with admiration when describing her thirty-years-a-slave great-great-grandmother, Margarett Booker, who lived fifty-years as a free woman in Barnesville, Belmont County, OH. Myrtle and Margarett both ran laundry businesses from their homes, with Myrtle earning $312 in 1940.[23]

"Kathy, just envision working five days a week washing and ironing clothes for prestigious doctors and lawyers in town. It was back-breaking work during a time before electric washing machines and dryers, but our female intrepid ancestors took pride in their accomplishments. Grammie Carter's ability to pay off her mortgage by 1930 was a feat that raised questions after her husband's death in 1909. Some relatives believed Columbus Delano, a wealthy former politician whose home Grammie lived in as a teen, may have influenced her financial situation (Figure 9).

Name	Race	Sex	Relat.	S	M	Occupation
Delano, C (70)	W	M			/	Farmer
" Eliz (65)	W	F	Wife		/	House
" Geo. B. (15)	W	M	G.Son	/		
" Ellen (4)	W	F	G.Daught	/		
Roy, Albert (45)	B	M	Servant		/	Servant
" Alice (37)	B	F	Servant		/	Servant
" Ellie (14)	B	F	Servant	/		Servant
Burris, Del (65)	B	F				
Moyce, Jas (17)	B	M	Servant			Servant

***Figure 9**: 1880 US Federal Census for Albert Roy, Knox, OH*

We took pride in our connection to Delano, because he advised President Lincoln to sign the Emancipation Proclamation, which freed slaves in Confederate states in 1863."

I interrupted, excited. "Isn't it thrilling to know our relatives lived around someone who had such a positive impact on African American lives in this country? We never learned anything like that in our school history books. That's why it's so important to study our lineage now, and learn how our family contributed to American history."

My mother nodded, adding, "Did you know that Delano was also the Internal Revenue Service *Czar*[24] in our Nation's Capital under President Lincoln?" I shook my head. "And I think his son, John Sherman Delano, worked in the same office, as a clerk. Columbus also served as U.S. Secretary of the Interior[25] under his cousin, President Ulysses S. Grant. But he got in trouble because of some underhanded money-related dealings with his cronies. I heard he did dastardly things against the Indians, like sending their children to schools that stripped their cultural identity.[26] However, he seemed to support Negro rights."

"So, Mom, do you think Columbus Delano was a good guy or a bad seed? Should we be glad or sad that Grammie worked for, and lived with him?"

"Well …" Mom stared into my eyes, "They say he brought Grammie and other Roy family members to Mount Vernon, after he left his DC job. It seems he treated our Roys well, letting them live with him in his enormous mansion, according to the 1880 Census[27] *but* …" She winked, then her voice trailed off.

"We kids sometimes rode our bikes out there to their former sheep ranch, off Martinsburg Road, a mile from downtown Mount Vernon. The house was a massive three-story structure with a lake in back and acres of land as far as the eye could see. The baa-baa of his herds of sheep echoed out to the road. I heard the Nazarene College bought the property in the 1960s, so I don't know what the property is like now."

After slurping a spoonful of jello, Mom continued. "Delano helped elect Abraham Lincoln, who many call the Great Emancipator."[28] So, I guess that makes him a good guy in my eyes. Yet…" Mom faltered again and her eyebrows lifted.

Hmmm, I wonder what Mom is hinting at. Many unspoken questions spewed from my creative brain, as she continued mincing her words.

"Mom" I nearly shouted, becoming impatient with her beating-around-the-bush dialogue. "I can't imagine why Delano would bring all those Black people hundreds of miles from Washington, DC to live in his posh home in tiny Mount Vernon." I paused a pregnant moment. "Oh … do you think Grammie is *biologically related* to the Delanos? Is that why the Roys were invited to live with them? Did he do the deed to plant *her* seed?" It's a phrase that I overuse because so many enslavers planted their own seed in Black women to *grow* their crop of enslaved people.

Mom shrugged, then winked again.

I got excited. "Do you think Columbus Delano, or his son John had a fling with Grammie's unnamed mother? Do you think Grammie's mom might have worked as a cleaning woman at the IRS or the Department of the Interior, or maybe at the Delano's private home?" Mom shrugged.

"Did the Delanos live near Alexandria, Virginia, where Grammie Carter was born?" Mom sat still, her lips slightly upturned at the edges, her eyes boring into my face, wanting me to say out loud what she believed. But I was tired of playing. "What do YOU think, Mom? Just tell me the truth!" I must have sounded manic with the intensity of my questions.

Mom shrugged again. "That would explain her mortgage-free house and those gorgeous stained-glass lamps. Kathy, you simply cannot imagine how they sparkled in the late afternoon, as the sun streamed in through the front windows." Mom looked beyond my face, perhaps thinking about the glorious colors from those lamps bouncing off the walls like a disco ball.

Returning from her reverie, she said, "This will be an interesting story for us to investigate together." Then she hesitated. "Just so you know, I already wrote a letter to the Delano family asking about Ella's birthright."

"You did what?" I nearly screamed, jumping out of my seat. Then, I checked my voice. "Umm, I don't think that's a good idea, Mom. Those rich folks might think you want money, or acreage, or something from them. I don't think White people like hearing that their famous ancestor may have had *relations* with the Black help. That might sully their lofty reputation."

Mom tilted her Chemo-bald head to the side. "You might be right, but we'll never know if we don't ask. I also sent a letter to the Division of Vital Records within the Bureau of Health Policy and Vital Statistics to find documents involving Ella's parents' names." (Figure 10)

To whom it may concern,

I am interested in finding more information about my paternal grandmother, Ella Roy (Carter, married name). Enclosed is her death certificate indicating she was born in Alexandria Virginia, 27 December 1866. I would like a copy of her birth certificate. Your records also indicated slave births started in 1853. I do not know if my grandmother was a slave or lived on a plantation. Would you please tell me how to get this information and the cost? I also need the township where she was born to get the enumeration district. Thank you for your help. Mary Marshall.

Figure *10: Mary Marshall's Letter to OH Division of Vital Records.*

After an agonizing wait of several weeks in early 2006, Mom's last full year on Earth, she received responses indicating the requested records were *not* available. Heavy sigh. We are not quitters, though. We tried again and the second time we succeeded, receiving a copy of Grammie's 1962 Death Certificate in the mail. Mom called me one Saturday morning in May, her voice especially cheery. She asked me to come over to work together on that long sought after document.

I told my thirteen-year-old son, Matt, to get dressed and eat breakfast. His brother had joined the Marines in 2003, at the beginning of the Iraq War, so Matt was the only child left at home. Sure, he was old enough to stay home alone, and he would have loved playing video games all weekend long, but his grandmother was *terminal*. I thought it important that we both spend as much time as possible with her while we could.

I gathered my notepad, pencil, and messy binder of genealogy documents, gobbled a bowl of microwaved oatmeal seasoned with butter and honey, then loaded Matt and my documents into our trusty blue Caravan. I steered the van northeast from former cow pastures near our south-of-Sacramento home. We drove toward Mom's house twenty minutes away, to her gated adult community near Stockton Boulevard and Mack Road. Matt hugged Mom, then made a bee-line for the sunroom, turning on the console TV for a morning of cartoons.

As usual, Mom spread our genealogy documents on the kitchen table near her computer workstation. She excitedly showed me Ella Carter's dDeath certificate which she had already mocked up with notations. (Today, those scribbles bring me precious memories of her handwriting, personal address, phone number, and memories of our visits.)

Time to get to work. We felt like Sherlock Holmes, examining an important piece of evidence for clues to help us solve the case. Mom's time was running out. We had to hurry. "Mom, Grammie's death certificate says she was born in Alexandria on 27 Dec 1866, one year after slavery ended in America." (Figure 11). She said, "It incorrectly says Grammie lived in Mount Vernon for 90 years, but that's not true. I believe she spent her earliest years in Virginia, and a few years in Springfield, OH, after she married."

Why do you suppose the middle name of "Mae" is in parentheses, with a question mark?" I asked.

Mom looked like a child who just got caught with her hand in the cookie jar. "Oh, I actually penciled that in because that's what someone told me. And I also added that her maiden name was Roy, based on what I had been told all my life."

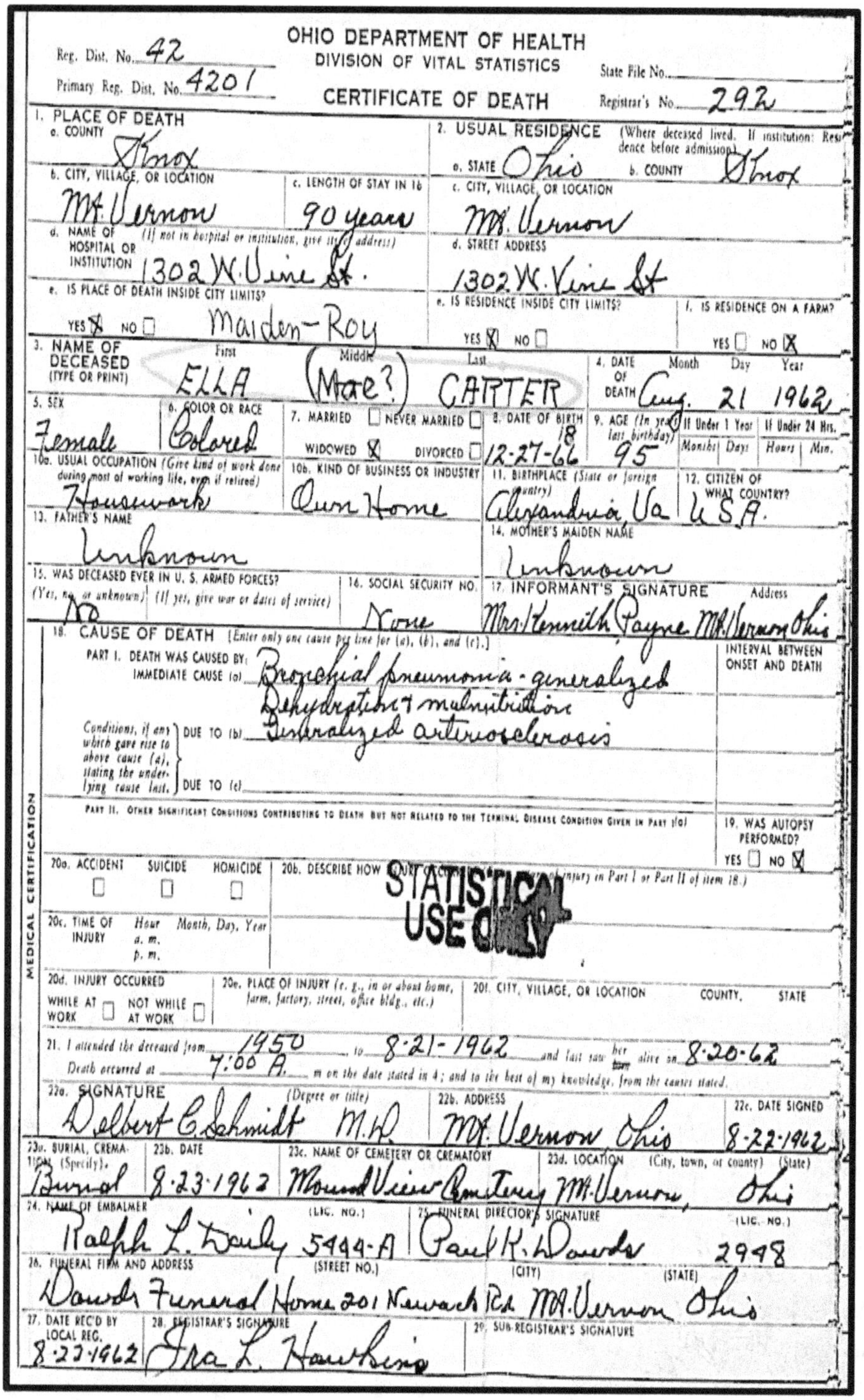

OHIO DEPARTMENT OF HEALTH
DIVISION OF VITAL STATISTICS
CERTIFICATE OF DEATH

Reg. Dist. No. 42
Primary Reg. Dist. No. 4201
State File No.
Registrar's No. 292

1. PLACE OF DEATH
a. COUNTY: Knox
b. CITY, VILLAGE, OR LOCATION: Mt Vernon
c. LENGTH OF STAY IN 1b: 90 years
d. NAME OF HOSPITAL OR INSTITUTION (If not in hospital or institution, give street address): 1302 W. Vine St.
e. IS PLACE OF DEATH INSIDE CITY LIMITS? YES [X] NO [ ]

2. USUAL RESIDENCE (Where deceased lived. If institution: Residence before admission)
a. STATE: Ohio
b. COUNTY: Knox
c. CITY, VILLAGE, OR LOCATION: Mt. Vernon
d. STREET ADDRESS: 1302 W. Vine St
e. IS RESIDENCE INSIDE CITY LIMITS? YES [X] NO [ ]
f. IS RESIDENCE ON A FARM? YES [ ] NO [X]

Maiden-Roy

3. NAME OF DECEASED (TYPE OR PRINT) First: ELLA Middle: (Mae?) Last: CARTER
4. DATE OF DEATH: Aug. 21 1962
5. SEX: Female
6. COLOR OR RACE: Colored
7. MARRIED [ ] NEVER MARRIED [ ] WIDOWED [X] DIVORCED [ ]
8. DATE OF BIRTH: 12-27-1866
9. AGE (In years last birthday): 95
10a. USUAL OCCUPATION (Give kind of work done during most of working life, even if retired): Housework
10b. KIND OF BUSINESS OR INDUSTRY: Own Home
11. BIRTHPLACE (State or foreign country): Alexandria, Va
12. CITIZEN OF WHAT COUNTRY? U.S.A.
13. FATHER'S NAME: Unknown
14. MOTHER'S MAIDEN NAME: Unknown
15. WAS DECEASED EVER IN U. S. ARMED FORCES? (Yes, no, or unknown) (If yes, give war or dates of service): No
16. SOCIAL SECURITY NO.: None
17. INFORMANT'S SIGNATURE: Mrs. Kenneth Payne Address: Mt. Vernon Ohio

18. CAUSE OF DEATH (Enter only one cause per line for (a), (b), and (c).)
PART I. DEATH WAS CAUSED BY:
IMMEDIATE CAUSE (a): Bronchial pneumonia - generalized Dehydration + malnutrition
Conditions, if any, which gave rise to above cause (a), stating the underlying cause last.
DUE TO (b): Generalized arteriosclerosis
DUE TO (c):
INTERVAL BETWEEN ONSET AND DEATH
PART II. OTHER SIGNIFICANT CONDITIONS CONTRIBUTING TO DEATH BUT NOT RELATED TO THE TERMINAL DISEASE CONDITION GIVEN IN PART I(a)
19. WAS AUTOPSY PERFORMED? YES [ ] NO [X]

MEDICAL CERTIFICATION

20a. ACCIDENT [ ] SUICIDE [ ] HOMICIDE [ ]
20b. DESCRIBE HOW INJURY OCCURRED. (Enter nature of injury in Part I or Part II of item 18.)

STATISTICAL USE ONLY

20c. TIME OF INJURY Hour a.m. p.m. Month, Day, Year
20d. INJURY OCCURRED WHILE AT WORK [ ] NOT WHILE AT WORK [ ]
20e. PLACE OF INJURY (e.g., in or about home, farm, factory, street, office bldg., etc.)
20f. CITY, VILLAGE, OR LOCATION COUNTY, STATE

21. I attended the deceased from 1950 to 8-21-1962 and last saw her alive on 8-20-62
Death occurred at 7:00 A. m on the date stated in 4; and to the best of my knowledge, from the causes stated.
22a. SIGNATURE: Delbert C. Schmidt M.D.
22b. ADDRESS: Mt. Vernon Ohio
22c. DATE SIGNED: 8-22-1962

23a. BURIAL, CREMATION (Specify): Burial
23b. DATE: 8-23-1962
23c. NAME OF CEMETERY OR CREMATORY: Mound View Cemetery
23d. LOCATION (City, town, or county) (State): Mt. Vernon, Ohio
24. NAME OF EMBALMER: Ralph L. Daily (LIC. NO.) 5444-A
25. FUNERAL DIRECTOR'S SIGNATURE: Paul K. Dowds (LIC. NO.) 2948
26. FUNERAL FIRM AND ADDRESS (STREET NO.) (CITY) (STATE): Dowds Funeral Home 201 Newark Rd Mt. Vernon Ohio
27. DATE REC'D BY LOCAL REG.: 8-23-1962
28. REGISTRAR'S SIGNATURE: Ira L. Hawkins
29. SUB-REGISTRAR'S SIGNATURE

***Figure** 11: Ella Roy Carter's Death Certificate, Knox, OH,1962*

"Wow, Mom. This says Grammie died at 96 years of age on the 21st of August in 1962 in Mount Vernon. The document described Ella Carter as a colored woman who owned her own home at 1302 W. Vine Street."

I looked up, both happy and a bit scared. I knew I would soon be alone, having to prove all those down-home stories with corroborating documents. As I read down to number 13 and 14, I sucked my teeth. "Darn! Her parents were listed as UNKNOWN."

"Yes, that's disappointing. But listen to this, Kathy. Someone told me Grammie had eleven children during her lifetime."

My innerds tightened, just thinking about how painful birthing eleven children would be. But my imagination soared on the clouds dreaming about the potential records we could find about each child.

Mom broke into my thoughts. "I only knew about Benjamin—"Bennie"—because he was a famous World War I hero. Of course, I knew my dad was Arthur, and his sister was Bessie, who lived next door to Grammie. We called Uncle Roy 'Peachy' for some reason.

"Let's see," Mom tapped her cheek with her index finger. "Uncle Richard's kids, Bobby and Dickie, were my favorite boy cousins. Oh, the fun I had beating them at marbles and tennis."

Mom stared into space, a beatific smile on her ravaged face. She must have been reliving fun moments with her family during the 1940s. "We'll have to figure out who those other kids were."

As Mom spoke, I began fixing tuna sandwiches, a quick-set orange-flavored jello mold with pineapple bits. Adding ice cubes to the boiled water/jello mixture and pouring it into a shallow pan, then placing it into the freezer, helps the jello set quickly. I also made Mom's favorite beverage: Crystal Lite iced tea and served with cookies made from her recipe for chocolate chip cookies.

As I worked, I uttered, "Oh, really?" and "She owned her own home?" and "Uh-huh," at natural intervals, while Mom verbalized what the Death Certificate was revealing. She acted surprised that pneumonia and malnutrition caused Grammie's death.

"Why is that strange, Mom?"

"Because her daughter, my aunt Bessie, brought Grammie into her home during the last five years of her life. I can't fathom why malnutrition was listed as a cause of death. Bessie was an excellent cook."

"Maybe Grammie was tired of living. She was almost one hundred years old, after all." All at once, I shuddered at my thoughtless statement. My mother was dying from breast cancer that metastasized to her brain. She was only 72 years old and desperately wanted to make it to 80. She pasted "80" signs all around her house as a plea to the Gods. I had to stop thinking about that all-too-soon inevitability and tune into what she was saying *in the here and now*.

Mom pursed her lips and huffed, "Or, maybe Grammie was so upset at what her sons did that she just withered away."

Now that was a juicy statement. "Mom, what did they do that was so awful that Grammie would lose the will to live?"

"I think they sold a lot of her priceless furnishings while she was living next door with Bessie." Mom glanced at the Death Certificate without speaking. The air was thick with words unsaid. I wondered what was rummaging through her head, but dared not ask. I *zipped my lips*, a phrase which Mom often used to suggest that listening was often better than running one's mouth.

Viewing that Death Certificate was helpful to be sure, but the piece of information we craved most—Ella's parentage—was listed as UNKNOWN.

"Anyway," Mom said, "I seem to remember someone saying Grammie was taking care of the Delano's disabled son ... or maybe it was a sick grandchild. And someone else thought Grammie was a nurse*maid* for the Delano's young granddaughter, Ellen, who was living with them.

Mom rummaged through our stack of genealogy documents, pulling out what she was looking for. "The 1880 Census reported that 'Ellie' was a servant living in the Delano home with fellow servants Albert and Alice Roy, a woman named Del Burris, and another Black servant named Jas (James) Moyce. I heard someone say Delano brought the Roys to Mount Vernon in the mid-1870s when he left his bigtime politician job in Washington, DC."

"Hey, Matt, lunch is ready." He came bounding in from the sunroom, next to the kitchen; he sat so he could still see the TV.

Mom asked him the usual questions adults asked sixteen-year-olds: "How are your classes? Who's your favorite teacher, and why? Have you thought about what you're going to do after high school?"

Then, out of the blue she said something that shocked us both. "I'd like you to have my car when I ... you know." Normally calm and introspective Matthew jumped out of his seat and embraced his grandmother, accompanied bye a heartfelt "Thank you."

None of us could speak for several minutes, eating our meals in silence. Each of us was probably thinking the same thing. Would Mom last long enough to find information about her wayward father before she died?

Meal finished, I put the dishes into the dishwasher, then set a plate of chocolate chip cookies on the table. "We need to find documents that will prove or disprove the family lore about both of your grandparents." I hoped our conversation would spark additional memories and new clues. I yearned to find something meaty for us history sleuths to chew on, but my mother remained silent, staring off into space. I wanted to get her mind off the cancer issue.

"Mom, do *you* think Delano is the reason Grammie Carter ended up in Mount Vernon, four hundred miles from her Virginia birthplace? Or do you think she and Albert and Alice traveled to Mount Vernon with other Black folks from Virginia, maybe with the Paynes and Fields with whom they married?"

She hunched her shoulders. "I still wonder whether Delano was *more than* just Ella's boss. He seemed to have treated our Roys *so well.*

I nodded. "You know, after our 1983 family reunion that Cousin Lavata skillfully arranged at Mohican State Park, she drove me to the Vital Records office in Columbus. I think it was the same building your sister, Betty, worked in. Anyway, Lavata showed me how to use the microfilm machine to read the 1880 Census to find our Roy family. While we were there, she said she thought Albert Roy owned a store, like a grocery store."

Mom cupped her hands and leaned her face toward me so that only I could hear her concerns. "Well, I don't know about that, but what I do think is that one of the Delanos *did the deed.*" Then she pointed to her crotch and laughed. "But it could have easily been one of his buddies in DC, or a family member, or a next-door neighbor. Who knows why White men do the things they do?" We both smirked.

"Why do you think a White man had anything to do with Grammie?"

"Don't you remember the black-and-white photograph of Grammie Carter I showed you? Her ultra-light skin color melded with her white clothing and white hair." Mom found the photo of Ella with her children and grandchildren. She compared that photo to her honey brown arm and to my light tan skin. She said, "It's pretty evident there was some cream in our African coffee–that's one of my most favorite of Mom's expressions. It's probably the origins of rape that many women—Black, Native, and White—have had to endure since time immemorial."

"Yep! That's truer than true," I nodded until my head felt like it would break off my neck. "I don't recall whether I ever told you this, Mom, but after our first family reunion, I became pen pals with Great-uncle George Booker. He and his wife, Geraldine, wrote to me that, 'From the age of six, Ella was raised by her mother's *brother*, Albert Roy, after her mother died in Virginia. Unfortunately, Geraldine never said who Ella's mother was."

After swallowing a piece of cookie, Mom said, "I think Grammie's obituary mentioned something about that, but I don't have a copy." We finished lunch in silence, but I yearned for more proof of Grammie's lineage. Who were Ella's parents, their ancestors, and enslaver(s)? How/when/why was Ella adopted by Albert? How did our Roys and Carters migrate to Ohio? How did Ella meet her husband? Who were his parents and their enslavers? Where were they living during their marriage? How did widow Ella pay off her mortgage and buy fancy furnishings?

    Five years later, in 2012 after I retired from my day job, I took my first of several DNA tests, hoping DNA testing would identify blood relatives who might have more family records to clarify the ancestry of Ella's Roy/Carter ancestral line. I am still searching for answers, 13 years later …

CHAPTER 3: Unsealing Grammie's Truths

What a fool! Even though I had already published eight family history books, attended many genealogy conferences, listened to family history podcasts, and delivered a dozen genealogy talks, I made a rookie mistake. I thought I had learned enough from family lore, my timeline of 300-plus historical events, and enrolling in an 18-week writing course. I thought I was ready to author an epic historical saga. That book would involve my Black Roy/Carter family, Native Americans, and Columbus Delano, who masterminded the relative success or demise of those two groups.

Seven months of dedicated effort in 2024 transformed my intensive morning-to-night research efforts into fifteen captivating chapters which outlined a three-part saga. My initial attempt aimed to craft a rousing historical narrative, weaving together tales of Black *contraband*[29]—freedom-seeking runaway slaves—Native Americans and their buffalo brothers, and the powerful people in Washington D.C. who attempted to eliminate the buffalo and, thus, the Native American culture.

Sadly, information about Grammie's parents, their enslavers, and her pivotal journey from Virginia to Ohio remained elusive. I did *not* want to fictionalize her life by making up stories of fantasy parents or pathological enslavers, etc. Time to start again, from scratch.

Many experts believe the first genealogy step is building a family tree. Start with oneself as the trunk of the tree, as shown on page ix. Then, find documents that prove your lineage. For example, a birth certificate should prove who your parents are. One branch of the family tree will be for your mother's family, and the other branch for your father's lineage.

The ideal is to find documents that prove each generation on the tree. There should be an unbroken line from you to each of your ancestors on the tree. Interviewing family is an excellent way to start, but adoptees may have to start start with a DNA test to find kin who may have family to interview.

Reunions and Revelations in The Homeland

All my maternal family lines migrated to Mount Vernon, in the latter 1800s. My mother inherited the legacy of Bookers enslaved in West Virginia, Roys in Virginia, and Williams in Maryland. At the outset, I did not know whether the Carters in DC had ever been enslaved. The histories of Myers and Crewetts are waiting to be revealed in my final family heritage book in 2026.

Online access to genealogical information is helpful, but it's also important to visit the land of one's ancestors. There's nothing like experiencing the sounds, smells, sights, impressions and feel of the homeland. Some records are only found in the city or state or county where your ancestors lived. One should investigate courthouses, libraries, historical centers and family member's home attics to find documents that may tell the tale. For descendants of enslaved Americans, that also means visiting the places where the enslavers lived and digging through their property documents.

I've visited Mount Vernon a few times in my life. The first was in 1958 when I was one year old. While I don't recall that specific occasion, I'm grateful to have a precious four-generation photograph that captures my maternal lineage (Figure 12).

Figure 12: Myrtle Booker, Pearl Williams, Mary Carter & Kathy, 1958.

My second trip to Mount Vernon is forever etched in my memory. The summer of 1967, Mom took my seven-year-old sister, Carrie, three-year-old brother, Greg, and my nine-year-old self on a thrilling three-day, cross-country Amtrak train adventure. We journeyed from Sacramento, California, through Nevada's high deserts. Seeing the glowing Salt Lake at night as we sped through Utah is still a unique memory. The unbelievably vivid red and orange tones of the Rocky Mountains that bank the Colorado River and Grand Mesa. We continued across the vast Midwest plains of Nebraska, north through Indiana, then east to witness the awe-inspiring Chicago skyline at night.[30]

From there, we switched to a rickety old train that chugged through picturesque farmlands, southeast to the endless cornfields of Mansfield, OH.[31] Under the twinkling stars, Mom's brother, Arthur "Sonny" Carter, drove us in his '57 Chevy to their family home at 101 West Walnut Street in Mount Vernon. We spent an unforgettable week connecting with my Grandma Pearl Williams Carter, along with several first cousins, aunts, and uncles. All were unfamiliar faces to us California strangers. Those cherished memories found their way into my first published book called the *Ancestors Are Smiling*!

Our closest maternal relatives greeted us at our first family reunion in 1983. Thousands of wooded acres surrounded a rustic conference center at Mohican State Park in Lucas, OH. The heartwarming gathering comprised of maybe 100 Carters, Bookers, Myers, Williams, Jenkins, Thomases and Walkers. We laughed and shared stories during three magical days of swimming, hiking, and chatting into the wee hours of the morning. My penpal from 1976, Granduncle George Booker was the scintillating Master of Ceremonies. Then, our family historian, Lavata (top right in Figure 13) provided every family with a 22-page, hand-typed reunion packet with relatives neatly listed by family line. Hers was a Herculean research effort that I treasure to this day.

***Figure 13**: 2003 Family Reunion in Columbus, OH*

After the 1983 reunion, Lavata drove me to the Vital Records office in Columbus. She taught me how to research my Roy family via microfilm records. I became an ancestor detective junkie, hooked after I found records from the 1880 Census containing my Roys and Carters.

In 2003, my Marshall family flew back to Mount Vernon for a poignant memorial service at Mound View Cemetery to honor all those we'd lost since our first reunion. My gregarious Great-granduncle George Booker led the service, a solemn reminder of passage of time.

My mother wrote in her memoir journal that, "We lived next to Cooper Bessemer, a steel-making plant which was at least a block wide and long. The sound of the horn, or ring that let the workers know it was time to leave, was deafening. Also, a really loud siren often blared from the building next to our house. At holiday time, the constant noise we endured every day came to a halt because they closed down the plant. This blissful quiet happened a handful of times a year. We never lived in a quiet place during the time we spent at Norton Street."[32]

Mom's family was once known for their longevity, with many elders living into their nineties. Grandaunt Reba Williams, Lavata'a mother, lived to be 107. Amazingly, she earned her high school diploma at age 106. That feat got a mention on Jay Leno's late-night TV show and article in Essence Mgazine! Good genes, right? Well ... Mom and her siblings died in their sixties and seventies, except for her youngest brother Dale. He is still alive and contributed very important DNA to this project. For 15 years, Mom's family lived in a company house on the foundry grounds. I suspect exposure to pollutants from the Cooper-Bessemer furnace and Glass Factory may have reduced their lifespans.

My fourth trip to Mount Vernon took place in 2009. I was overjoyed that my younger son Matt joined me while his older brother, Isaac, was stationed overseas with the Marines in Iraq. We flew to Atlanta, Georgia, to visit my first cousin Julie. We embarked on a scenic, nine-hour drive north, passing through the lush forests of Tennessee and Kentucky, heading to a family wedding in Columbus, OH. The morning of the wedding day, I borrowed my cousin's van and made a quick detour to Zanesville, OH, for a Myers/Lett family reunion before returning to Columbus for the evening nuptials. Coincidentally, my parents met on a blind date at the skating rink in Zanesville, in 1952, on Monday, designated as "Negro Night."

The fifth trip was an impromptu journey to Columbus in 2012, triggered by paternal Cousin Ted Canty, whom I met through genetic genealogy (DNA). When he discovered I had a living, sharp-minded, then 105-year-old Grandaunt Reba, he urged me to visit her *immediately* to capture her invaluable oral history. I videotaped and audio-recorded oodles of family stories from Reba. Then her daughter, Lavata drove me and Cousin Julie on a memorable car trip to view the family homestead in Mount Vernon. She showed us the Williams house where Mom spent her first 15 years of life and I videotaped the house and her stories. Oops! Later iterations of my computer operating system rendered those valuable videos defunct.

> **TIP: Transcribe oral/video history into typed narratives and save new copies of the videos annually. Technology changes over time and can render older video and audio recordings unusable. I learned this the hard way, after losing important video interviews with my elders.**

Uncle Dale Carter, Mom's only living sibling, drove me to the State Archives in Columbus, OH. It turned out to be a phenomenal repository. Not only did we find historical texts about my family from Mount Vernon, but we also stumbled upon shelves containing a few books from Maryland. Yes, there it sat—a book with an index containing two men with the elusive family name of Otho Williams. That discovery marked a pivotal moment which led to my second published book, *Finding Otho: The Search for Our Enslaved Williams Ancestors*.[33]

> **TIP: When taking a genealogy trip, be on the lookout for documents that might be useful for other book projects. I never dreamed of finding useful books about Maryland in the Ohio State Archives.**

My sixth trip to the family homeland was an extended stay at the charming Mount Vernon Inn in November 2023. Cousin Joe Booker introduced me to several heretofore unknown cousins who became indispensable sources of family history: Kenora Davis, JoAnn Fields, and Joyce Myers. My formerly enslaved Booker family is sensitively portrayed in *The Mystery of Margaret Booker: One Woman's Triumph Over Slavery*.[34]

For three days in 2023, I explored the crowded depths of the incredible Knox County Historical Society Museum,[35] stepping *way back* in time. They crammed artifacts about Mount Vernon's history from the early 1800s to the present, including memorabilia from the places where Mom's family worked, played, married, worshipped, and resided. For example, the 1871 *Atlas of Knox County, Ohio*, indicated who owned which land parcels, so I could track how families migrated through the various townships over the years.

The Museum also held period clothing, books, and machinery from the industries which attracted my ancestors from Virginia, West Virginia, Maryland, DC and other places. What a captivating journey through the vibrant history of Knox County!

Residents are encouraged to bring their historical items to the museum instead of throwing them away. Thousands of pieces of memorabilia grace the spacious Knox County Historical Museum.

Museum volunteers like Jim Gibson brought me a steady stream of exciting evidence that documented my family's presence in Knox County, OH. Who could believe the Museum stored the Masonic sword owned by my formerly enslaved two-times great-grandfather (2xGGF) Joseph Booker? Many thanks to his grandson, Joe Booker, who donated that important artifact, along with Joseph's photograph (Figure 14).

Figure 14: Kathy Holds 2xGGF Joseph Booker's Masonic Sword.

I felt such pride in 2xGGF Joseph's accomplishments, considering his enslaved beginnings in Beverly, Randolph County, West Virginia. His son, postal carrier and musician George Booker, also played a part in Knox County history. Professor Howard Sacks[36] interviewed George in his *Way Up North in Dixie* book about Black musicians Ben and Lew Snowden (originators of the song "Dixie").

"The Community Within,"[37] was my favorite display. It was a partnership between Kenyon College faculty, students, and the local African-American community. Professors Emeritus Ric Sheffield[38] and Howard Sacks were the masterminds behind that project celebrating family, social life, work, and church, also online in the *Digital Kenyon African American History Archives* (https://digital.kenyon.edu/knoxcobha/).

My Aunt Norma Carter worked at the high-class Rudin's Department Store whose huge turquoise/copper clock used to border the Public Square (Figure 15, left). My mother Mary dressed mannequins and painted sales windows after school at Ringwalt's Department Store from 1949 to 1952. This glimpse into *my* family's history time-traveled me back 75 years.

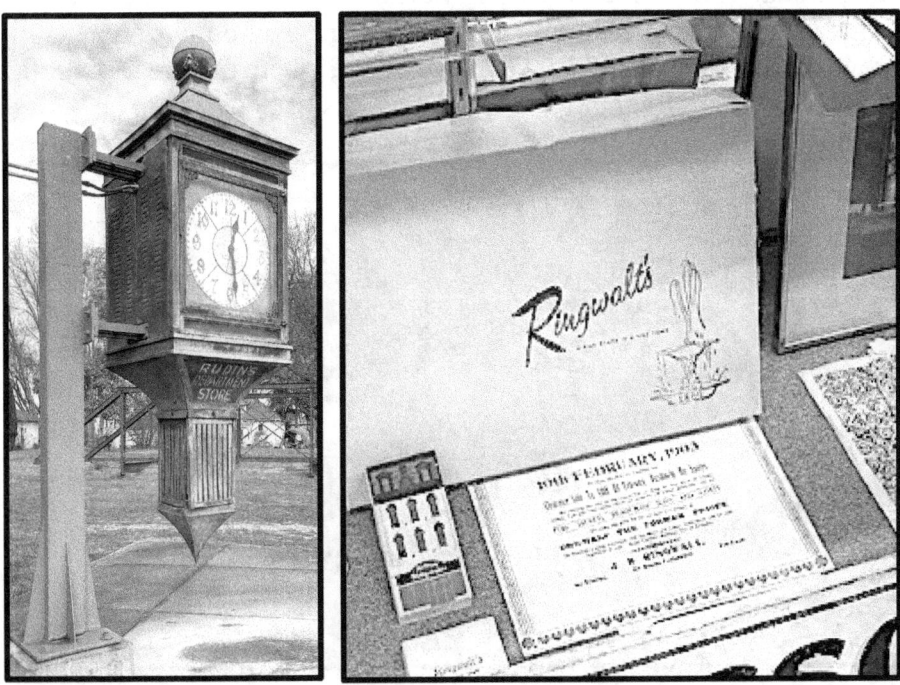

Figure 15: Where Aunt Norma & Mother Mary Worked in the 1950s

Who could believe one of the books in the Knox County Museum Book Store described a typical day in the life of my two-times Great-granduncle, Albert Roy? Yes, it's right there on page 102 in Lorle Porter's *Politics and Peril in Mount Vernon*,[39] which is chock-full of local history.

A hidden storage room in the center of the Museum also held an unpublished diary called *Buckeye Born,* written by Katherine Braddock, the daughter of one of Albert's employers in the late 1800s. Museum guide Jim Gibbons let me review the typed manuscript which described Albert's hardworking reputation for the real estate mogul, John Sellers Braddock. Although the *Politics and Peril* dates contradicted Albert's work history in Katherine Braddock's memoir, that charming diary and *Politics and Peril* were a viewfinder into my family's life during the 1800s. See more in Chapter 9.

A black, wheeled postal cart, which may have been used by my penpal-postman, Granduncle George Booker, stood next to a bright yellow car.

Believe it or not, the museum held comedian Paul Lynde's yellow Thunderbird (Figure 16). And guess what? I found an unusual connection between the Lyndes and my family. Paul's father, Hoy Lynde, was the Sheriff of Knox County, OH. He lived in Martinsburg in 1930, near politician Columbus Delano's former home, now the Mount Vernon Nazarene College. Hoy grew up for a time at 307 W. Gambier Street, where my great-grandfather, Robert Carter, was a servant in 1884. Six Degrees of Separation, eh?

Figure 16: Paul Lynde's Thunderbird at Knox Historical Museum

Visiting the Knox County Museum gave me incredible views of the place where all my maternal lines intersected. I could have spent weeks there. Instead, I left several of my family heritage books with Jim Gibson, hoping to enhance Knox County Museum's repository of Black history. I also left several of my heritage books at the Mount Vernon Public Library.

All around the outside of the building are remnants from the many factories that brought willing workers to Mount Vernon during the industrial age. Black men were given opportunities to succeed. My 2xGGF, Joseph

Booker, and great-grandfather, Otho Williams worked as machinists for Cooper-Bessemer (Figure 17). I'm standing next to equipment that might have been serviced by my Carter ancestors!

Figure 17: *Cooper's Foundry Machinery Knox Museum, OH, 2023*

A Pajama Party Gone Wild

After landing in Columbus, Ohio, in November 2023, I spent several hours at the Ohio State Archives, looking through Columbus Delano's personal letters from DC, old deed maps, and histories. Then, I drove 80 minutes east, toward Springfield. I looked forward to meeting up with second cousin JoAnn Fields, at second cousin Kenora Hogan Davis's posh home.

I had spoken with Kenora on the phone several times, and she's the one who sent me the wonderful photograph of Ella Roy on the cover of the book. JoAnn was already there. What a joyous occasion with friendly and fun family historians! We love our genealogy folks!

My cousins brought out scads of family photographs and documents, and they allowed me to photograph them for this book. We all know the importance of saving family records for future generations. But I was basically a stranger they were trusting to use the photographs with integrity. I tried to scribble their pearls of wisdom, but sometimes I videotaped the treasures they brought forth.

I finally saw a copy of Ella Roy Carter's obituary (Figure 18), a precious find I wished I could have shared with my mother.

> Obituary
>
> Mrs. Ella Carter left without parents in infancy, was adopted by the late Albert and Alice Roy, an uncle and aunt. She was born in Alexandia, Virginia, December 27, 1866 and moved to Mt. Vernon, Ohio at the age of six.
>
> On December 4, 1884 she was joined in holy wedlock with Mr. Robert Carter by Rev. Benjamin H. Lee. To this union eleven children were born. William, Alice, George, Bengamin, Roy, Robert, Charley, Bessie, Ralph, Richard, ~~~~, and Arthur. Her husband and six children preceeded her in death. Servivors are four sons Roy, Richard, Ralph, and Authur, and one daughter Mrs. Bessie Payne. Also she leaves 10 grandchildren, 18 great-grandchildren, and 2 great-great- grandchildren. She became a widow in 1909 after which she worked very hard to raise her family and proved to be a wonderful mother and grandmother. She remainded quite active up until the last two or three years.
>
> She was a member of Wayman Chapel A. M. E. Church which she had attended faithfully for every service or function from the age of six. She was a member of the Senior Stewdress Board for many many years, and also served faithfully at all church socials or suppers and in any capacity when needed.
>
> She was a charter member of the Ben Carter Post 349 American Legion Auxiliary, which bore her deceased son's name. She was the beloved Gold Star Mother and Auxiliary Chaplin, and always active and the most beloved and honored of all members. She was also a member of the Gold Star Mothers of Knox County Chapter.
>
> Mrs. Carter departed this earth, at the home of her daughter, Tuesday, August 21, 1962, at 7 a.m., at the age of 95 years, 7 months, and 24 days. She will be sadly missed by all of her relatives, friends, and neighbors who all knew her as a quiet, kindly person with a ready smile and slight nod of the head and serving her god well.

Figure 18: *Grammie Carter's Obituary, Mount Vernon, OH, 1962.*

I assumed Ella's daughter—affectionately called MomBessie—submitted the personal information for Grammie's official obituary. That long-awaited information clarified on the first line that:

> *Ella was left without parents in infancy and was adopted by Albert Roy and his wife, Alice, who were her uncle and aunt.*

But the obituary did *not* specify who Ella's parents were. Nor did it say how, when, or why Ella and her adopted parents left Alexandria for Mount Vernon, at some point in the 1870s. Most of our known family members incorrectly maintained in their online trees that Albert and Alice were Ella's blood parents, but they were not.

It would take another year of aggressive sleuthing before I could deduce who Ella's mother was (Chapter 3), and three months after that to form an educated guess about her birth father (Chapter 12).

The obituary described Grammie Carter as an active member of the Wayman African Methodist Episcopal (AME) Chapel, which *she attended from the age of six until her death in 1962.*

If those dates are correct, it could mean Ella was in Mount Vernon as early as 1872. The Reverend James A. Rawls came to Mount Vernon from Virginia in 1865, conducting worship meetings in people's homes. In 1874, he and his congregation organized as the Wayman Chapel of the African Methodist Episcopal (AME) Church. Two years after that, they erected the church building at 102 West Ohio Avenue (which, I believe, used to be called West Front Street before the terrible flood of 1913).[40] There were two churches in town that served as an important respite for Black folks who lived there as one percent of the Mount Vernon population.

That fabulous obituary indicated that Ella married Robert Carter on the fourth of December in 1884. Unfortunately, it gave no clue as to whether Robert was born in Mount Vernon. It did not spell out how the lovebirds met. There was no clear information about what transpired between their marriage ceremony and Robert's death, which left Ella a 43-year-old widow and mother of six living children by 1909.

The obituary provided a goldmine of information found nowhere else—the names of *all* Robert and Ella's eleven children. Glory be! I had originally guesstimated when the children were born from 1885 to 1908, but eventually found a Birth Record inside one of the family Bibles which contained the actual birthdates (Figure 19).

Sadly, Baby William, Alice, George, and Charlie were stillborn, or died before the 1900 Census. Benjamin/Bennie was born in 1892, followed by Roy in 1894, then Robert in 1896. Bessie was born in 1901 followed by Ralph in 1903, then Richard Albert in 1906. Last but not least was my grandfather, Arthur Taft Carter, born in 1908. (More in Chapter 15).

ELLA ROY & ROBERT CARTER'S KIDS' BIRTHS:

- William H. Carter, 4 July 1886
- Alice A. Carter, 4 Dec 1887
- George Carter, 2 Feb 1890
- Benjamin Andrew Carter, 1892
- Roy Carter, 20 March 1894
- Robert Jr. Carter, 13 Dec 1896
- Charley Carter, 27 Feb 1899
- Bessie R. Carter, 1 Feb 1901
- Ralph Carter, 8 Jun 1903
- Richard Albert Carter, Jan 1906
- Arthur T. Carter, 2 May 1908
  (Kathy Marshall's grandpa)

Figure 19: Ella & Robert Carter's Children's Births

Robert Carter's obituary was clearly a bonanza, but the time for *gathering* background documents was over. I unleashed my inner author, ready to write the secrets surrounding Grammie Ella Roy Carter, Grandpa Arthur, and the unknown generations that preceded them.

Let's learn about the prominent politician who lived in Mount Vernonio, and who employed servants named Ellie [Ella] Roy, Albert and Alice Roy, Delcenia Burris, and James Moyce.

CHAPTER 4: Life on a Sheep Ranch[41]

Thanks to the Mount Vernon Nazarene University (MVNU), I had one of the best days of my life on November 6, 2023. They requested former student and long-time MVNU archivist, Walter Baughman, to give me a tour of Columbus Delano's former LakeHome property which MVNU purchased in the 1960s. The Delano's three-story manor house now serves as the MVNU Administration Building. Walter showed me *everything* in and around the manor house, including where my family worked as live-in servants in 1880. You cannot imagine how many photos and videos I took, sharing my emotional feelings about treading where my Roy family lived and worked almost 150 years ago in videos and this book. Figure 20 shows LakeHome in 1871.

Figure 20: Columbus Delano's LakeHome Manor, Martinsburg Rd.

I saw the modern inventions built into the Delano's 1871 home, like the indoor flushing toilet, spacious tiled shower, an intercom system built into the walls, and indoor lighting throughout the house. Inventions we take for granted these days were brand-new in the 1870s, at least for rich some folks. Many of the exquisite wooden moldings and wallpaper inside the house are original.

During that experience of a lifetime, I sat in the parlor where many parties were given, and marveled at the *tiny* kitchen my family may have used to prepare small and huge meals for ordinary dinners and fancy events. I imagined a pre-teen Ella standing in the stately dining room, invisible, as the Delanos ate their meals. She must always be at the ready to get the family whatever they needed.

I assumed that Ella helped Aunt Alice cook the meals; assisted Alice's mother, Delcenia, with the washing and ironing; helped Uncle Albert with the kitchen garden out back; and cared for the Delano's young granddaughter, Ellen. I mused that Ella became proficient at reading and arithmetic by studying with the Delano's teenage grandson, George.

All of these thoughts crowded my brain as Walter toured me around the peaceful pond visible from Ella's bedroom window. He showed me the stables where the Delano's priceless Percheron horses and sheep were held. He pointed at the ice house beyond the pond, and we examined the beautiful gardens. It was more than I could imagine.

Walter also showed me around the pristine MVNU campus. My favorite place was the Achives room where I snappped dozens of photos from my smart phone, capturing snowy Christmases, balmy sunsets, and life events in the 1800s in Mount Vernon.

Everyone at MVNU bent over backward to give me one of the most memoriable experiences of my life. And guess what else? We learned that my 1976 pen pal, Granduncle George Booker, had been on staff at the college!

Please enjoy this glimpse into a different time and place, where my Roy ancestor's lived among the richest of the rich in Knox County, OH. This chapter is based on an unpublished, bare bones booklet of the first tour Columbus Delano gave to visitors from Washington, DC. I wrote it as though it happened in 1878, when my Roys may have lived there. So, relax, and enjoy a tour of the Delano's LakeHome property, led by Columbus and his wife Elizabeth, with several mention of their servants, my ancestors.

The Delanos Give a Home Tour

I've been looking forward to unveiling my good fortune with the world. It's time to show off our brand new *LakeHome Manor*, situated on Martinsburg Road about a mile from downtown Mount Vernon in Knox County, OH.

Our first guests began arriving around one o'clock to my little oasis, away from the maddening pace in Washington, DC. A slight breeze carries the fragrant scent of roses and gardenias, and the brilliant azure sky promises an outing of delightful discoveries. The distant bleating of sheep and mooing of my Hereford cows will set the stage for an unforgettable gathering.

"Welcome to our little slice of heaven! I hope you enjoy your time with us today," I greet each visitor with open arms. "I hope you had an enjoyable trip to our little burg. We've been giving tours of our modernized home since 1871 when the house was built. You took the Baltimore and Ohio railroad from Washington, DC? Some of our visitors come from the the Indian territories, others as far away as Cuba and England. As you can imagine, I know a lot of people after having been a lawyer, banker, Internal Revenue Service commander, and President Grant's Secretary of the Interior.[42]"

My wife, Elizabeth Leavenworth Delano, stands next to me. Her piercing blue eyes and auburn hair braided atop her head like a crown add three inches to her petite frame, as well as lending an air of royal exuberance. "Welcome to our home," she says, as she shakes the man's hand and gives his wife a hug. We usher our visitors through the front door into our Italianate-style mansion.

"Let me show you to your rooms and let you freshen up a bit after your long trip," she tells our out-of-state guests. When they enter the main hall, they notice the impressive staircase spindle crafted from various types of wood topped by a shiny golden horsehead symbolizing grace and strength.

Pointing at the wall, Elizabeth explains, "We imported this bamboo-inspired wallpaper from Cuba after a fascinating business trip there last year. The tropical beauty of that charming place is impossible to describe," she enthuses.

I reach over and press a tiny button on the wall. "Albert, please bring the guests' suitcases upstairs." A moment later, they hear a deep male voice respond, "Certainly. I'll be right there."

Our guests are speechless. They look at one another, then the button, then back at me. "Is that magic?" The man asks, tentatively.

I laugh. "No, it's called a speaking tube. Instead of yelling my order, I simply press the button and speak like a civilized human being. My voice can be heard on the third floor where the servants sleep, the kitchen, the pantry, and our bedroom, where the tubes are installed."

Our guests merely shake their heads in wonderment as Elizabeth guides them up the stairs. She opens a door on the second floor to reveal a spacious indoor bathroom. The room sparkles with white porcelain tiles. But the guests seem most enthralled by the flush toilet and the indoor shower—modern marvels in the 1870s and 1880s that most people could only dream about.

"You can't imagine the blessed simplicity of merely turning a handle, then feeling warm water flowing down your body, instead of waiting for servants to bring up pail after pail of heated water for a tub bath," Elizabeth explains proudly. "Eventually, these home improvements will become available to all of us in the *upper strata*."

"May we try it out later this evening?" The portly husband asks, his black handlebar moustache quivering as he speaks.

Elizabeth beams with pride. "Well, why don't you freshen up now, while we wait for everyone else to arrive? There are towels and washcloths in that cabinet over there, and there's a bar of soap on the sink. Your bedrooms are just down the hall. Let me show you. Oh, if you need anything at all, just press this button on the wall, then speak what you need. The servants will be happy to accommodate you."

"Columbus recently brought most of our servants here from Virginia. Colored people weren't generally treated well there, as I'm sure you know. We prefer to be as polite to them as we would be to anyone else." The guests glance at each other, perhaps surprised at Elizabeth's benevolence.

"Come downstairs to the parlor when you are ready. We'll have a buffet lunch for you to sample. My husband will give you the grand tour once everybody arrives.

"Oh, wait. Let me show you a feature that no property owner should be without, since you are standing right here anyway." That surely piqued their interest. A few steps away, near the top of the polished mahogany wood stairs was a door, narrower than most, but otherwise bearing the same intricate white molding as everywhere else (Figure23). Elizabeth beams as she turns the doorknob and flicks on a switch. Light from an unknown source floods the narrow opening to reveal steep stairs. "For the servants. They can go about their work almost invisibly, without disturbing us. This stairwell goes up to their quarters on the third floor, downstairs to the kitchen, then continues down to the basement where they wash and iron our clothes." The guests ooh'ed and aah'ed anew at the modernity of the house.

Servants Alice Roy and her mother, Delcenia Burris, are dressed alike in crisp, black uniforms with frilly white aprons tied around their waists, as is Alice's adopted daughter, Ella Roy. Their hair is braided in two plaits arranged on top of their tan heads, milkmaid style, to ensure no hair drops onto the feast they are busily preparing for a light lunch before the tour.

Ella shined the silver, then set the buffet table inside the dining room. She artfully arranged hors d'oeuvres on an oblong wooden platter at one end of the buffet. Luscious blueberries and sliced, home-grown apricots and peaches—picked by Ella that morning—lay next to a platter of aged and creamy cheeses from Mr. Delano's cows, Merino sheep, and goats. Ella set small, white ceramic plates imported from Belgium at the right edge of the table, along with folded white napkins and tiny forks. An assortment of crackers and breads, ice tea and lemonade completes the light lunch. Guests can sample whatever they wish before venturing on a grand tour of the property. Everything has to represent the industry of Mr. Delano's ranch.

It was nearly two o'clock. Albert finished depositing the guests' suitcases in their respective rooms for the night, and they had freshened up and dressed in casual clothes. Some were in the parlor drinking wine and enjoying Ella's hors d'oeuvres. Some sat on a leather sofa in the lavish parlor (Figure 21).

Impatient, Columbus sat in a leather chair between the black Steinway grand piano and a massive stone fireplace. He was eager to showcase his beloved LakeHome farm to his esteemed visitors.

Some guests dared touch the unusual buffalo rug in the center of the room, curious about its backstory. Delano explained, "As Secretary of the Interior, I sometimes traveled across the middle of America, through Indian Country. I joined a buffalo hunting party near Yellowstone," then he pretended to shoot a rifle toward the buffalo rug. "Then, I recommended that President Grant proclaim it as the first National Park in 1872." The female guests looked shocked, but the men looked excited.

Figure 21: Kathy Marshall in the Delano's Parlor, 2023.

"*You* mean *you* shot that beast *yourself*? What a champ!" The men punched Columbus playfully on the shoulder. One fellow even beat his chest like a gorilla. The men were jealous, wishing they had killed the beast themselves.

Other guests admired the varied and sundry artifacts the Delanos collected during their trips: cigars from Cuba, seashells and Native Indian pipes from Canada, and paintings from Europe. They even had some carved, wooden African masks. Quite the eclectic collection.

"All right, my good friends," Columbus clapped, "It's time to commence the estate tour." He strode out the front door onto the expansive south porch, then took a deep breath of fresh air, feeling a sense of pride and satisfaction as his guests surveyed the lush surroundings. He squatted, brushing his hand across the lush grass. "My gardeners meticulously maintain about fifteen acres of lawn, flowers, bushes, and trees," he said nonchalantly, casually picking a piece of grass from his fingernail as he stood up.

The women bent over to touch and smell the vibrant rhododendrons and geraniums by the front door, as their host continued. "The red and pink roses over there are a special variety from England that can withstand our cold winters; they bounce back every year, prettier than the last. The maples and ash over there"—pointing—"are especially brilliant in the fall. The mighty oak, Ohio buckeye, and hickory trees enhance the picturesque setting, don't you agree?" All heads nodded in admiration.

Columbus led the group to a small reflection pond glistening in the sunlight, home to bass and trout. An ornate gazebo stood at the east end of the pond. "This is our favorite spot for quiet reflection, reading, painting, fishing, or just napping. And sometimes the servants bring Elizabeth's bridge ladies a fine lunch in the gazebo."

A statue of a regal dog, crafted with exquisite detail, faced the house from its perch on a short peninsula in the pond. Nearby, a sundial stood as a testament to the passage of time.

A red-haired woman dressed in a hunter green dress was in awe. "It's so serene here. I could sit by this lake for hours, enjoying the ducks and birds and fish. Indeed, this *is* a little slice of heaven." Their host beamed from ear to ear.

Before the tour continued, coachman James Moyce readied several large carriages, each pulled by two handsome Percheron horses acquired from France. They were ready to transport the guests in comfort around his 300-acre farm. James's curly brown hair was contained under a black top hat, his hands sweltering in gloves that matched his black suit. But his infectious smile signaled to the guests that he enjoyed working with the horses, as well as showing them around.

Across Martinsburg Road were three impressive barns where Mr. Delano raised his prized flock of Merino sheep and goats, and a piggery supplying pork for the family's use. Nearby barns housed imported horses, showcasing his dedication to excellence in livestock management. He even served as President of the National Association of Wool Growers.

The next stop on the tour was the LakeHome Mill (Figure 22). As everyone piled out of the carriages, Columbus began extolling the virtues of his mill. "As you will soon see, this is a state-of-the-art facility." His finger started pointing as he walked the crowd through the building. "It includes a 40-barrel grist mill and an elevator. Over here, the workshop contains an eight-horsepower engine, forge, anvil, drill, saws and other tools that we need to keep the machinery running at tip-top shape.

Figure 22: Delano's LakeHome Mills Flyer from 1880.

"Our mill efficiently grinds different types of grains to feed all my livestock, plus some." Walking his guests outside, he continued. "In back, over there, is the Miller's cottage, and on the other side of the road, almost hidden among the trees, is the gardener's cottage. There are also a couple of tenant houses along the banks of the creek. Everything and everyone works together to make LakeHome a success." Columbus grinned at his tourist friends.

The final destination was the dairy barns, where Mr. Delano proudly introduced his guests to his award-winning herd of black-nosed Jersey cows. "The newspaper describes my cattle as 'the finest herd of Jerseys to be found outside of Tennessee, a testament to Mr. Delano's commitment to quality and excellence in agriculture.'" His guests clapped in response. Once the outdoor tour was over, James ensured the horses were fed, brushed, and cozied in their stalls for the evening.

In the undersized kitchen, hustle and bustle was the name of the game as Alice and Delcenia put the finishing touches on meal preparations. Everything had to be perfect. Ella ensured the table settings and chairs were spaced perfectly. The water and wine glasses stood like soldiers in perfect lines. The fresh flower centerpiece perfectly perfumed the air. The carafes of water and bottles of wine were perfectly arranged down the middle of the table. They were nearly ready for the dinner to begin.

Columbus escorted his guests back into the manor house for an intimate house tour before the grand banquet. They followed him up the stairs and into the Delano's personal bedroom. As one would imagine, it exuded an air of sophistication and comfort. Its windows, bordered by intricate white moldings (Figure 23), looked onto the manicured front lawn. Their huge bed was covered in an embroidered white quilt imported from Europe. All was as pristine as a manor house should be.

The two grandchildren's rooms were spacious and beautifully decorated, the white shelves filled with books, model ships, and stuffed animals. Columbus shared, "After making up the beds every morning, my second girl, Ella, sometimes sits in that rocking chair practicing her reading skills on our four-year-old granddaughter, Ellen. I've even caught my grandson, George, studying basic mathematics with Ella."

"Well, isn't that progressive of you to educate your Negroes," a bearded fellow said, nodding his approval and adding, "It's the Christian thing to do." Others dipped their heads in agreement, then continued exploring.

Columbus said, "Well, after all, as you know, I was the one who seconded the nomination of Abraham Lincoln for the 1860 Presidential election. And I was among his inner circle who helped convince him to sign the Emancipation Proclamation." Wagging his finger, "I believed then and still do today that it's *our* responsibility to extend benevolence to people who haven't had a fair chance in life. As you saw, I fully entrust the care of my precious horses to James. And Albert—the tall fellow with muttonchops—has demonstrated an excellent work ethic while managing my mill store. In fact, I'm thinking about financing a restaurant downtown and having him run it. His wife, Alice, and mother-in-law, Del, are whizzes in the kitchen, as you will experience tonight. Enough chit-chat. Ready to go upstairs to see the servant's quarters?" Some guests flinched, a horrified look on their faces, but they merely shook their heads. "Nobody? Well, what about going downstairs to see the modern lighting and power equipment I installed in the cellar?"

Figure 23: Typical Exquisite Woodwork at LakeHome.

A couple of fellows said, "Count me in!" The rest elected to retire to their rooms and change into evening attire, their stomachs growling for the promise of a delicious meal.

The clock neared 6:30 p.m. Some of the guests gathered in the parlor around the inviting, massive stone fireplace. Its orangey flames danced a lively polka and cast a cozy glow throughout the room. Columbus' low voice was heard throughout the house on the speaker tube system. "Time for dinner." Dressed to the nines, the guests traipsed down the stairs, or from the parlor, into the spacious dining room with hunting dogs on the foresty wallpaper. Elizabeth encouraged them to sit wherever they liked. A floor-to-ceiling picture window looked out onto the placid lake, ducks flapping their wings as the sun set. In the distance, they could see large white greenhouses which the Delanos said produced a variety of vegetables during the year. Beyond that were apple, peach, apricot, and walnut orchards.

Delano mentioned that a petite stone structure with a cupola about 100 feet from the duck pond, served as an icehouse. Albert had chopped off chunks of ice for their eating and drinking festivities and he ensured the guests' beverage needs were met.

The meal included ham from Mr. Delano's prized Berkshire hogs, potatoes with gravy, homemade blackberry jam on biscuits, peas and carrots picked that morning, and apple pie made from orchard apples planted in the early 1800s by Johnny Appleseed himself. Yes, that is a fact. With Ella's help, cooks Alice and Del brought out platters and plates and bowls of deliciousness for the guests to sample. Their hosts beamed with pride at the moans of joy and compliments their staff received.

"Don't blink, Old Man," Mount Vernon's most successful real estate mogul John Sellers Braddock said, "I might just steal your staff from you."

After the hearty supper, the guests returned to the parlor for lively discussions ranging from the complexities of politics, to the marvels of the modern innovations at the LakeHome farm.

Around 10 o'clock, the Mount Vernon locals began to leave, the spring air carrying the scent of hickory logs burning in the mansion's fireplaces. Columbus escorted them to their carriages, which James had readied. Yawning, the out-of-town folk slipped upstairs to their rooms. After ensuring the sleepover guests' comfort, Mr. and Mrs. Delano moseyed up to their bedroom, ending what had been a satisfying day.

But the staff were still busy cleaning up after the evening's revelry. Alice readied the kitchen for tomorrow's breakfast, asking Albert to make sure there was adequate bacon in the smokehouse. Del gathered the ingredients for pancakes and raisin bread rolls. Ella would be in charge of assembling the breakfast fruit plate and setting the breakfast table before the guests came down the stairs.

The servants finally gathered in their third floor living area, engaged in conversations amongst themselves, looking forward to a restful six-hour night in their cozy quarters. They would be up early in the morning to stoke the fireplaces and prepare breakfast for the overnight guests and the Delanos.

Ella walked to her bedroom, knelt to say her prayers, then nestled her lithe body under a colorful calico quilt. Her bed was positioned in front of an arched picture window which overlooked the lake. If she stared long enough, she could spy a sliver of moonlight and a few stars through the dark canopy.

This was Grammie's home as a teenager, and these were her people. Contented, she closed her eyes and dreamt about candy raining from the sky. Or maybe she floated on a big red balloon in a warm sea surrounded by shimmering fish. A glowing face peeked out from the clouds, coming closer and closer. "Mommy, is that you?"

When African Americans delve into their family histories, as my mother and I did, it is common to learn that their ancestors were not lawyers, bankers, or other professionals. Instead, they took pride in the prominent individuals for whom their ancestors worked. If your Black ancestor worked for a wealthy, renowned person, it conferred a sense of shared prestige upon you as well. In Mount Vernon, there were several affluent, notable figures like Columbus Delano, real estate mogul and bridge builder John Sellers Braddock, and C.F. Cooper and foundry which hired Black folk.

The Delano family arrived in Mount Vernon in 1808, and through sheer determination, Columbus become a lawyer, banker, then politician. He generally supported Black rights. However, as Secretary of the Interior, he allowed almost every buffalo/bison in America to be slaughtered. He allowed Native American children to be stolen from their families and forced to attend retraining schools that *killed* the Indian culture within them. His personal wealth surged during his tenure in DC from $60,000 in 1871 to $200,000 by 1875. Columbus Delano was a complex man who, on the whole, my family held in *very* high regard because he seemed to support Black folk's rights. Through association, the African American community held our Roys in high esteem.

The fact that Grammie worked for an important man like Columbus Delano seemed to answer a lot of questions. Were Ella's fine furniture and mortgage-free house connected to her employment with the Delanos?

Did Columbus Delano or his son plant the *seed* that produced Ella? Is that why he brought the Roys to his fancy sheep farm after Ella's mother died in 1874? Did Delano force 14-year-old Ella to wear that magnificent silk dress displayed on this book cover, as he performed one of his many stump speeches in the Public Square?

My family's stories about the Delanos are fraught with mystery and intrigue, to be sure, but how many of them are true? All I know is that I was blown away on my visit to LakeHome in 2023. I stood inside what may have been Ella's bedroom on the third floor, overlooking the duck pond. I imagined Ella dreaming about the mother she could barely remember. Did she wrestle with ghostly thoughts while spending her toddler years in dark places in Alexandria, while her mother toiled? (Hence, the eerie opening paragraph in the Prologue.) Data documents are critical, certainly, but it's the stories that make people want to know more about their ancestors.

And I craved to know the what and the where of Grammie's younger years. Who were her parents, and where was Ella living before she moved to Mount Vernon?

CHAPTER 5: Charting Ella's Lineage

During the first years of the 21st century, my mother's eyes lit up as we tried to find information about her father, Arthur Carter, and his mother, Ella Roy Carter. Like detectives hot on the trail of a wanted bandit, we chased every lead, determined to unveil the secrets hidden within Grammie Carter's family tree.

One sunny Saturday morning in 2006, I picked Mom up and took her to breakfast at Mimi's Louisiana-style restaurant, before bringing her to my house for a rousing day of research. Several documents lay on my black-stained Ikea table, awaiting our scrutiny. Mom said, "The name *Susan Roy* has been echoing through my memory banks. Could she be the key to unlocking Grammie's past? Look, this 1880 Census shows a Susan Roy living near Elizabeth City, in Southfield, Virginia … wherever that is."

I looked through my copy of the *North American Road Atlas Map of Virginia*. "Hmm, Elizabeth City is next to the edge of the Chesapeake Bay, near Fort Monroe."[43]

"Fort Monroe?" Mom squinted. "What does that have to do with our Roys?"

Twenty years ago, public awareness of Fort Monroe—located near present-day Hampton at the southeastern edge of Virginia—was limited. This site is notable as the location where the first Angolan Africans brought to English-speaking America arrived on the *White Lion* ship in 1619. They were indentured servants. In the following decades, chattel slavery became established throughout the English-speaking settlements that later formed the United States. In 2019, scholars marked the four-hundredth anniversary of these events at the mouth of the Chesapeake Bay.

At the beginning of the 21st century, it was not widely known that thousands of individuals seeking freedom during the Civil War, who escaped to Union-held territory, were referred to as "contrabands of war." While interpretations of this term vary, most Union Army personnel did not return these individuals to Confederate enslavers. Locations such as Fort Monroe, Freedmen's Village in present-day Arlington, and various Union camps served as places of refuge for those escaping enslavement. The classification of escapees as "contrabands of war" contributed to President Lincoln's decision to issue the Emancipation Proclamation in January 1863, which allowed approximately 180,000 Black men to serve in the United States Colored Troops (USCT). Many historians consider the contributions of USCT soldiers significant to the Union's success in the Civil War.

When my mother and I researched our family history over twenty years ago, we were unaware of these historical details. We frequently visited the local library to access early online genealogy resources, including FamilySearch.org. The name Susan Roy remained memorable because my mother believed it had relevance to our family lineage.

A Goldmine Finds Roys

In 1865, the Federal government created the Bureau of Refugees, Freedmen, and Abandoned Lands,[44] a federal agency that helped formerly enslaved people and poor Whites after the Civil War. Imagine a treasure chest overflowing with untold stories, hidden away for 150 years, just waiting to be discovered. Those "Freedmen's Bureau" records represented a treasure trove for African American genealogy.

Run by the military, the Bureau chronicled the lives of freed people for seven transformative years. This trove included marriage registers, hospital records, bank accounts, census lists, labor contracts, food and clothing rations, letters transporting people to other states for work, rental agreements for tenement housing, and much more. Compiled across fifteen states and the District of Columbia (DC), these records offer a glimpse into the lives of freedmen and freedwomen during a critical period of transition in America.

However, most people have no clue those documents existed. Those revealing military records remained largely inaccessible, hidden within the depths of the National Archives[45] since 1872. Their handwritten pages are filled with stories but lacked the organization needed for efficient research. The daunting prospect of sifting through countless documents deterred even the most determined genealogists, like me.

But a beacon of hope emerged in 2016. FamilySearch International, the world's largest genealogy organization, appointed African American Thom Reed to head a monumental effort to index[46] the Freedmen's Bureau Records. About 19,000 people volunteered to transcribe 1.8 million names of former slaves and White immigrants, from Civil War-era records, into a digital format that computers anywhere in the world could access. A genealogical wellspring!

While still under the leadership of the first Black President, Barack Obama, *FamilySearch.org* donated the digitized records to the Smithsonian National African American Museum of History and Culture in DC. My inner detective couldn't wait to search these enticing records. My fingers itched to uncover the secrets buried within. Holding my breath, I navigated to the

Smithsonian's Freedmen's Bureau Online Portal,[47] then typed **Ella Roy** into the search criteria boxes.

A record materialized on my computer screen with lightning speed, and I jumped out of my seat, snapping my fingers in triumph. The name "Ella Roy" appeared on the seventh line of the hospital record[48] in Table 1, dated 31 Dec 1866, at the "East Cap Hill Bk's [East Capitol Hill Barracks] four days after Ella's birth (Figure 24). I later learned the barracks were on the grounds of the U.S. Capitol building itself, at 8th and I Streets SE.[49] The barracks housed Union soldiers during the Civil War, and freedmen after the war ended.

Described as "Col" (colored), Ella had a sickness that warranted $1.00 in unnamed supplies. Eliza Heacock was the agent on Ella's behalf.

\multicolumn{9}{c}{1866 Freedmen's Bureau Hospital Record}
Date	Name	Residence	Race	Cause	Service	Food	Clothing	Agent
Dec 30	Charity Lewis	South	Col	—	$1.00	$1.00	$2.00	Bartlett
Dec 31	Allen Johnson	Uiontown	Col	Sickness	$2.00			JS Dore
Dec 31	ELLA ROY	East Cap Hill Bk's	Col	Sickness		$1.00		Eliza Heacock

Figure 24: Ella Roy, 31 Dec 1866 Freedmen's Bureau Hospital

I didn't know what that document meant. Superintendent? Agent? East Capitol Hill Barracks? Wouldn't "East Capitol" mean "District of Columbia (DC)" instead of Alexandria, Virginia, where Ella's Death Certificate indicated she was born? It's important to check geographic maps to understand how City and County boundaries may have changed over time.

***TIP:** Check maps from the time period you are studying. For example, county boundaries between Alexandria, the District of Columbia, and Arlington changed during this time from being independent cities or part of the Virginia Commonwealth. I learned that my search might be more fruitful in DC and Arlington rather than Alexandria as we know it today.*

A wave of excitement washed over me. This hospital record was the first potential confirmatory evidence of Ella's whereabouts a few days after her birth. But I needed more direct proof that this record was for my Ella Roy. Is it possible that Ella Roy was born here in the Freedmen's Hospital? Founded in 1862, it was the first hospital to aid in the medical treatment of the formerly enslaved. Later, it became the major hospital serving the African American community in DC. The hospital founded on the grounds of Camp Barker at 13th and R Streets in Northwest DC, was replaced by a new building in 1909 at Bryant and 6th Streets, then becoming a teaching hospital for Howard University Medical School.

For months, I presumed Ella was born at the L'Ouverture Hospital in Alexandria, because her Death Certificate said she was born in Alexandria. I researched files, walked those streets in 2024, and questioned experts. Where, exactly, were the "East Capitol Hill Barracks?" From maps of that time period, I deduced that most Freedmen's Bureau records for my family were *actually* pointing to the Freedmen's Bureau DC office, not in Alexandria. Therefore, I presume that Ella was born in the DC Freedmen's Hospital, living in the East Capitol Hill Barracks in DC, not today's City of Alexandria.

> **TIP: Understand that Freedmen's Bureau records may have been filed in offices near where your family lived. Check the Mapping the Freedmen's Bureau website for Bureau offices in the vicinity. Freedmen's Bureau offices in Alexandria and DC housed important records for my Roy/Carter families.**[50]

To address poverty and unemployment among freedmen, the Bureau designated buildings as tenements for 350 families in DC, and for 100 families in Alexandria. The moderate rent charged to freed folk was less than what they paid previous landlords for their sub-par shanties. Five hundred fifty acres near Alexandria were rented for tenements, as well as small lots in Arlington. Monthly reports provided tenants' names, occupations, family size, room numbers, rent rates, payments, and arrears. Could I find Ella's family there?

I scrutinized the 31 Dec 1866 hospital document. Surnames like Reid, Jackson, and Brown had already popped up in my DNA match lists (See Appendix B for a DNA guide), indicating we shared a common ancestor. Were those hospital roommates part of Ella's F.A.N. club, a term coined by genealogist Elizabeth Shown Mills to indicate Friends, Associates, and Neighbors: people who might be associated with your family? I looked at the lineage trees of all the people with those surnames from the hospital records. Then, I looked for DNA matches with those same names, seeking more evidence of where and with whom Ella Roy was living after birth.

TIP: Search the records of all names listed on family documents. Notice other pertinent surnames who could be Friends, Associates, and Neighbors (FAN Club) to clue you to additional records to investigate.

Intrigued by Agent Eliza Heacock's connection to Ella, I turned to Google for information about her. A simple search revealed that Heacock was not just any government agent. In 1862, famous feminist Lucretia Mott wrote to her sister that, "the Alexandria freedmen are now claiming attention and that the Association was preparing to send the **Heacock sisters** as teachers to Port Royal"[51] in **Caroline County**, VA." Little did I know at the time that Caroline County would become a research place of interest for this project.

Eliza Heacock was a Quaker champion for educating Black people. Records place her in DC around 1866. By 1868, she was teaching at the Freedmen's Village, built on Confederate General Robert E. Lee's former property (now the site of Arlington Cemetery). Discovering Eliza Heacock's nexus to Ella provided a glimpse into my future great-grandmother's early life, suggesting she was born into a community that prioritized education and uplift for people of color during the difficult post-Civil War period.

In 2024, I went back to the Smithsonian Freedmen's Bureau portal and entered "Roy" as the surname. Two hundred records appeared—too many to study! *Maybe I should more carefully review that 31 Dec 1866 hospital record for Ella Roy [NOTE: That standard date format may be read as the 31st of December in 1866].*

I clicked on the "Previous Record in the Roll" button to see if other women surnamed Roy received treatment at the hospital in December. Bingo! On 27 Dec, the day Ella was born, a colored woman named Jane Ray (or Roy) received treatment for an unnamed sickness. Her supplies and clothing totaled $3.00. The 16-17 Dec 1866 page also listed Jane Roy. Glory be! Was Jane Roy my great-great-grandmother?

TIP: Always remember that many people were illiterate before 1870, so names may have been spelled differently. Plus, latter-day transcribers may have mistyped the family name. I found our names spelled Ray as often as Roy. Research all spellings of names.

Someone named Jane Roy was housed in "Bet 21–A22 SH". Was that an abbreviation for a birthing room, or where she slept? It was different from the "East Capitol Hill Barracks" where infant Ella lived. *Wouldn't Ella's mother live in the same barracks as her newborn? Was Jane Roy the correct mom?* I searched for the Roy and Ray surnames in every hospital record in Alexandria during the December 1866 time period.

The 13–14 Dec page listed an Agnes Roy, living in the East Capitol Hill Barracks, where Ella dwelt after birth. My fingers trembled as I found Agnes Roy received clothing worth $2.62. I also discovered that Agnes Roy's agent was Eliza Heacock, the same as infant Ella Roy. Never give up the search!

Could I find more direct evidence that would solidify that Agnes Roy was Ella's mother, instead of Jane Ray? I believe so. A 22 Dec 1866 hospital record said Agnes Roy received $2.00 in groceries. She resided in the East Capitol Hill Barracks and Eliza Heacock as her agent, just like infant Ella Roy. The same barracks and agent found on multiple documents makes it more likely that Agnes *was* Ella's mother, not Jane Roy. Interesting: Agnes is described as being White on the 14 Dec 1866 hospital record (Table 1). Was that a typo or did a light-skinned Agnes give birth to a pale Ella? Later, I observed that on all other records, Agnes is described as mulatto or colored.

Date	Name	Residence	Race	Cause	Supplies	Agent
14Dec	Betsey Jackson	Gay St.	White	Health	$3.25	A.P. Black
14Dec	Emma Hoffman	E. Cap betw 9&10	White	No job	$2.50	Maggie Wright
14Dec	Julia Mack	3 St betw C&D	White	Sickness	$2.00	Maggie Wright
14Dec	Lucinda Thomas	3 St. near D	White	Old/infirm	$3.00	Maggie Wright
14Dec	**Agnes Roy**	**E. Cap Hill Barracks**	**White?**	**Sickness**	**$2.62**	**Eliza Heacock**

Table 1: Hospital Records for Residents Treated on 14 Dec 1866

Figure 25 indicates Agnes and Ella Roy were *received* into the Freedmen's Village between 1 March 1 and 27 April 1867.[52] Does this **prove that Agnes**

and Ella were close kin? Not exactly, but it simply lends more credence that it is possible they are connected.

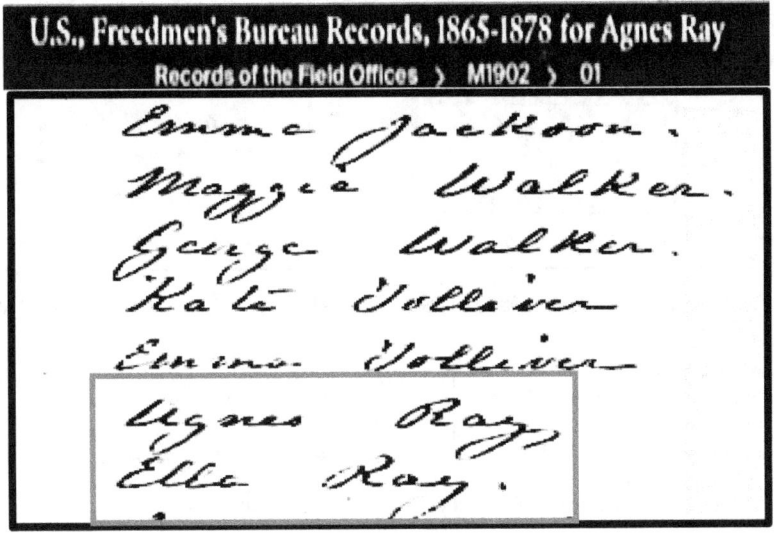

Figure 25: *Agnes and Ella Roy were received March to April 1867.*

Further, the 22 April 1867 "Record from the Field Offices" letter in Figure 26 indicated that Lydia Stull, Matron of "The Home," wrote to the Assistant Commissioner that she and Agent Eliza Heacock thought Agnes was a diligent worker and a woman of good character who would do a good job for the new employer in Boston. On 23 Apr 1867, Matron Stull "requests transportation for Agnes Roy, freedwoman, and infant child to Boston, Massachusetts." In another letter, Matron Stull says she [Agnes or Ella?] "may go with the Scott children when transportation has been obtained. I think Miss Lowell would be much pleased with her. P.S. This woman [Agnes] and her child [Ella] are now dependents of *The Home*."

Did Agnes and/or baby Ella ever travel to Boston? The bottom box in Figure 26 only shows Agnes. Why isn't infant Ella included? And, why does it say *cancelled* in tiny print? Does that mean baby Ella was sent by herself, or with the Scott family who were referenced in a previous transportation letter? The mystery thickens.

I could not find Agnes or Ella in any 1870 Census anywhere. There was a 22-year-old *white* Agnes Roy living in Boston in 1870, but she wasn't my Agnes. I was perplexed and needed to seek another tactic.

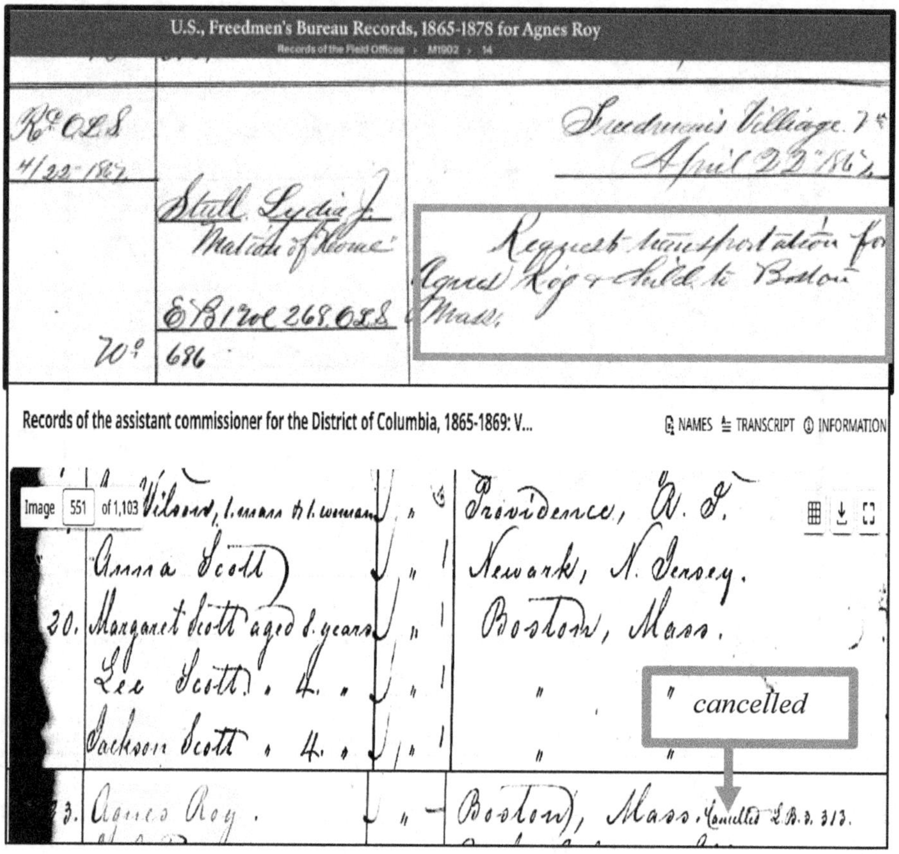

Figure 26: Transportation for Agnes & Child to Boston, 22 Apr 1867

So, now that I had a first and last name for Ella Roy's likely mother, Agnes Roy, I went back to the Smithsonian web portal and typed **Virginia** as the location, **Agnes** as the first name, and **Roy** (and also *Ray*) as the surname. Huzzah! Appearing on my computer screen was a Labor Contract between Agnes Roy *and child*, two weeks before Ella was born. (Figure 27).

The employer was Slave Trader Walker R. Millan. The original handwritten occupation on his 1860 Census said *"Slave Trader,"* but the transcriber somehow (!) mistyped *"Wagon trader"*).

TIP: Double check all transcriptions against the original handwritten information. I would have missed an important clue had I accepted the mistyped wagon trader instead of correct slave trader occupation.

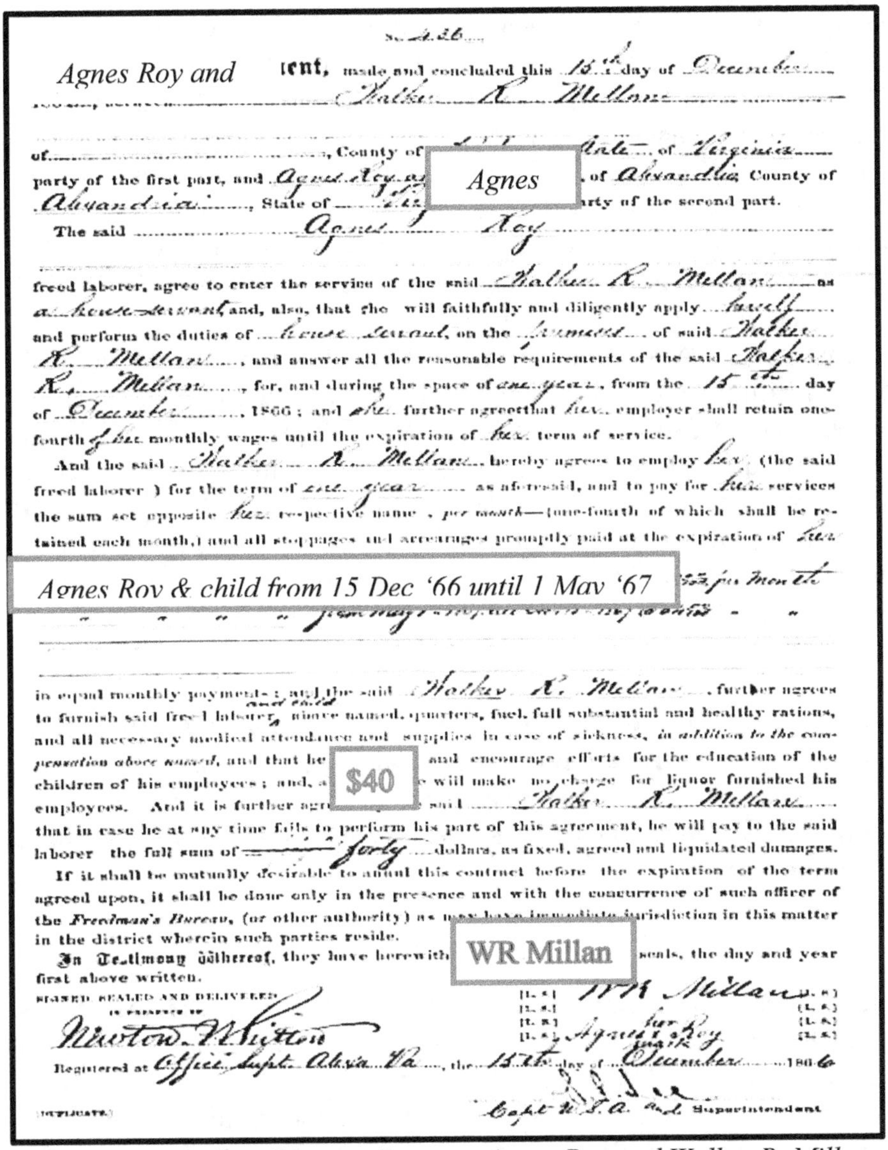

Agnes Roy and ...ent, made and concluded this 15th day of December ... Walker R. Mellan

of ..., County of ... State of Virginia party of the first part, and Agnes Roy ... Agnes ... of Alexandria County of Alexandria, State of ... party of the second part.

The said Agnes Roy

freed laborer, agree to enter the service of the said Walker R. Mellan as a house servant and, also, that she will faithfully and diligently apply herself and perform the duties of house servant on the premises of said Walker R. Mellan, and answer all the reasonable requirements of the said Walker R. Mellan, for, and during the space of one year, from the 15th day of December 1866; and she further agrees that her employer shall retain one-fourth of her monthly wages until the expiration of her term of service.

And the said Walker R. Mellan hereby agrees to employ her (the said freed laborer) for the term of one year as aforesaid, and to pay for her services the sum set opposite her respective name, per month—(one-fourth of which shall be retained each month,) and all stoppages and arrearages promptly paid at the expiration of her

Agnes Roy & child from 15 Dec '66 until 1 May '67 ... per month

" " " " from May 1 ... until 15 ... 4 dollars

in equal monthly payments; and the said Walker R. Mellan further agrees to furnish said freed laborer and child above named, quarters, fuel, full substantial and healthy rations, and all necessary medical attendance and supplies in case of sickness, *in addition to the compensation above named*, and that he ... $40 ... and encourage efforts for the education of the children of his employees; and, a... will make no charge for liquor furnished his employees. And it is further agr... said Walker R. Mellan that in case he at any time fails to perform his part of this agreement, he will pay to the said laborer the full sum of forty dollars, as fixed, agreed and liquidated damages.

If it shall be mutually desirable to annul this contract before the expiration of the term agreed upon, it shall be done only in the presence and with the concurrence of such officer of the *Freedman's Bureau*, (or other authority) as may have immediate jurisdiction in this matter in the district wherein such parties reside.

In Testimony Whereof, they have herewith ... WR Millan ... seals, the day and year first above written.

SIGNED, SEALED AND DELIVERED IN PRESENCE OF Newton Whitton

WR Millan [L. S.]

Agnes her mark Roy [L. S.]

Registered at Office Supt. Alexa. Va., the 15th day of December 1866

... Capt. V.R.C. ... Asst. Superintendent

(DUPLICATE.)

***Figure** 27: A Labor Contract Between Agnes Roy and Walker R. Millan.*

Agnes was supposed to be a house servant for the Millans, starting the 15th day of December, 1866. Agnes *and child* would earn three dollars per month. Then, from May 1, 1867, until December 15, 1867, Agnes would earn four dollars per month. The contract indicated that, "Agnes agrees her employer shall retain one fourth of her monthly wages until the expiration of her term of service. She will faithfully and diligently apply herself and **perform the duties of house servant on the premises of said Walker R. Millan.**" The contract did not specify whether "premises" meant his home in Fairfax County or his workplace at the former Slave Pen in District 6 in Alexandria, VA.

Several Freedmen's Bureau documents clearly indicate that Agnes never fulfilled the first half of the work contract with Millan. Agnes and Ella were sheltered in the Freedmen's Village at least through late April 1867. I found no evidence that Agnes and Ella ever went to Boston, nor ever actually worked for Millan. But... does the work contract insinuate that Walker Reid Millan might have been Agnes Roy's former employer/enslaver? Not necessarily, but it's a tantalizing lead to investigate.

Interesting. A similar Work Contract was also issued on 15 Dec 1866 between Millan and a laborer named Benjamin Taylor. However, Benjamin's pay was one measly dollar a month. Was Benjamin my Agnes's father, son, sibling, or husband? My stomach roiled. Some employers were rich as thieves. Yet, they paid their former slaves a mere pittance to perform the same exhaustive farming or servant duties they were forced to perform *for free* during the long period of bondage. "That really chaps my hide," as disgruntled cowboys used to say.

> ***TIP:*** *Note that some Work Contracts issued after the period of enslavement were between the former enslaver and their enslaved property. Check the land, property, and probate records of the new employer to learn whether they were a former enslaver who owned your family member.*

The Bottom Line

I am thrilled! The Freedmen's Bureau information presented in this chapter proves to my satisfaction that Agnes Roy was my future great-grandmother Ella Roy's mother.

I believe the soon-to-be-born Ella was the child referenced in Walker Millan's 15 Dec 1866 Work Contract, but I found no evidence that Agnes ever fulfilled that contract.

Further, I was unable to prove whether that Agnes or Ella were ever sent to Boston to work, according to several transportation letters from 1867.

My research plan was clear: find one more generation. But like many of us, we sometimes go down the rabbit hole to explore more possibilities. I wondered whether Agnes had any family living with her at the Freedmen's Village, and I wanted to learn what her life was like before she became pregnant with Ella.

CHAPTER 6: Alexandria, A Mother's Shadow

Glory be! I had a dark chocolate and port wine celebration at my house when Freedmen's Bureau records proved Ella Roy's mother was Agnes Roy, my two-times great-grandmother (2xGGM). I thirsted to learn more about Agnes's life before she became pregnant with Ella in March 1866.

The years between 1863 and 1865 were a tumultuous time in America, but especially in Alexandria, Virginia, which was marked by the Civil War and its aftermath. For African Americans, this period brought both immense hope and enduring challenges. Imagine the thrill of newfound freedom after decades of bondage. Yet, this newfound liberty was fragile. Its promise was often tempered by the harsh realities of a society still grappling with racial prejudice and economic inequality, like now.

Life in Alexandria provided many stark contrasts—the joy of being free on the one hand, but continued hardship on the other. As the war raged, many African Americans found work as laborers, cooks, or domestic servants, often for Union soldiers or White families. Others sought opportunities in the contraband camps throughout the American South, where they could find shelter, food, and a sense of community. Yet despite their newfound freedom, Black folk continued to face significant obstacles. Many individuals were not permitted to own property or access education due to existing discriminatory policies at the time. Segregation was the norm, limiting Black folks' access to public facilities, decent jobs and housing. Post-slavery wasn't much better than before.

Amid the challenges, a spirit of toughness, strength, and hope prevailed. African American communities formed churches, schools, and social organizations to support one another. They established businesses, bought land, and endeavored to build a better future for themselves, their families and their community. Several Black neighborhoods in Alexandria before the Civil War, included: The Berg, Colored Rosemont, The Bottoms (The Dip), Cross Canal, Fishtown, Hayti, The Hill, The Hump, and Uptown.[53]

Could I locate where Agnes Roy was living and working before she became pregnant with Ella in March or April 1866?

During a May 2024 genealogy trip, I met with several experts who helped me learn about the rich African American history in DC, Alexandria, Fairfax, and Manassas in Prince William County—nearby places where my Roys and Carters may have lived. Char McCargo Bah, creator of the reverent Contrabands and Freedmen Cemetery Memorial,[54] provided me with a <u>partial 1865 Alexandria Census</u>[55] which listed an Agnes Ray (Roy?) living in "District 6", wherever that was.

As shown in Table 2, Agnes was an enslaved resident prior to 1863, unable to read, a mulatto, and over fourteen but younger than twenty years of age.

Oh, no! Not a chart! Guess what? Statistics and history become interesting when *we* have a personal stake in their findings. Agnes Ray/Roy, was one of the 674 females living in District 6, as verified in this <u>1865 Alexandria Census</u>.

This was not a normal Census. Residents were divided by surname within District, not by address, so it's impossible to know which people were close neighbors. And because many people were still illiterate, we cannot be sure of the correct spelling of their surnames. I wondered whether William and Lucinda Row listed before Agnes Ray, were actually Roys, or just typos. Were those "Rows" from Spotsylvania or Caroline County, Virginia, as noted by our DNA matches and other Freedmen's Bureau records?

Agnes became pregnant with my great-grandmother, Ella Roy, around March 1866, but I think the information in this 1865 Census is valid for Agnes. Unfortunately, most of that invaluable Census was burnt or unavailable, so there is no complete account of Alexandria's entire colored population of 8,743 Black folks. Thankfully, the surnames starting with Q through Y were rescued from a fire, in addition to some "B" surnames. The previous chart shows Rosses, Redmonds, **Roy**als, Rows, **RAYS**, Redmons, Reynolds, and **ROYS** who were living in District 6. Oh, happy day when I spied an **Agnes Ray** in this list! (see the first shaded box in Table 2). Could she be *my* two-times great-grandmother?

I thought it interesting that most of these people were listed as mulatto, which indicates they looked like they were of mixed race. There were eleven males and ten females in the partial listing. Eight were fourteen years of age or under, seven were between 14 and 20, and six were between 20 and 50 years of age. Twelve had been enslaved prior to 1863, including Agnes, and nine were free. Eleven were *residents* of Alexandria, not *runaways*. Five were laborers. Only five could read, and the rest were illiterate. I was thrilled to have this information about part of the community in which my 2xGGM lived at the end of slavery.

Agnes Ray was listed after William and Lucinda Row in District 6. Were the Rows and Rays/Roys from the same family and, if so, had they always lived in Alexandria or did they migrate there from some other part of Virginia, Maryland or DC? I doubted that Agnes was alone in the world, so was it possible she was related to Minor, Millie, Ellen and Smith Roy who were listed at the bottom of the 1865 Census? Clues.

Was Ella's unknown father one of the 3,766 black men living in Alexandria during 1865? Or was Agnes's *Baby Daddy* the Caucasian Sheriff Walker Millan who signed a Work Contract with Agnes? Did Ella's father have the last name Roy, Ray, Row or Rowe? Were people with those names blood relations to Agnes? Am I getting closer to the truth or still spinning my wheels?

1865 Alexandria Census - "R" Surnames (Partial)

R Names [Incomplete]	Color				Sex		Age					Pre-War or Pre-1863 Status			Job		Literacy		No. of District
	Black	Mulatto	Quadroon	Octoroon	Male	Female	14 and under	Under 20, over 14	Under 50, over 20	Under 70, over 50	Over 70	Slave	Free	Resident of Alexandria Co.	Laborer	Mechanic	Able to read	Unable to read	
Ross, Benjamin		x			x		x					x						x	6
Ross, Henry		x			x		x					x						x	6
Ross, William		x			x		x						x	x	x			x	6
Redmond, Annette		x				x	x					x		x	x			x	6
Royal, Hester		x				x	x						x					x	6
Row, William		x			x			x					x					x	6
Row, Lucinda		x				x			x				x					x	6
Ray, Agnes		x				x	x					x	x					x	6
Redmond, William		x			x			x				x						x	6
Rector, John		x			x		x						x	x				x	6
Ray, Malinda	x					x		x				x						x	6
Ray, Delia	x					x	x						x	x			x	x	6
Reynolds, Lewis		x			x			x				x			x			x	6
Reynolds, Annie		x				x	x					x						x	6
Reynolds, Edward		x			x			x				x						x	6
Renolds, Ephraim		x			x				x			x		x	x			x	6
Renolds, Cynthia		x				x			x			x	x					x	6
Roy, Minor		x			x				x			x	x	x	x		x		6
Roy, Millie		x				x			x				x	x			x		6
Roy, Ellen	x					x	x						x	x			x		6
Roy, Smith	x				x		x						x	x			x		6

Table 2: "R" Surnamed Blacks in Alexandria Census, 1865.

Was Benjamin Taylor—who signed a contract with Walker Millan on 15 Dec 1866 Ella's Daddy? There were 75 Black Taylors in the 1865 Census, but none had the name Benjamin.

Could the 1865 Alexandria Census finally provide a cornucopia of answers? It is an eerie, yet beautiful thought that some of my relatives might be amongst those counted on the previous chart. *Where, exactly, was District 6 located anyway?*[56]

The Infamous District 6 in Alexandria, VA

WHAT? As I was writing this page, I accidentally clicked the 1865 Census hyperlink. The enumeration sub-District *boundaries* for Alexandria City and County appeared. District 6 encompasses the area that borders the center line of King Street to the center line of Wolfe Street ... that's where Agnes Roy was living in 1865. I couldn't visualize where that was, though. (Figure 28)

District 1	Center line of Montgomery Street to town's northern boundary
District 2	Center line of Montgomery Street to center line of Wythe Street
District 3	Center line of Wythe Street to center line of Oronoco Street
District 4	Center line of Oronoco Street to center line of Queen Street
District 5	Center line of Queen Street to center line of King Street
District 6	Center line of King Street to center line of Wolfe Street
District 7	Center line of Wolfe Street to center line of Gibbon Street
District 8	South of center line of Gibbon Street to Fairfax County line
"District 9"	All of Alexandria County outside of town limits *except* Freedmen's Village

Figure 28: Alexandria African American 1865 Census Districts.

My fingers danced over the keyboard as I Googled a map of Alexandria. I used color to illustrate the rough boundaries from descriptions on the 1865 Census link. The light yellow shading in the top quarter of the following map approximated the District 5 boundary between Queen and King Streets. **District 6 encompassed the blue shading in the center of the map, including King, Duke, and Wolfe Streets.** The bottom pink section designated District 7 as Wolfe Street to the center of Gibbon Street (Figure 29).

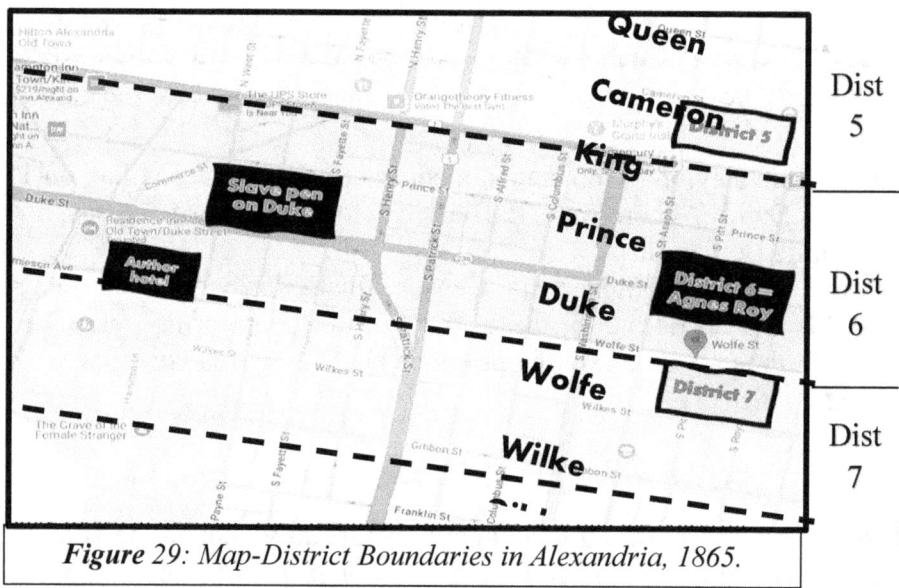

Figure 29: Map-District Boundaries in Alexandria, 1865.

"**So what?**" as esteemed genealogist, Dr. Shelley Murphy would say, prompting us to analyze what the data tell us. Here's what ...

For nine glorious days in May 2024, I stayed at the Residence Inn, two blocks from **1315 Duke Street in District 6**. That's where the aforementioned Walker Reid Millan—with whom Agnes signed a Work Contract in December 1866—may have conducted his slave trading business during the late 1850s.

When Millan joined the Confederate 4th Calvary in 1862, maybe that's when Agnes escaped from his grasp. The infamous "Slave Pen" located in District 6 was originally run by the notorious slave traders Isaac Franklin, John Armfield, and Rice Ballard, from 1828 to 1836.[57] Their horrific reign is painfully described in *The Ledger and the Chain: How Domestic Slave Traders Shaped America*, by Joshua D. Rothman. The building is now called the "Freedom House," but I still think of it as the Slave Pen, since that's what it was called when my ancestor may have worked there.

Freedmen's Bureau documents indicate Agnes Roy was living and working in Alexandria's District 6, somewhere between Wolfe and King Streets, where the Slave pen was located at 1315 Duke Street. **Perhaps** Agnes was working for, and living in Millan's living quarters above old Slave Pen-turned jail in the 1860s.

How could I prove whether Agnes had to work in that horrible place when she was enslaved? Was she prey to some man who impregnated her there without her consent? An estimated 3,750 enslaved people *were* exported from that Slave Pen to Natchez, Mississippi, and to New Orleans, Louisiana. Does my Ella have unknown siblings who died in infancy or were sold Down South from the Slave Pen[58]? (Figure 30).

Was Agnes a laundress, cook, domestic, or *breeder*? Did she suffer mental and physical abuse at the hands of Millan, or did he treat her well? Did Ella spend her first years playing in the former Slave Pen while her mother worked there? Is that why Grammie Carter resisted talking about her earliest memories? Did the ghosts of Millan's formerly enslaved victims enter Ella and Agnes' nightmares? (Hence, this Prologue's first paragraph.) I shuddered to imagine the horrors of that place where my family *may* have toiled.

In 2024, I slept at the Residence Inn in District 6, a block and a half from Millan's old Slave Pen haunt, now called the Freedom Hoouse Museum (Figure 31). I hoped my *spirited* ancestors would tap my shoulder and point me toward the corridors where they existed over 150 years ago. I wanted to breathe the air my Roy ancestors breathed, as I imagined them walking amongst the vibrant trees along Duke Street. I toured the Slave Pen Hellhole and studied the many Afro-American history tours offered in Alexandria. Are the pieces of Agnes' puzzle finally coming together?

History of 1315 Duke Street

The Franklin and Armfield Slave Pen at 1315 Duke Street was one of the largest slave trading companies in the country and is listed on the National Register of Historic Places.

The three-story brick building with mansard roof was built as the residence of Robert Young, Brigadier General of the second Militia of the District of Columbia. By 1828, it was leased by Isaac Franklin and John Armfield and used as a "Negro Jail" or slave pen for slaves being shipped from Northern Virginia to Louisiana. Franklin and Armfield were active until 1836, exporting over 3,750 slaves to cotton and sugar plantations in the Deep South. Later, other firms continued trading in slaves here. A sign seen in Civil War period photographs has the name of Price, Birch & Co. During the Civil War the building and its surrounding site were used as a military prison for deserters, the L'Ouverture Hospital for black soldiers and the barrack for contraband-slaves who fled the confederate states and sought refuge with Union troops.

Figure 30: Former Slave Pen

Figure 31: Present-Day Freedom Center Museum

The fact that an Agnes Ray lived in District 6 of Alexandria, which includes the Slave Pen, *and* she signed a Work Contract with former Slave Trader Walker Reid Millan, gives **credence to my theory that Agnes Roy worked for, and probably had been owned by Walker Millan prior to 1865.**

And ...

Walker Millan signed a Work Contract with Benjamin Taylor the same day as Agnes Roy! Was Ben related to my Agnes? Maybe a father, brother, or son?

Who Were Agnes Roy's Employers?

I don't doubt that Agnes Roy worked hard her entire life. That was always expected of Black people, whether they were enslaved or free, man, woman, or child. According to the 1865 Alexandria census, Agnes was enslaved in 1863—likely born to an enslaved mother. Thus, she likely had a boss/enslaver from her first breath. That supposes Agnes' mother had been enslaved, since the status of the woman was legally passed on to her children, according to the Virginia Law of Hereditary Slavery. In that Act, "Negro women's children to serve according to the condition of the mother," passed by the General Assembly in the session of December 1662, Virginia's colonial government attempted to better define the conditions by which people were enslaved or free. This was a reversal of the usual common law presumption that the status of the child was determined by the father. The act enabled the reproduction of one's own labor force.[59]

Shocking! Freedmen's Bureau files uncovered a disturbing letter[60] from November 1866. (Figure 32). It involved Agnes Roy, one month before Ella's birth It sounds like Agnes was working for a Mrs. DeMariel, who accused her of stealing, or losing clothing for which she was responsible. The colored schoolteacher, Mrs. Miles, confirmed the allegation. Agnes requested her wages, but Mrs. DeMariel refused to pay because of the lost clothing/property. This document indicates Agnes was working at "The Farm" at the Freedmen's Village as of September 1866, three months before Ella's birth.

Based on the complaint, I imagined that Agnes was employed as a washerwoman. Surprise and pride filled my heart at how she reacted, indignant to the accusation that she stole clothing. I imagined that someone may have set her up to be disciplined, but in the back of my mind, I wondered whether Agnes took and sold the clothes to get enough money for food. We'll never know.

The letter inferred that Agnes might "go to the courts" to get the money that was rightfully hers. Does that mean she was an assertive firecracker who would fight for her innocence? I could not find what happened to the case, except that on 22 Apr 1867, the Matron of "The Home," Lydia Stull, wrote a glowing note about Agnes to a prospective boss in Boston: *"I think Miss Lowell Would be much pleased with her."* Does that mean Agnes was declared innocent of the accusation?

> *In accordance with your instructions, I called on Mrs. DeMariel with the enclosed papers, refute referring to the case of **Agnes Roy** (cold). Ms. DeMariel reiterated her statement contained in her letter, stated September 25, 1866, enclosed herewith. Her statement is sustained by that of Mrs. Miles, the colored schoolteacher at the farm. Ms. DeMariel declares she will pay nothing more. She cannot say positively that Ms. Roy is dishonest but states that clothing in her charge and for which she was responsible was lost or stolen. I am inclined to think the difficulty about wages arose from a misunderstanding as to the terms of the agreement when it was made, a mistake not unlikely to occur under the circumstances. **I am of the opinion that if Ms. Roy resorts to the courts she will fail to establish her claim, though she doubtless considers it just, the weight of testimony is against her.** Very respectfully, your servant, B Cat. A.AG*

Figure 32: Complaint Letter Against Agnes Roy, 3 Nov 1866.

Regarding employers after enslavement, Agnes signed a Work Contract with Walker R. Millan in December 1866, but a number of Freedmen's Bureau transportation letters indicated Agnes and Ella were to be sent to Boston or *The Home*. I found no evidence one way or the other that Agnes ever worked for Millan *after* 1867. But I still wondered whether Millan had been her *former* enslaver. The 1850 and 1860 Censuses support that possibility, as revealed in Chapter 11. An unexpected Freedmen's Bureau record pointed my inquisitive brain toward a totally different place—Prince William County. Sadly, Agnes and Ella were *nowhere* to be found in 1870.

What Have We Learned About Agnes Roy?

Mulatto Agnes Roy lived in Alexandria as of the end of 1865. She was enslaved in 1863, living in District 6 between King, Duke, and Wolf Streets— the same District where the infamous Slave Pen was located where Walker Millan worked in the late 1850s (and perhaps in the 1860s). Millan may have been Agnes's former enslaver and, even though he signed a work contract with her in December 1866, she may never have actually worked for him after slavery.

CHAPTER 7: Solving the Washington DC Roy Puzzle

This genealogy project has been exhausting and inspiring at the same time. Every documented answer to a research question brought to the surface more confounding questions to investigate. I *am* covering a lot of ground, finding a plethora of documents that could prove or disprove my theories. But it's hard.

It's difficult for me to believe that Agnes Roy was taking care of newborn Ella by herself in the East Capitol Hill Barracks, or in Alexandria's District 6. I had so many questions to sleuth, like:

- Did Agnes live on her own or did her family live nearby?
- Who was Ella's father? Was he working at the Freedmen's Village, or living close by in Alexandria as of March 1866 when Ella was conceived?
- Was Ben Taylor Agnes' father, husband, brother or son?
- What happened to Agnes and Ella after 1867— the last time they were noted together in Freedmen's Bureau Records?
- Did Walker Reid Millan employ Agnes in Alexandria and/or was he her former enslaver at the Millans' extravagant Oakley plantation in Fairfax, Virginia, and/or was he her biological father or Baby Daddy?
- Did Agnes's family migrate to Alexandria during the Civil War from another place in Virginia, Maryland, District of Columbia (DC), to Ohio?

I began looking more closely at the Freedmen's Bureau records for Roys, Carters, Jacksons, Paynes, Fields, and Hackleys—people with those surnames migrated to Mount Vernon by the 1880s (Appendix C). Maybe they all came from the Freedmen's Village, barracks, The Home, DC, or Alexandria.

I spied a *Name Index to Tenement Book*[61] that noted which of the former contrabands at the Freedmen's Village would qualify for one of the tenements being built after the Civil War (Table 3). Agnes Roy/Ray is listed after someone named Clarence (?) Ray and Rebecca Ray. Are they related to our Roy family? Could Clarence (spelling?) be Ella's father, sibling, cousin or husband? Who was Rebecca Roy, listed a few names above Clarence? Were they all connected to my Agnes (and Ella) Roy?

I could not find a "Clarence Roy" or "Clemence Roy" in any indexed Freedmen's Bureau record. But I found an 1870 Census record from Richmond, VA, with a Rebecca Roy (24) living with a 55-year-old Ella Roy (Rebecca's mother?) and four other Roys. But that does not tell me much. It looks like another dead end.

I found scads of Freedmen's Bureau records with Roys in Richmond, Hampton, and Fort Monroe where the first Africans arrived in 1619, but I could not determine their kinship with my family.

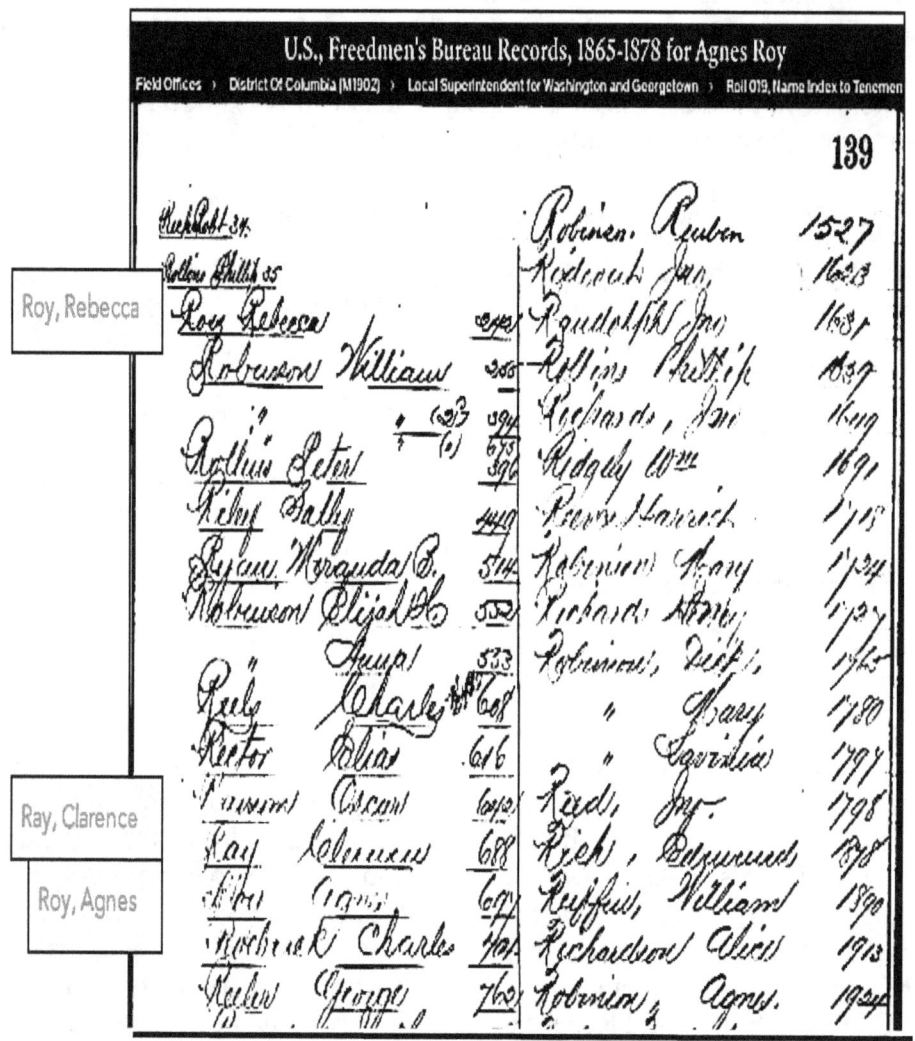

Table 3: *Freedmen's Bureau Name Index to Tenement Book.*

TIP: Check all names on documents surrounding your family to learn whether they are relatives or friends whose records should be examined.

Can We Find More of Agnes's Family?

I met my first mandate to find Ella's mother—Agnes Roy—but I hoped to find more of her Roy ancestors. My 2xGGM Agnes and 1xGGM Ella Roy were living in the East Capitol Hill Barracks in 1866 and 1867. I theorized that Agnes was not in Alexandria or the Freedmen's Village by herself. Perhaps her parents or other relatives lived with or near Agnes in DC or Virginia.

My first go-to genealogy resource is normally the Census. So, I looked for women named Agnes and people with the surname Roy in DC. Can you believe what I found!

An 1870 Census[62] located a 75-year-old Peter Roy in DC's Ward 6. Living with him were his wife AGNIS (60), daughters Lucey (22), Ella (no transcribed age), Lousa (12), and son Jesse (18), as shown in Figure 33. Could that Agnis born in 1810 be the mother of my 2xGGM Agnes, born in 1847? Boy, oh boy, was I excited to find more possibilities!

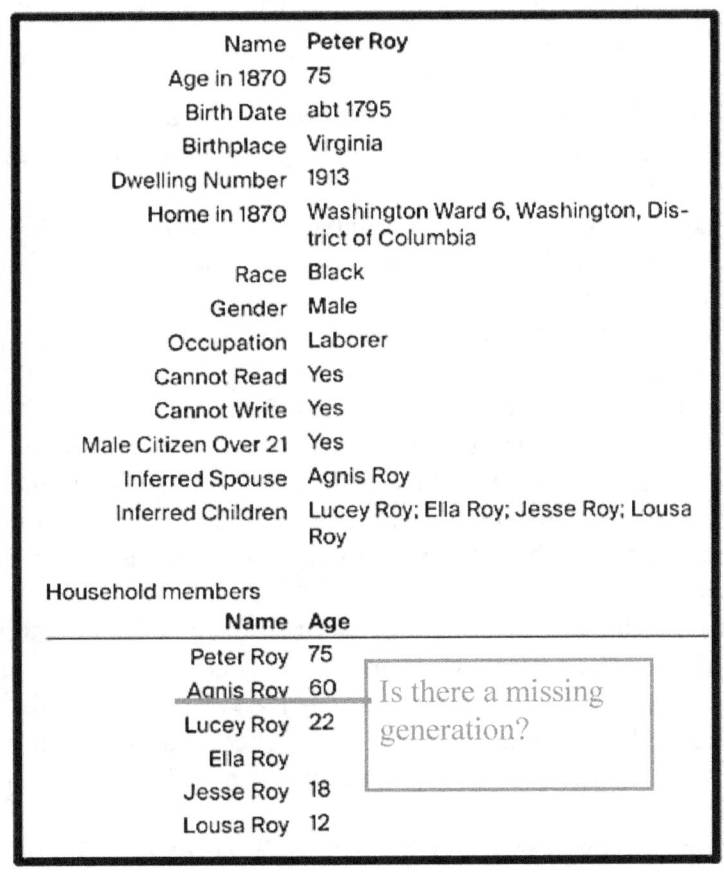

Figure 33: Roys in DC in 1870 Census.

NOTE: I shall continue to spell DC Peter Roy's wife who was born around 1810 as AgnIs, to differentiate her from my 2xGGM, AgnEs Roy who was born around 1847.

I had not planned to search for more generations than Ella Roy's parents in this book project, but I felt *so close* to finding more relationships that I jumped headfirst into the rabbit hole to find more relatives. Discovering someone named Ella and Agnis Roy in the same household with these DC Roys certainly was worth drooling over. Especially since I couldn't find my four-year-old Ella anywhere else in Virginia or DC in 1870.

But this revelation was confounding. Most of my DNA relative's trees indicated that Peter Roy's wife was Matilda, not Agnes, and they lived in Manassas, Prince William County (PWC), VA. Were these DC Roys related to me and my DNA matches in Manassas? Upon closer inspection of the original handwritten 1870 Census, I learned that the Ella in the 1795 Peter Roy's family unit was 20 years old and working as a servant. So, she was *not* my four-year-old Ella Roy living with her great-grandparents as I had hoped. Heavy sigh.

Keep your spirits up, Kathy. You have only scratched the surface of this ancestral puzzle. You've got to determine whether or not DC politician Columbus Delano came into contact with your family while they lived in DC. Now, get to work!

My 2xGGM Agnes Roy would have been about 23 by 1870, a year older Lucy Roy. It is *plausible* my Agnes Roy was Peter and Agnis's daughter, and that my four-year-old Ella was their granddaughter.

But it's important to consider every possible angle. Where were my Agnes and Ella living in 1870 if not with Peter Roy in DC or at the Freedmen's Village? Was Agnes working for Walker Reid Millan in 1870 at his family home in Fairfax, VA? Or, was she working at the former Slave Pen on Duke Street in Alexandria? Or, was she cleaning, washing, or cooking for Columbus Delano in DC? Or, was she playing homemaker for Ella's unnamed Daddy? This led me on a mad chase for more evidentiary records for my *black ancestor detective* arsenal.

Thank goodness for DC City Directories. I found Roys residing in the DC from 1865 to 1887. From 1865 to 1870, Black folk were listed as col'd (colored) in the DC Directories. Then, in 1871, the individuals listed with an asterisk were Black people. A Peter Roy worked as a sawyer in 1865, a laborer in 1869, a shoemaker in 1870, and a laborer in 1871. Were they all the same Peter? My Peter Roy?

An Agnes Roy was listed in 1871 as a servant at "1306 C Street nw" (northwest). Was that record for Peter's 61-year-old wife, Agnis, or my

2xGGM Agnes Roy? Wouldn't Peter and Agnis Chew Roy be living in the same place? Prior to 1870, the City Directory rarely listed wives' names if they were *merely* housekeepers. Therefore, I believe the Agnes listed as a servant in 1871 was Peter's daughter, a live-in servant at 1306 C nw (Figure 34).

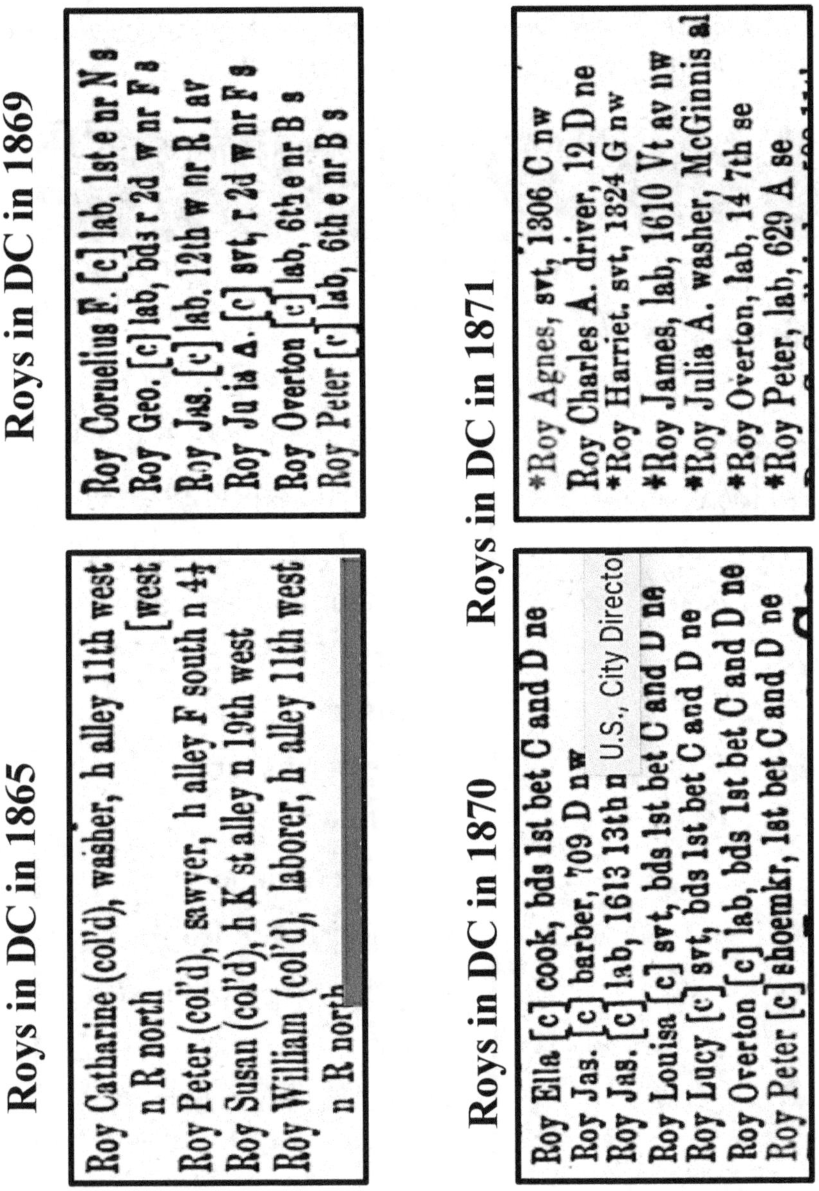

Roys in DC in 1865

Roy Catharine (col'd), washer, h alley 11th west n R north
Roy Peter (col'd), sawyer, h alley F south n 4½ [west
Roy Susan (col'd), h K st alley n 19th west
Roy William (col'd), laborer, h alley 11th west n R north

Roys in DC in 1869

Roy Cornelius F. [c] lab, 1st e nr N s
Roy Geo. [c] lab, bds r 2d w nr F s
Roy Jas. [c] lab, 12th w nr R I av
Roy Julia A. [c] svt, r 2d w nr F s
Roy Overton [c] lab, 6th e nr B s
Roy Peter [c] lab, 6th e nr B s

Roys in DC in 1870

Roy Ella [c] cook, bds 1st bet C and D ne
Roy Jas. [c] barber, 709 D nw
Roy Jas. [c] lab, 1613 13th n U.S., City Directo
Roy Louisa [c] svt, bds 1st bet C and D ne
Roy Lucy [c] svt, bds 1st bet C and D ne
Roy Overton [c] lab, bds 1st bet C and D ne
Roy Peter [c] shoemkr, 1st bet C and D ne

Roys in DC in 1871

*Roy Agnes, svt, 1306 C nw
Roy Charles A. driver, 12 D ne
*Roy Harriet, svt, 1824 G nw
*Roy James, lab, 1610 Vt av nw
*Roy Julia A. washer, McGinnis al
*Roy Overton, lab, 14 7th se
*Roy Peter, lab, 629 A se

Figure 34: Roys in DC City Directories in 1865, 1869, 1870 & 1871.

Next, I checked Freedman's Bureau Bank Records. As shown in Figure 35, Peter's daughter, Lucy Roy (22), recorded a bank record in Washington, DC on 29 April 1871. The record validated that Lucy was born in 1849 in Spotsylvania, VA, from which several of our Roy DNA matches' family came. Those Spotsylvania Roys migrated to DC, Alexandria, and Manassas.

Oh my! Poor Lucy was a widow at age 22. I wondered who her husband was. It doesn't look like they had any children.

NOTE: This record clearly states that Peter and Aga (Agnis) Roy were Lucy Roy's father and mother, not her grandparents.

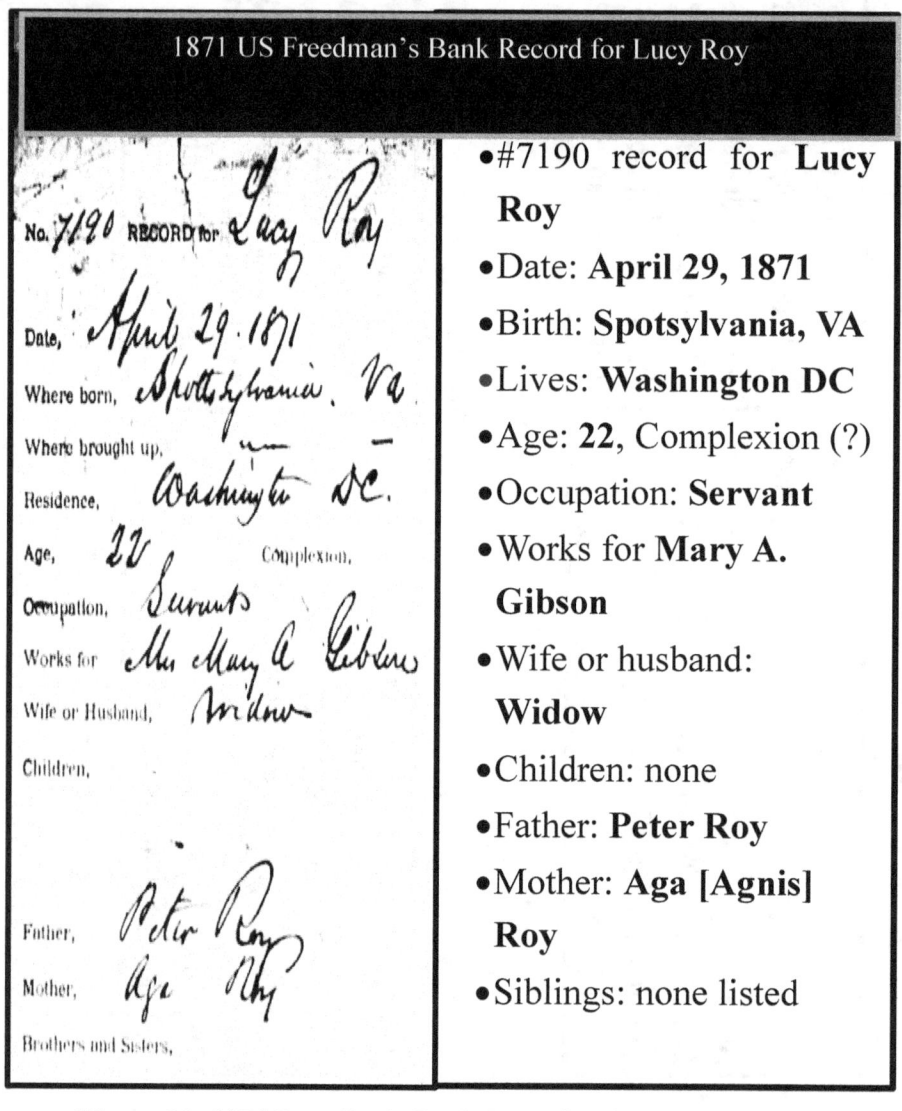

Figure 35: 1871 Lucy Roy's Bank Record with Peter & Aga Roy.

Lucy's father was listed as Peter Roy and her mother as Aga, which is a nickname for Agnis/Agnes.

I loved seeing that Lucy signed her own name on the bank record, indicating she could read and write.

This document suggests it is *possible* the Peter Roy family living in DC in 1870 was related to Roys who migrated from Spotsylvania, VA.

This bank record offered more celebrate-with-port-wine surprises!

> **TIP: Freedmen's Bureau Bank records often contain information about the account owner's birthplace, residence, age, occupation, employer, marital status, children, father, mother, brothers and sisters.**

Who Was Mary A. Gibson?

Lucy Roy's 1871 Bank Record stated she was a servant for Mrs. Mary A. Gibson. When trying to find out exactly where Mary lived, I came across a beyond-thrilling piece of information. According to the <u>Congressional Record #5510</u>–House, 12 June 1871, the Committee on Invalid Pensions was referred the bill (H.R. 7247) to increase the pension of Mary A. Gibson. She was the widow of Commander William Gibson, US Navy, who died in 1887. Mary had been receiving a $30 per month pension ever since, but she requested her pension be increased to $50 due[63] to her husband's bravery and service to the country. The precise wording of the bill follows:

*Be it enacted, etc., that the secretary of the interior [who was **Columbus Delano**] be, and he is hereby, authorized and directed to place upon the pension roll, subject to the provisions and limitations of the pension laws, the name of Mary A. Gibson, widow of Commander William Gibson, United States Navy, and pay her a pension of $50 per month from and after the passage of this act; and this pension shall be in lieu of what she is now receiving.*

Why is this a fantastic find? Columbus Delano was Commissioner of the *Internal Revenue Service* (IRS) until 1870. Then, President Grant appointed him as the US Secretary of the Interior until 1875. I read 400 of Delano's personal letters and his public biography suggests he sometimes bent the rules for his friends and acquaintances. That's precisely why his cousin, President Grant, requested Delano to step down from his post in 1875.

I wonder if Delano was personal friends with Mary Gibson or her family members. Did they run in the same social circles? Did Delano or his wife ever come to Mary's house and, if so, could he have met servant Lucy? Was Agnes ever at Mary Gibson's helping to clean or working for mary's friends? Is it possible that Agnes came in contact with Delano when her daughter Ella was four or five years old when Agnes Roy was living or working at 1306 C Street NW in 1871? I think so.

Did We Prove a Roy Nexus to Columbus Delano?

The 1871 DC City Directory indicated that Columbus Delano was the Secretary of the Interior—his address was "cor K and 12th nw." Does that mean his building was at the corner of K Street and 12th Street northwest (Figure 36)?

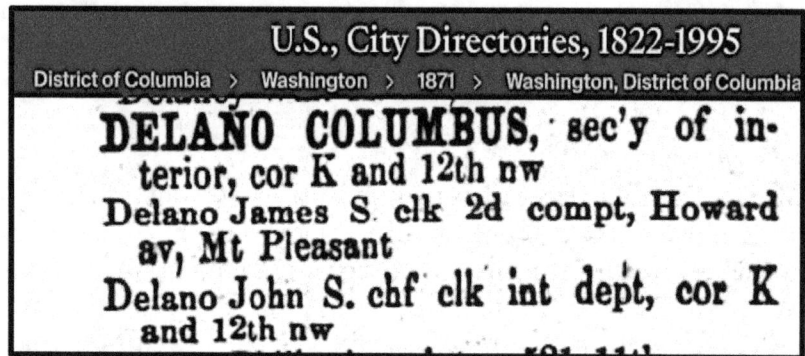

Figure 36: DC Directory for Columbus Delano in 1871

I am a visual person so I needed to see all these addresses on a map. Was it within the realm of possibility that my Roys—especially Agnes—could have come into contact with the Delano family in DC? The map in Figure 37 approximates where my Roy family and Columbus Delano were living or working in DC in 1871.

The streets in Washington, DC are divided into quadrants—northwest, northeast, southwest, and southeast—with the Capitol Building roughly in the center. For example, "A" Avenue (the encircled #2 on the map would be closest to the Capitol, and "Y" (past the #6 circle) would be the farthest away. I identified how close the Roys (circles #1 to #6) were to Delanos (circle #7) on the map.

According to the "Ward 6 Heritage Guide," the US Department of the Interior [where Columbus Delano worked between 1870 and 1875], was located in DC's Ward 6. It includes the Anacostia and Potomac rivers and is home to many historic districts, including Capitol Hill, and Mount Vernon Triangle.[64] Peter Roy, his wife Agnis/Aga, their children, and my Agnes Roy's family lived in Ward 6 in 1870-71.

Figure 37: Map-Proximity of Roys to Columbus Delano in DC: 1871

For example, Circle #1 includes people named **Ella** (cook), Louisa (servant), **Lucy** (servant), Overton (laborer), and **Peter** (shoemaker). Hmm. An Overton Roy married Jane Grimes in 1867. I found Overtons in Spotsylvania.

Circle #3 contains Agnes Roy and Harriet Roy in 1871 and

Circle #7 was where Delano worked in 1871 (12th & K nw), which is about 12 blocks away. Definitely within walking distance.

The map helped me visually assess that it *was* possible that my Roys were in direct contact with Columbus Delano in DC. Now I know that my theory has legs. It is certainly *possible* that Columbus Delano had a connection to my Roys, and brought them to his home in Mount Vernon, when he left DC in 1875. Note: His manor house was built in Mount Vernon in 1871, so, theoretically, he could have brought the Roy to Mount Vernon before 1875.

Truthfully, I found no direct evidence that my Roys arrived in Mount Vernon before 1880, only suppositions that somehow the Albert and Alice and Delcenia may have hooked up with Agnes and Ella and Columbus Delano. My mother's story about Delano bringing her Roys to Mount Vernon is plausible. The story about a genetic relationship to the Delano's is less clear.

A Tangled Web of Roys in Virginia and DC

Peter Roy seems to be a common ancestor name, passed down through generations of our DNA matches' family trees. The Peter Roy found living in DC from 1865 to 1880 was born in 1790 or 1795. A Freedmen's Bureau record said he married a woman named Agnis Chew in 1827 in Spotsylvania, VA, about 60 miles southeast of DC. That Agnis was born around 1810. Now, this is where it gets tricky …

As already mentioned, several DNA matches to our family's super-testers note a Peter Roy in their trees. That Peter was born between 1805 and 1814, and he married someone named Matilda. Table 4 compares the Peter and Agnis/Agnis Chew ancestral couples in Washington DC. Table 5 shows the Peter Roy and Matilda ancestral couple in Spotsylvania, VA.

In 1871, the elder Peter Roy lived near what is now the intersection of 6th Street southeast and Independence Avenue in DC (circle #1). Peter and Matilda and several other Roys were listed on an 1862 list of **runaway slaves** from enslaver Nancy Rowe in Spotsylvania County, Virginia, which is about 35 miles south of DC (See Chapter 8). Little pieces of the puzzle are starting to come together.

I plugged "Roys born in Alexandria, Virginia between 1800 and 1880" into DNA matching programs like Ancestry.com, and FamilySearch.org's full-search text editor, to learn out where our Roy name came from. I tried to find Agnes and Albert's slave owner(s) with a Roy/Ray/Rowe last name, but I had little luck *proving* where our Roy name came from.

Our DNA matches with a Peter and Matilda Roy ancestral couple also had a son named Joseph Roy who married Hattie Moore. I wondered if that Joseph was Albert and Agnes's brother, or first cousin who lived in 1870 Manassas. Their birth and death dates varied, but most matches said Peter and Matilda were born in between 1805 and 1814 and died after 1880.

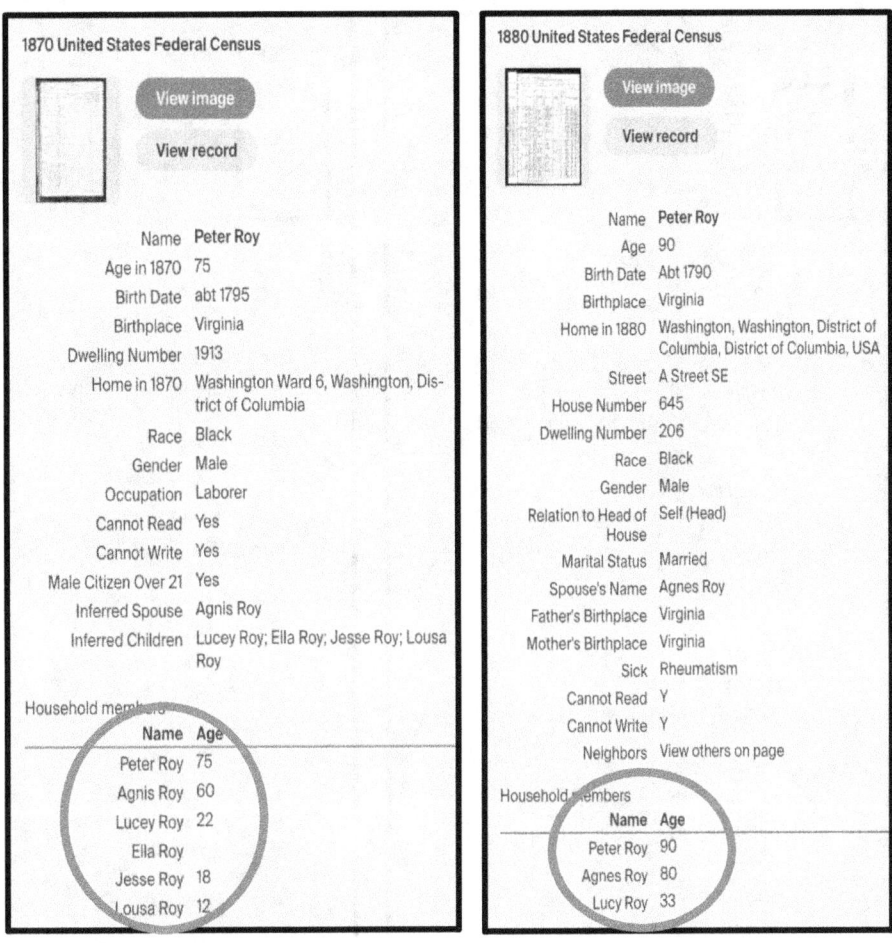

Table 4: Peter Roys in 1870 and 1880 in DC and Spotsylvania, VA.

None of those matches contained an Agnes or Albert Roy in their trees. Darn!

Joseph and Hattie Roy named one of their kids *Albert* William Roy, another *Agnes*, *Nellie* and *Mellie* (similar to Ella/Ellie), and another *Alice* (Albert's wife). So, it seems likely their Roy family was somehow connected to mine. Yet we have several DNA matches who have Peter Roy and Matilda from Spotsylvania and DC, and we and a fellow named Tony G. have Peter Roy and Agnes Chew from DC, as shown in Table 5. So, those Roys *may* be related to my family.

Confusion reigns! In all cases, except my family and Tony G., Peter Roy's wife is always listed as Matilda and they were from Spotsylvania, VA. In my and Tony's trees, though, numerous documents in DC confirm that Peter's wife was Agnis (or Aga, or Agnes, or Susan Agnes). Chapter 8 attempts to sort out these important relationships.

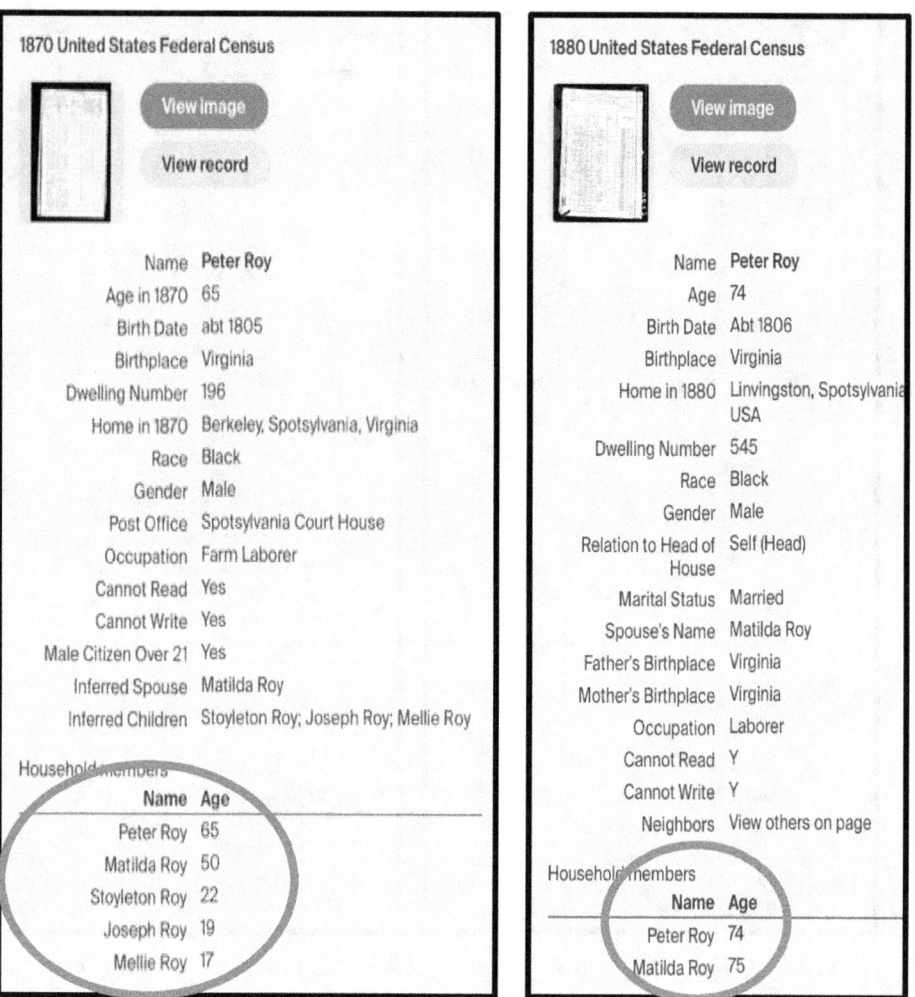

Table 5: Peter Roys in 1870 and 1880 in Spotsylvania, VA.

A Long-Lost Brother Surfaces

The magnanimous Freedmen's Bureau repository delivered a sweet gift which unleashed a plethora of answers, as well as additional questions about our Roy family. A 1853-1911 Virginia Death Register found an 1874 death record for an Agnes Roy who was born in 1847 (Figure 38). She was a 27-year old unmarried farmer who died from consumption. Her parents and birthplace were listed as *unknown*. Is that because she was sold as a youngster and never knew her parents? Or was it that whoever provided the death information knew nothing of her parentage? Or maybe it was simply politically incorrect to tell tales about a possible White father and Black mother?

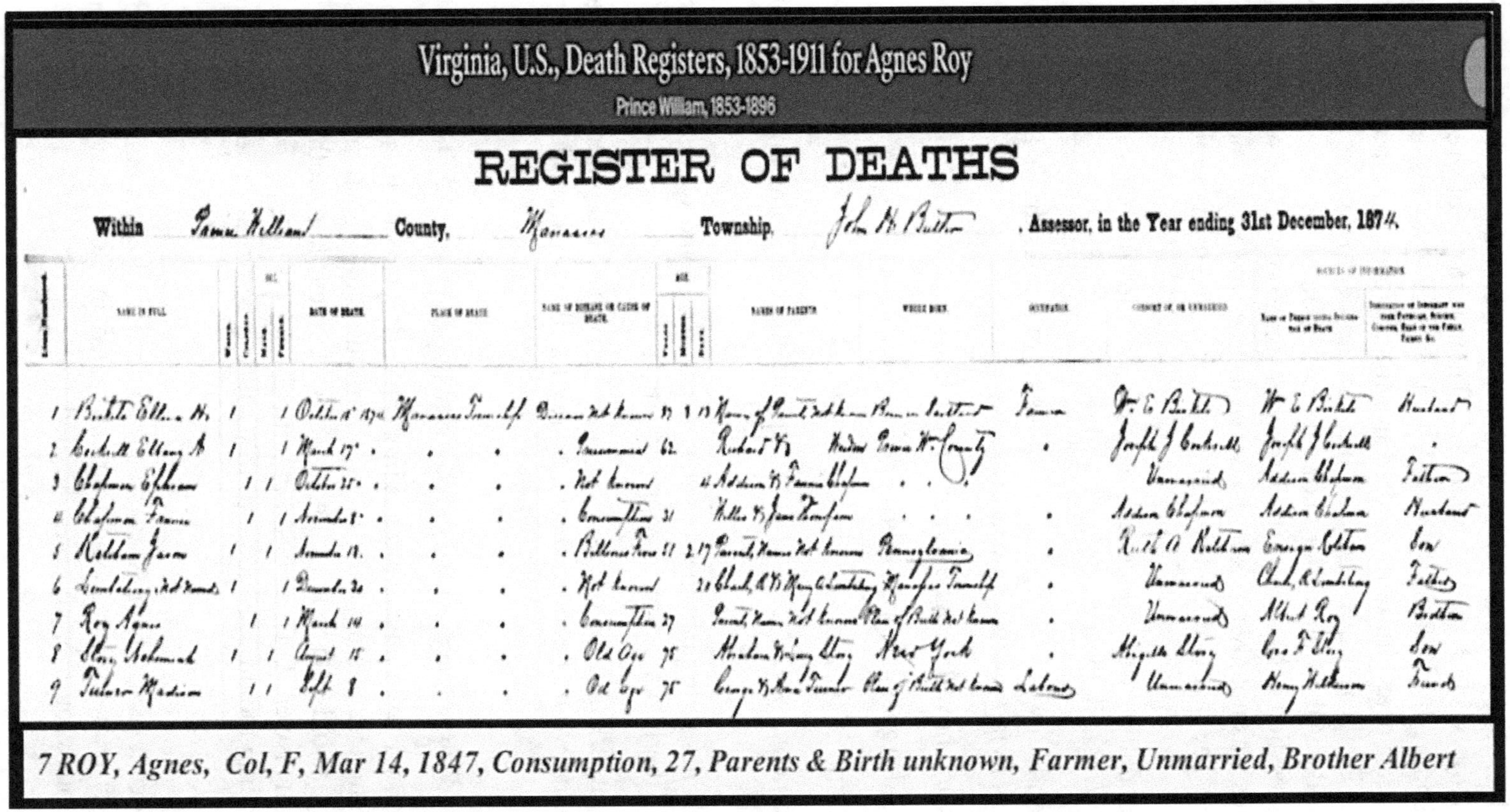

Figure 38: 1874 Manassas Death Register for Agnes Roy

7 ROY, Agnes, Col, F, Mar 14, 1847, Consumption, 27, Parents & Birth unknown, Farmer, Unmarried, Brother Albert

The brightest spot on that Prince William County Death Record verified that **Albert Roy was Agnes's brother!** That factoid cleared up a family misconception that Albert Roy was Ella's father, because she seemed to have lived with, or near him until he died in Mount Vernon. Nope. Albert took on the role of Ella Roy's guardian, just like my mother told me so many years ago. But *when* did Albert take charge of Ella? As soon as she was born in 1866 or when Agnes died in Manassas in 1874, or at some point in between those dates?

Agnes was not always a house servant, like Millan's 1866 Work Contract suggested. The fact that Agnes died a farmer raised many more questions:

- Why and how was Agnes in Manassas 39 miles from her former residence at *The Home* in the Freedmen's Village?

- Why and how did she end up 35 miles from Alexandria's District 6 where she was living when Ella was conceived?

- When and how did Agnes migrate to Manassas by 1874?

- Why did Agnes become a farmer?

- What kind of farming did she do and with whom?

- Did someone give Agnes land or was she sharecropping and, if so, for whom?

- Was Agnes living near her brother, Albert Roy, who was a farmer, likely at the Liberia plantation in Manassas in 1870?

- Most importantly, who was taking care of Agnes' daughter, child Ella Roy, who would become known by my family as Grammie Carter?

Where was Ella Roy Between 1868 and 1874?

The search for solid answers regarding the early years of Ella Roy has proven to be a complex and elusive journey. In particular, the question of where seven- or eight-year-old Ella was living in 1874, the year her mother passed away, remains unanswered. This period is critical not only to Ella's story but also to understanding the broader context of her family dynamics and connections.

Another death record from Manassas revealed that Joseph and Hattie Roy had a baby girl named Agnes who tragically died in 1875, just shy of her first birthday, one year after my 2xGGM died.

Further exploration of Joseph and Hattie's lineage revealed that they had another child, a son named Albert, likely named after his Uncle Albert. By 1900, young Albert was residing in Mount Vernonio, alongside his Uncle Albert, Aunt Alice, and cousin Ella Roy. This familial gathering illustrates the continuous thread of connection among the Roy family members in Virginia and Mount Vernon, emphasizing the importance of these ties in understanding Ella's life and heritage.

Another child of Joseph and Hattie was named Alice, presumably honoring Albert Roy's wife. These connections are pivotal as they serve as paper trail evidence that the PWC Roy family is likely related to my ancestors: Agnes, Albert, Alice, and Ella Roy. Such familial links are crucial in piecing together the puzzle of Ella's lineage and her place within this intricate family network.

However, despite these discoveries, the mystery surrounding Ella Roy's whereabouts between 1868 and her mother's death in 1874 remained unresolved.

Was Agnes farming alongside Albert, but simply went unrecorded in the 1870 Manassas Census? Were Agnes and Ella living with the William Jackson family who lived in Manassas? The lack of confirmatory documentation leaves many unanswered questions regarding Ella's formative years and her family's circumstances of that time.

Given the fragmented nature of historical records, it seems plausible that Albert and Alice took responsibility for baby Ella during her infancy, as suggested by Ella's obituary. This theory not only highlights the potential support system within the family but also underscores the enduring bonds that were likely crucial to Ella's upbringing amidst the challenges faced by her family.

In conclusion, the quest to understand Ella Roy's early years reveals a tapestry woven with familial connections, heartache, and resilience. While many questions remain unanswered, each piece of information gathered strengthens the narrative of her life and the legacy of her family.

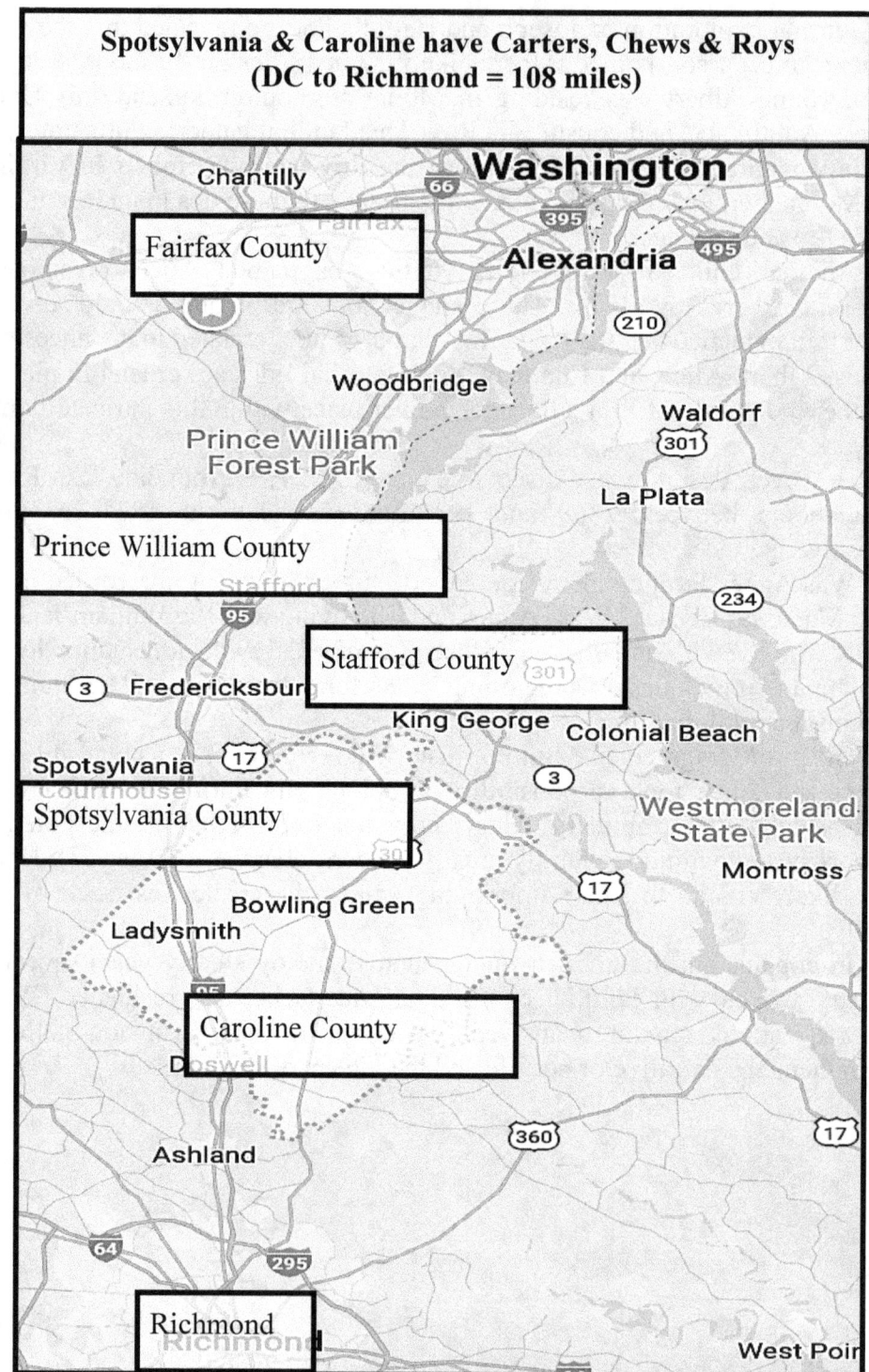

Figure 39: Map of Pertinent Virginia Counties.

CHAPTER 8: Tidewater Trio of Spotsylvania, Caroline & Stafford

Several Freedmen's Bureau records indicated that my Roys came from Spotsylvania and Caroline Counties, but I had no idea where those places were. So, I developed a simple map. Figure 39 highlights Spotsylvania, Caroline, Prince William, and Fairfax Counties, all of which are located near Washington, D.C., and Alexandria to the north, and Richmond to the south. According to Freedmen's Bureau and Bank Records, it appears that Peter Roy and Agnes Chew originated from Caroline and Spotsylvania Counties. This leads to an interesting question: Did the Carters, Roys, and Chews know each other before they all ended up in Freedmen's Village around 1865-66?

To dig deeper, I decided to look at family trees that included people with the surnames Carter, Roy, and Chew from Caroline County. You won't believe my reaction when I discovered that a White woman named Judith Carter had a father named John Carter and a mother named Hannah Beverly *Chew*, born in 1736 in Spotsylvania! It's important to note that enslaved individuals often took on the last names of their enslavers. Were Agnis Chew's blood relatives owned by Chew enslavers? I suspected that Peter Roy and Agnes Chew were likely Ella's grandparents or great-grandparents, but I still need to figure out how and why they made their way to freedom in Washington, DC by 1871.

The 1870 Census turned out to be a treasure trove of information. I compiled all the residents from Spotsylvania County into a spreadsheet, sorting them by surname: orange for Roys, red for Jacksons, and blue for Robinsons. By re-sorting the data by household number, I could identify close neighbors—though they might not have lived right next to each other, they were certainly in proximity. Table 5 highlights the most relevant names I found.

While examining the census, I looked for friends, associates, and neighbors who might have married into our family. For instance, the Paynes were living near the Roys in 1870 and later married Carters. In our DNA match lists, the Robinsons and Gaskins were also closely linked to the Roys in Manassas.

Additionally, a woman named Sarah Stapleton shares a first name with one of our distant Roy ancestors. All these surnames seem to connect in Spotsylvania, and I'm eager to prove or disprove whether they migrated together to DC and/or Prince William County.

I also noticed the surname Jackson appearing frequently in our DNA matches.

Tracking the Enslavers

What about the enslavers? Elliott and Joseph DeJarnette are listed on the top white line of Table 6 They were farmers worth $35,000 ($350,000 in 2025 dollars) and they lived *very* close to my Roys.

1870 SPOTSYLVANIA COUNTY CENSUS

29	195	196	Dejarnette	Elliott H	31	1839	Male	White	Farmer	20000	900
4	199	200	Dejarnette	Joseph S	45	1825	Male	White	Farmer	15000	800
20	72	73	Jackson	Thomas	50	1820	Male	Black	Farm Laborer	500	100
21	72	73	Jackson	Mary	45	1825	Female	Black	Keeping House		
23	14	14	Lewis	Millie	21	1849	Female	Mulatto	Servant		
4	51	52	Lewis	Emma	43	1827	Female	Black	Keeping House		
8	192	193	Payne	Agnes	24	1846	Female	White	At Home		
11	192	193	Payne	Albert S	19	1851	Male	White	Farm Laborer		
12	192	193	Payne	Jackson	15	1855	Male	White	At Home		
16	79	80	Roy	Ann	28	1842	Female	Black	Keeping House		
17	79	80	Roy	Hawes	4/12		Male	Black			
34	196	197	Roy	Peter	65	1805	Male	Black	Farm Laborer		
35	196	197	Roy	Matilda	50	1820	Female	Black	Keeping House		
36	196	197	Roy	Stoyleton	22	1848	Male	Black	Farm Laborer		
37	196	197	Roy	Joseph	19	1851	Male	Black	Farm Laborer		
38	196	197	Roy	Mellie	17	1853	Female	Black	At Home		
10	69	70	Robinson	Sarah	60	1810	Female	White	Farmer	960	200
14	69	70	Robinson	James	30	1840	Male	White	Farm Laborer		
28	242	244	Stapleton	Sarah	24	1846	Female	Black	Keeping House		
1	198	199	Ware	Clara	35	1835	Female	Black	Domestic Sent		

***Table 6**: "FAN Club" Data in the 1870 Spotsylvania, VA, Census.*

Brother Elliott owned 2200 acres of land and 500 enslaved persons to work his 875 acres in Spotsylvania. Their "Pine Grove Forest" plantation house features colonial architecture with Corinthian columns flanking the front and rear porches. Their 20 rooms included a basement, first, and second floors. Like most large homes, their kitchen was located about 50 feet from the main house to reduce the chance of fire in the main house. The manor house sat on a hill, with spacious grounds surrounded by large oak, walnut, and hickory trees.

Elliott Dejarnette was one of the most wealthy men in that section of Virginia, according to the *Fredericksburg Star* newspaper in 1888. I imagined countless Black and White feet trudging up and down the stone steps during a hundred years of its existence. Did the Dejarnettes enslave my Roys?

What's this? The 1860 Census contained William and Mildred WALLER who owned 119 slaves. Their Waller ancestors were colorfully described in Alex Haley's blockbuster book *Roots, the Saga of an American Family* (1976). It became the first TV miniseries in 1977, showing the world the horrific truth of American slavery. We gasped, cringed, cried, yelled, and cursed the exceptionally cruel Waller's treatment of stolen-from-Africa teenager, Kunta Kinte, in 1767.

Waller descendants were listed a couple Census pages before the DeJarnettes in the 1870 Census, close to Black Roys, Carters and Chews. And yes, I did find several fourth cousins who matched my supertester's DNA and who descended from Wallers in Spotsylvania and Caroline counties. Figure 40 contains a list of enslaved people from the DeJarnett family given to the Wallers, and some have the family names I'm looking for! Are the Peter, Matilda, Stapleton and Jacob my kin who I found living in Manassas, PWC?

> ... Of my daughter Mary Hampton who intermarried with Doct Nelson S. Waller [of Kunta Kinte fame] her present husband the following property together with the future increase of the females from the date of this will towit. Temple & his wife Fanny & George, G, little MATILDA and all her children except JACOB, towit Moses, PETER, Haws, STAPLETON, Joe, Nelly & Washington & Isbell & child William + twenty seven hundred dollars ...
>
> Source: Spotsylvania, Virginia, Will Book Vol U-V, 1852-1858, p. 347, for Elliott DeJarnette.

Figure 40: Mary Hampton (m. Waller) Will Mentions Roys, 1857.

This unexpected finding flooded my senses with a new appreciation for the *Roots* miniseries! I could now visualize what *my* enslaved ancestors *may* have experienced, dressed like, behaved like, and endured from their pious masters in Spotsylvania County in the 1700s. That made Kunta's experience even more real for me after finding this extraordinary information!

I found more treasures as I examined Spotsylvania's enslavement records.[65] Enslaved people with my family's names appeared, but which ones were for *my* family? I settled on Figure 40 that contained several familiar names on one document: Matilda, Peter, Stapleton, and Jacob. Note: A Jacob Burroughs lived with Albert and Alice Roy in Manassas in 1870. More of these names were found in Freedman's Bureau records. Do these records *prove* the DeJarnettes, Wallers, or Mary Hampton were our enslavers? DNA does find some genetic connections, but more research is needed to come to firm conclusions.

TIP: Did you find wealthy people living near your Black family in the 1870 Census? They may have been your family's enslavers prior to 1866. Check their probate documents for your enslaved family names.

Voting with Their Feet

In July 2025, I visited charming Old Town Fredericksburg, which was part of Spotsylvania County before 1879. Strolling down the well-maintained streets flanked by charming historic buildings, I was transported back to the 1700s. I envisaged the hustle and bustle of horses and carriages, women in long dresses and bearded men wearing top hats ambling past the Lewis Store on Caroline Street and stopping at one of the many eateries.

The history of White people living in Fredericksburg, Spotsylvania, and Stafford Counties is well-documented, both before and after the Civil War. But what is most fascinating to me are the texts that reveal daring migrations of the thousands of freedom seekers who voted with their feet.

Figure 41: Enslaved People "Migrating" from Fredericksburg to DC.

Figure 41 from the Library of Congress shows enslaved people crossing the Rappahannock River at Tinpot Ford, just below the Orange and Alexandria Bridge, visible in the background. It is often used to illustrate slaves' efforts to achieve freedom.

Perusing the *Spotsylvania Memory Blog*[66] brought forth an astounding document (Figure 42). The names of about twenty enslaved people who *voted with their feet* to claim their freedom (i.e., ran away). Were my ancestors among them?

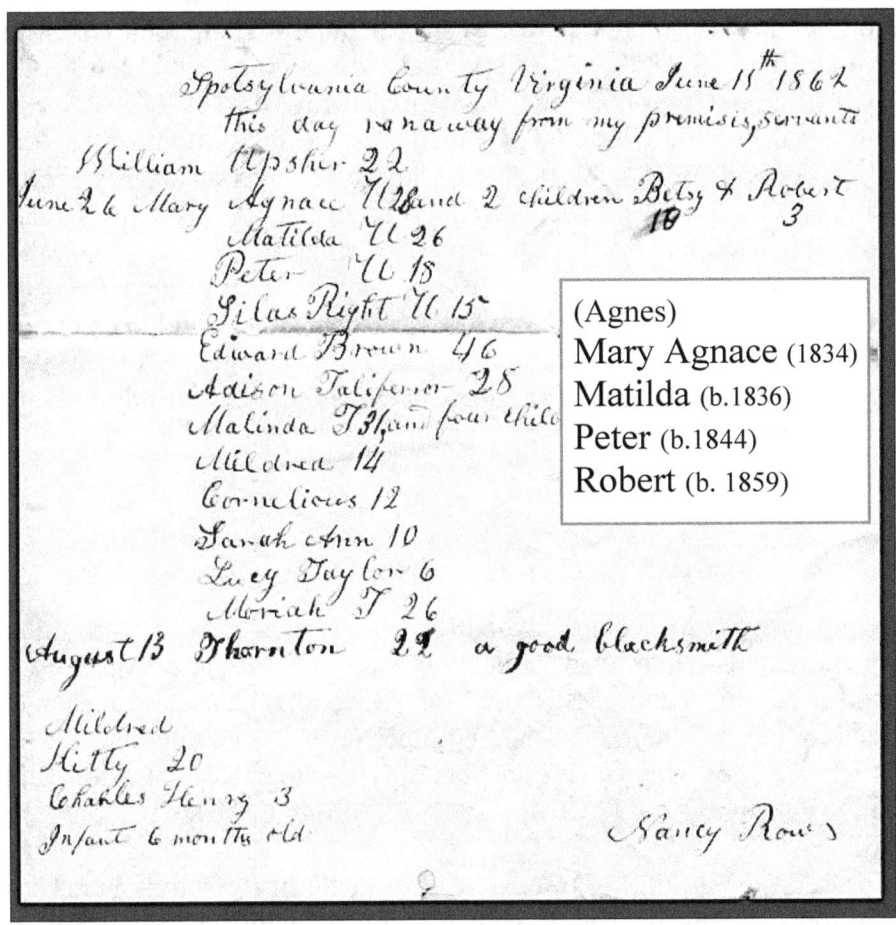

***Figure 42**: Runaways from Nancy Rowe's Estate, Spotsylvania, VA*

Enslaver Nancy Rowe's 1862 estate contained the familiar names of Mary **Agnace** (age 28, b. 1834), Matilda (age 26, b. 1836) and Peter (18, b. 1844). I found those names in later generations of our DNA matches family trees. Was Matilda the sister of Mary Agnace (Agnes)? If so, were her children—Betsy

(10) and Robert (3)—siblings or cousins of my great-grandmother Ella Roy? Was Mary Agnace the missing generation between Agnis Chew (born around 1810 and living in DC by 1870) and my 2xGGM Agnes Roy born around 1847? Or am I mistaken, chasing after rainbows that only exist in my imagination?

When did Nancy Rowe obtain her enslaved property? Her husband, Absolom Rowe/Roe, owned a large estate at 801 Hanover Street in the still-beautiful town of Fredericksburg. An inventory and appraisal of his estate in 1855 included all his earthly possessions including livestock, farm equipment, household furnishings, 889 acres of land, cash and bonds, and twenty-five slaves appraised at $14,375 (worth $533,000 in 2025). There was no evidence that Absolom, or his wife, Nancy Rowe, ever considered freeing their enslaved property. So, on June 18, 1862, the intrepid individuals voted with their feet.[67] (Figure 41). Did these **Rowe**s provide our family's **Roy** surname?

I also noticed that the Clara WARE mentioned at the bottom of Table 7 was likely enslaved by WEIRS (Wares?), the largest enslavers in nearby Prince William County. Grammie Ella's Uncle Albert lived a few Census lines away from enslaver Edgar Weir at his family's Liberia Plantation in Manassas, PWC. That 1870 proximity suggests that some of our direct line Roys may have been enslaved by Weirs. Was my family connected to the Rowes and/or Weirs is further discussed in Chapter 11.

I got greedy. On a roll of genealogical successes, I tried to find the Holy Grail that would prove the truth of our Roy heritage.

Was Stafford, Virginia, Our Point of Freedom?

The depth and breadth of several evidentiary documents proved to me that Agnes Roy was Ella Roy's mother, hence, my 2xGGM. Teenager Agnes Roy was enslaved as of 1863, according to the 1865 Alexandria Census. Agnes may have traveled to the Freedmen's Village with her probable parents, Peter Roy and Agnis Chew. They may have caravanned with other Roys, Carters and Paynes from Spotsylvania and Caroline County, through Stafford County, in around 1862.

Time passed quickly during the hustle and bustle of the Civil War, with thousands of formerly enslaved contraband entering the nation's capital. Agnes Roy birthed baby Ella Roy on 27 December 1866, when she was about 19. The young mother and her baby lived in the East Capitol Hill Barracks with (or near) Peter Roy and his wife Agnes Chew, who lived in the same barracks. Other Roys, with the given names of Peter, Matilda, Overton and Stapleton, settled thirty miles south of DC in Manassas, PWC. That's a nifty recap of facts, but so what?

I was intrigued to learn that Stafford County, VA, was steeped in African American history. Nestled next to the Potomac River, about 35 miles south of Washington, DC, it is just south of Marines Headquarters in Quantico, along Interstate 95.

By some ancestral serendipity, my eldest son—who was newly retired from a career in the Marines—moved his family to Stafford. Glory be! Every genealogist studying African American history knows the goal is to get their research back to the East Coast—specifically Virginia, where the first Angolans were brought to the future English-speaking America. My son and grandchildren were living in Black History central! I read as much as I could about his new home, wondering if we had roots there.

Stafford County had a population of about 4,200 enslaved Blacks, 350 free Blacks, and 5,400 Whites. A Stafford resident wrote that "The Best male Negroes sold for $1,500 and the Best Field Girls from $1,300 to $1,350."[68] I wondered whether those pronouncements applied to my Virginia ancestors.

On a frosty day in January, my teenaged granddaughter, Jazmine, and I decided to embark on an adventure to Fredericksburg's Rappahannock Central Library to uncover more secrets about our Virginia past. We discovered the end-all book about the lives of enslaved people and their masters in *A Different Story: A Black History of Fredericksburg, Stafford, and Spotsylvania*.[69] Bingo!

We learned many pertinent facts about slave life. For example, all enslaved people had to leave town by 10 AM on Sundays, or they would get punished with five painful lashes on their backs. The enslaved couldn't sell anything without their master's written permission. But the most surprising thing was learning that some enslavers allowed their human property to hire themselves out, just like they were free. This broke the law but gave enslaved people a little taste of freedom. With every page we turned in that book, our curiosity grew, and the mysteries of the past started to come alive in our imaginations.

Although no major battles took place in Stafford, both Confederate and Union troops occupied the county in intervals from 1861 to 1865. When Union forces appeared there in the spring of 1862, their presence enabled 10,000 self-emancipating freedom seekers to march on the Trail For Freedom.[70] They crossed the Rappahannock River, traveled north through Stafford to Aquia Landing, and then on to contraband camps in Washington, DC.

The story of these freedom seekers is personified through the engrossing memoirs of John Washington, a man in bondage who would write his personal story. He described his flight to freedom from Fredericksburg in *A Slave No More*. I read the whole book in a couple of hours, it was so engrossing.

Aquia Landing was also a stop for kidnapped free Blacks like Solomon Northup whose life is documented is his book, *12 Years a Slave*. He was a free man forced into bondage in 1841, but wrested back his freedom in 1853, both times by passing through Aquia Landing.

As I stood at that historic site with my children and grandchildren in 2024, we paid homage to those brave souls. I wondered if our Roys and Carters stood at the same spot, gazing up the river toward freedom. It was so emotional! I have goose bumps just thinking about the hordes of people longing to be free and voting with their feet! I was determined to impart to my grandchildren that history becomes real when you know your place in it, and can see what your ancestors like Albert Roy did to help make the world what it is today.

CHAPTER 9: Albert Roy's Enduring Legacy

Figure 43: Albert Roy (1838-1931) & Wife Alice Burrows (1847-1913).

Yes, this book is primarily about my Great-grandmother, Ella Roy and her secrets. But it was difficult to find anything about her, at least initially. Sadly, that is a common occurrence when trying to find historical documents about women of any race.

So, I concentrated on looking for records pertaining to her guardians, Albert and Alice Roy (Figure 43). Perhaps finding where Albert Roy was in time and place, I would find stories about Ella too.

Over the past forty years, I have discovered probate and real estate records involving Albert Roy. Even without fully understanding the legalese in those documents, one could easily surmise that Albert Roy was no stranger to financial transactions. Census records verified that he owned several properties over the years (Appendix D). I wondered if he had purchased Grammie's house at 1300 West Vine Street.

During our normal Saturday visit, after hitting a few balls, Mom clarified a story she had heard about her grandmother's younger years:

"Ella lived in Mount Vernon, OH, at age 14 (at least) until she died in 1962. I need to know who her mom and dad were. She stayed with Albert and Alice Roy on E. Gambir St. in Mount Vernon. Apparently she was born in Virginia as were the Roys. Alice had no children and could not be her mother. The Roys were shopkeepers for the famous person, Columbus Delano, a rich White man, who lived in Mount Vernon. He was an attorney and did other political type activities. I do not know the connection between the Roys and the Delanos. Ella fits in there somewhere."

Ella Roy Carter's 1962 obituary said she was "left without parents in infancy and was adopted by the late Albert and Alice Roy, an uncle and aunt. Ella was born in Alexandria, Virginia, December 27, 1866, and moved to Mount Vernon, at the age of six." I wanted to learn whether Albert had anything to do with Ella's upscale lifestyle that my mother and Cousin Kenora remembered so vividly.

Over the decades, I examined newspapers, visited the Mount Vernon County Recorder, and searched online for every possible document involving Albert and Ella Roy. Then, I investigated the people he did business with to learn whether they were part of Albert's FAN club. Maybe that information would shed light on when and why my Roys came to Mount Vernon in the first place. Maybe exploring Knox County, OH, documents could reveal how Ella obtained her supposed wealth.

On a 2003 reunion trip, I found an unusual record on the RootsWeb's WorldConnect Project for Mount Vernon at the Genealogy Society building. It said, "Albert and Alice (Roy) came to Knox County evidently to be servants for Columbus Delano … In 1900, Albert and Alice own a restaurant and a home (no mortgage) and had two nephews living with him."[71]

Yes, I considered the possibility that my Roys were already living in Mount Vernon before Columbus Delano hired them to work, but I tried to uncover every rock that might *prove* the truth.

Who Were Albert Roy's Employers?

Thankfully, there were quite a few deeds, newspaper articles, and other records about Albert Roy in Ohio, including two unexpected mentions of him in books held at the Knox County Historical Society Museum in 2023.

Their docents mused that the dozen or so published books in their store might have some information about my Black family members. I scoffed, never once imagining that any of the one-percent Black population in town would be included in history books.

I filed through to the Table of Contents in Lorle Porter's brilliant *Politics and Peril, Mount Vernon, OH in the Nineteenth Century*. It displayed chapters with headings like "Builders and Bloomers, The Hobby of Politics, This is Tyranny, Family Genealogists, Political Figures, and The Lincoln Trolley: the Wheel of Death." Then I looked into the back for an Index. I gasped! An Albert Roy was assigned to page 201 in the "Will the Bitterness Fade?" My fingers fumbled to the page, hoping against hope to find something interesting and useful. I was not disappointed. The first paragraph of Chapter 13 was about the ultra-rich Braddock family and their servants, as follows:

"On a March morning in 1879, Annie Monahan put the finishing touches on the family's breakfast at the John Sellers Braddock home at 189 West High Street. Ella Grimm, the second girl, finished hanging the wet laundry on the line behind the eight room brick house. Albert Roy, a former slave, finished his meal, and set out to take the family's cows to pasture along the B&O tracks next to Braddock's Mount Vernon Bridge Factory. Roy was employed as a groomsman, stable boy, and yard man; he also attended the family's fruit trees and Mrs. Braddock's gardens."

What a a remarkable picture of a typical day for Albert Roy, summarizing his knowledge, skills and abilities. On another page, Ms. Porter indicated that:

"In 1880, John Cooper, co-owner of Cooper's Iron Works, sold his 20-room mansion called 'Thistle Ridge' to John and Margaret Braddock. The beautiful three-story, blue slate mansard-roofed home at 189 West High Street overlooked Cooper's factory at Sugar and Sandusky Streets."

Politics and Peril has more juicy tidbits, "The servants handled the domestic routines so that Margaret (Braddock) could engage in her social duties, and her own political causes, chief of which was temperance. For Annie Monahan, Ella Grimm and Albert Roy, there are rooms on the third floor of the Braddock home were far warmer and safer than in their previous lives."

I sat back in my chair trying to process what I had just read. Was that an accurate description of what Albert's life was like during an average day in 1879? A vision crossed in front of my eyes. Albert was dressed in a dapper black uniform with crisp white shirt. His dark, fluffy, mutton-chop sideburns and moustache framed a slightly tanned face. His intelligent, deep-set brown eyes conveyed an air of competence and confidence. He was obviously a trusted part of the Braddock household. But where was his wife Alice living, if Albert slept on the third floor of the Braddock's huge home? And where was Ella?

My sizzling neurons conjured up a slew of additional questions: Was the Ella Grimm working as a "second-girl" cleaning the Braddock's bedrooms actually *my* Ella Roy? [I later learned Ella Grimm was a 19-year-old White woman with a young child.]

That story in *Politics and Peril* was dated 1879, one year before my Roys were listed as servants in the 1880 Census at the Delano's LakeHome property. Does that mean Delano did not bring the Roys back home with him in 1875 when he left DC for good? Were our Roys only living for a short time with the Delanos when the Census taker came around? Was the 1879 date with the Braddocks incorrect?

I did not find more of my family surnames listed in *Politics and Peril,* but there were some interesting entries about other African Americans. First was Knuck Harris, a free Black man who purchased lots 123, 124, and 125 in 1810 for $8 (p. 23). Next, John and Judah Bird rescued an Indian child whose mother had been attacked and killed by a White man (p. 37). In 1870, Ben and Lew Snowden—the famous Black musicians—attempted to vote in the Morris Township, but were turned away (p. 182). At Morey's soap factory, black men named Judge Larre and Samuel **Jackson** boiled soap from lard (p. 79).

The book also mentions several topics related to the county's divisive thoughts about slavery, as well as a mention of the US Colored Troops. The book also mentioned that in 1866, Columbus Delano asserted that Confederate rebels could not have been overthrown without the assistance of Black troops. Honestly, that's more information than I was expecting to find about Black folk in that wondrous, chock-full book of Mount Vernon history.

Those 1879 and 1880 dates in *Politics and Peril* were a bit of confounding for my research. The Census indicated Albert Roy was working for the Delanos, yet *Politics and Peril* had him working for the Braddocks. I need to pinpoint where my Roys were at precise time periods.

Jim Gibson at the Historical Society surprised me with an unbelievable data source he thought would solve my data dilemma. He disappeared inside a back room, then reappeared after a few minutes with a sheaf of papers stapled in the corner. He presented for my scrutiny a copy of the unpublished *Braddock: Buckeye Born* diary which was referenced in *Politics and Peril*. The diary was written by daughter Katherine Orrinda Braddock. What luck!

Katherine described accompanying her father when he inspected their new Thistle Ridge home. It was huge, filled with awe at the grand double parlors and the Italian-made marble mantles which dominated all the rooms. The diary also mentioned the trips her family took to New York, to their favorite store, *Tiffany*—well-known for fine jewelry, china, silver, and *stained glass lamps*.

As mentioned in the Prologue, cousin Kenora, who had dusted the furniture in Grammie Carter's house every Saturday in the 1940s, recalled that Grammie had several beautiful Tiffany lamps in her mortgage-free home. My mother said the same thing. How did Grammie obtain such wealth?

Our family historian, Lavata Williams, mentioned it was common for Black folk in Mount Vernon to own their own homes, thanks to the decent-paying industrial jobs available to them in town. But rare was the person who had those priceless lamps and beautiful furnishings. Did Albert or Grammie buy them from the Braddocks when they left Mount Vernon for Arkansas in the 1890s, or did they just give Albert or Ella the lamps to avoid the travel hassle?

Katherine Braddock wrote on page 24:

> *"New service was procured for our home that fall. Kate Keefe, a Roman Catholic born in Ireland, became our cook. She remained with us for eighteen years. Her edict that she would not allow children in her kitchen is the main reason that Sister and I never learned to cook. Father **procured Albert Roy**, an ex-slave. He was one of the most industrious and painstaking Negroes. He took servant Peter's place and remained with us for ten years. One Saturday morning in December 1882, Albert Roy came up to Miss Shaw's studio, just after I had begun my lesson. He brought the carriage to take me home because Grandfather Braddock had died in Illinois."*

Here's the confounding part of the story. The 1880 Census indicates Albert, Alice, Ella, and Delcina were working for and living with Columbus Delano, two miles from the Braddock house. Which dates are correct? Did the Roys work for the Delanos or the Braddocks after they left Virginia? *Politics and Peril* entries placed Albert Roy with the Braddocks in 1879. Katherine Braddock's diary placed Albert Roy there by 1882 and she said he worked for their family for ten years. Which dates are correct?

    I wanted to do my due diligence, as tasked by the Genealogical Proof Standard, so I Googled the author's name and Bingo! found her telephone number. I called Lorle Porter at home at the end of my 2023 trip to Ohio. After praising the 90-year-old's informational book, I dared to ask whether the 1879 date factoid—out of the many thousands of facts she had in her fabulous book––might have actually been 1881 instead of 1879? Then our family's theory that Delano brought our Roys to Mount Vernon in 1875 when he retired would make sense.

    I'm afraid my question stressed out the dear lady more than anything else because she prides herself on doing impeccable research. I assured Ms. Porter that her travail was nothing but awe-inspiring, thanked her again for the powerful lead she gave me, then hung up the phone. Perplexed and jazzed at the same time.

    Those two sources about Albert Roy were enlightening yet confusing. What does it mean by "ex-slave, Albert Roy, being 'procured'"? That term usually means to purchase something. Slavery was over in 1865, so was Albert *sold* or traded by the Delanos to the Braddocks immediately after the 1880 Census was taken? Was my mother's belief that Columbus Delano brought Ella, Albert and Alice to Mount Vernon in the mid-1870s wrong? Was the 1880 Census placing the Roys as servants in the Delano's home a fluke? Did Delano "give" Albert Roy to the Braddocks immediately following the 1880 Census taker's visit? Did Albert continue working for the Braddocks until 1890 or so before they moved their prosperous real estate business to Little Rock, Arkansas? During the ten-year period from 1881 to 1890 were Alice and Ella also working for the Braddocks, or the Delanos, or were they housekeepers taking care of their own home?

I would perhaps never know for sure how and when my family arrived in Ohio, but I chose to target as my #1 theory that: Columbus Delano brought Albert, Alice, Ella, and Del on the train with him from DC in 1875 and they worked for the Delanos through 1880, then Albert worked for the Braddocks until 1890 when they left for Arkansas.

Less popular was that my Roys arrived in Mount Vernon, on the train with other Black families from Virginia or DC, such as the Paynes, Hackleys, and/or Fields.

The Property Monger

Within the quaint town of Mount Vernon sat the bustling, mortgage-free home of 52-year-old Albert Roy and his 53-year-old wife, Alice Burris/Burrows. Despite not having any living children of her own by age 39, Alice was surrounded by the warmth of friends from the small Black community.

Living with Albert and Alice Roy as of June 1900 were servants named Grace Rouse (19) and Leona Jackson (17) whose unnamed father was born in Virginia. Ella Roy Carter's nine-year-old son, Bennie Carter, and namesake nephew Albert Roy (24) from Manassas, were living with Albert and Alice. Albert seemed to be a caring family man, even though, or maybe because, he had no children of his own (Table 7).

According to the 1898 Mount Vernon City Directory, Albert Roy was working at a restaurant located at Three East Vine Street, and his home was nearby at Gay and Gambier. Does this factoid apply to Ella's Uncle Albert Roy or his nephew, who was also named Albert Roy?

The 1900 Census confirmed that the elder Albert owned a restaurant at 229 Main Street, a few blocks from his home at 104 West Front Street.

I could not find the name of his restaurant, but it seems he had a clientele that included jurors, as verified in an 1897 newspaper entry which indicated Albert Roy was paid $3.50 for juror suppers.

Guess what? As of 2023, a quaint business called "Paragraphs Bookstore" shared Albert's former restaurant's address. Wouldn't "Paragraphs" be the perfect place to sell copies of *this* book once published? (Figure 44).

Table 7: 1900 Census for Roys in Mount Vernon.

Figure 44: Site of Albert's Restaurant on Main Street in MV, OH, 1900.

One sunny afternoon after visiting nearby Kenyon College, I became immersed in the Deed room at the downtown Knox County *Recorder*. I had seen all of these records online, but touching the heavy, bound deed books brought more gravitas. I took lots of photos with my smart phone, striving to follow the money: Who bought what property from whom and for how much?

The first time I found a deed transaction involving Albert Roy was in Book 80, in 1883, on pages 529-530. Albert paid $1,200 to L.P. Rosa for a five-acre plot in the *Walker's Addition*. I found an interesting record for an Alice M. Elliott, deceased in 1897. Albert Roy bought her home in Coshocton Township in Knox County, OH.[72] Appendix D contains a sampling of the legal records I found which involved the Roys. I examined Sanborn Maps from the Library of Congress, dated 1882.

How did Albert earn enough money to buy his 1883 property? Did Delano, deceased in 1896, leave Albert some money to purchase the 1897 property? Or, had Albert made plenty of his own money from his own smarts, after years of working for the uber-rich Delano and John Sellers Braddock? The 1900 Census taker lists the Black Hill family right after the White Elliott family who lived nearby on West Gambier Street. Page 35 in the Census recorded a one-month-old White girl named Mary E. Elliott, born the previous month.

This document from 1897—the year after Columbus Delano died—may explain those Tiffany lamps! Did Albert share his wealth with Ella and other family members? I believe the likely answer is YES!

The Family Man

It was indeed a blessing that Ella Roy was raised by her capable Uncle Albert and Auntie Alice who were obviously family-loving people. They willingly served as adoptive parents to Ella before she married in 1884, and moved to Springfield, OH, with her husband until about 1906, when she moved back to Mount Vernon with her children. Alice and Albert invited their nephews Albert and Bennie Carter to live with them, and they lent Ella a helping hand with housing and the rest of her children.

So, who were the two servant girls, Grace Rouse and Leora Jackson, also living with Albert and Alice in 1900? The name Jackson tickled my brain; could Leora be related to a man I'm theorizing might be Ella's father? I wondered what kind of servants the girls were. Did they work for Albert and Alice in the restaurant, cooking or cleaning, or as personal servants in their private home? If the latter, does it mean Albert and Alice were financially well off in the decade after Columbus Delano died in 1896?

"Surprise, surprise, surprise!" as country hick Gomer Pyle often uttered in a Southern drawl on the 1960s TV show of the same name. Guess who *could* have babies, after all? Yes. Alice's upstanding hubby, Albert Roy. In May of 1899, Albert Roy was accused of bastardy by a single woman named Sadie Hill (Figure 45). Maybe 60+ year old Albert wanted his genetic line to continue. I found no evidence that an infant lived in Sadie Hill's house on Front Street[73] between present day West Gambier and Ridgewood Avenue. That's a few blocks from the Public Square near Albert's restaurant. Did Sadie give the child up for adoption, or did some other family member raise it?

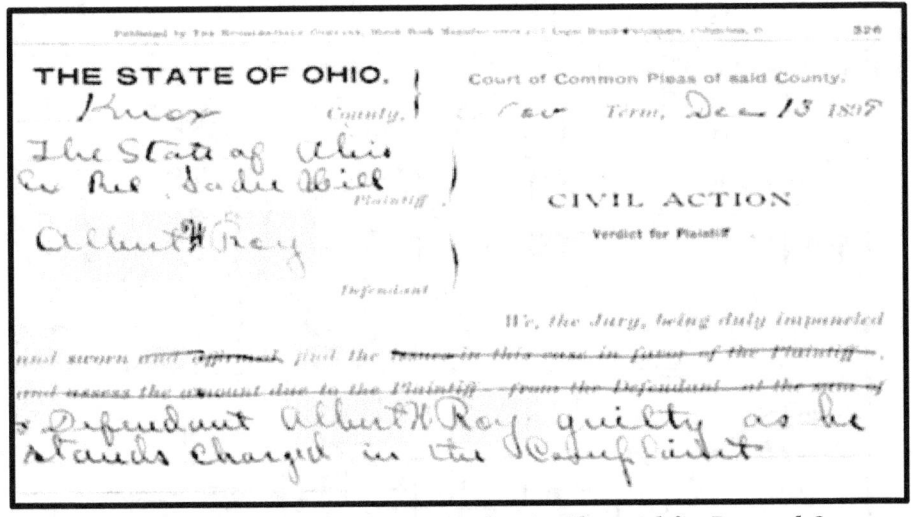

***Figure 45**: Is Albert Roy Guilty As Charged for Bastardy?*

Albert wasn't tarred and feathered, and his restaurant business seemed to be successful even in light of the public announcement of bastardy. This made me wonder whether the infant's Baby Daddy was actually the 24-year-old nephew Albert W. Roy who was living with his Uncle Albert and Aunt Alice?

The City Directory for 1903 had two entries for Albert Roy; one address listed as "Restaurant, 229 South Main, off Public Square." (Figure 45)The second address was "h 11 E. Gambier." There were several entries for Albert's nephew, Albert W. Roy, but by 1908 he was living in Akron, OH, and died there in 1923.

In 1910, Albert was living with Alice, his wife of 47 or so years, at 104 West Front Street. Alice was the landlady with three roomers: Benjamin Carter—Ella's oldest living child who became a World War I hero—and Oliver Ivory and Ernest Ford, who were "off-bracers" at the glass factory.

By 1910, Albert was no longer working at the restaurant. He was a laborer for an unnamed private family and had a mortgage on his home. An eleven-person Sites family lived on the back side of Albert's multi-family dwelling at 104 1/2 West Front Street (in Appendix D, those were lots 213 & 214).

Newly widowed Ella Roy lived next door with her children Bessie, Ralph, Richard, Roy, and Arthur, as well as a roomer named Mary Tiffin. In another household at that address were Margaret and Robert Sharp, and their children Mabel and Bernard Mayle.

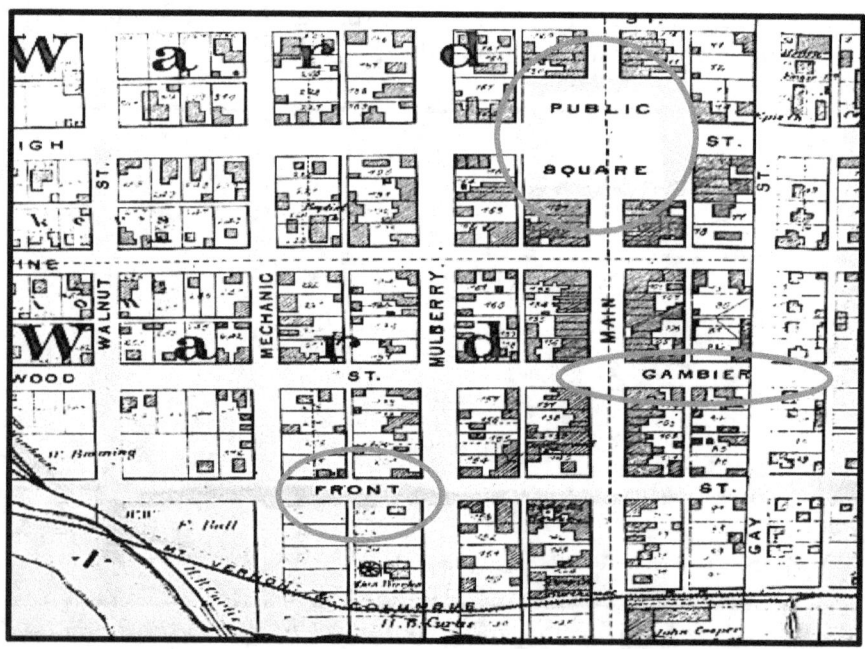

Figure 46: Map-of Downtown Mount Vernon, ca. 1900.

I researched all these new surnames but didn't find blood connections. That did not mean they weren't close friends who might have traveled together from Virginia to Ohio after slavery's end.

The West Front Street moniker disappeared from maps around 1913, changing its name to West Ohio Avenue. Aha! That meant Albert's property was right next door to the Wayman AME church where all of my family members worshipped from the 1880s until the 1970s. Nowadays, there is a large grassy rectangle where Albert's house likely sat next to the now-defunct church.

Albert's Death Certificate Leads to More Questions

I examined the usual genealogical reports, like Census, death records, and City Directories. Each newfound record was a blessing and a curse, resulting in a few answers along with more questions. For example, Albert's Death Certificate (Figure 47) described him as colored, married to Alice Roy, and living at 134 West Ohio Ave (records from 1900 through 1920 said he lived next to the Wayman AME Church at 104 West Ohio Avenue). Albert was born in Virginia on 10 April 1838. He died 20 May 1931 from senility and was buried in Mound View Cemetery on 23 May 1931. So, what's unclear about that?

Different documents list contradictory birth years for Albert: 1838, 1840, 1845, 1847, 1848, and 1849. All said he was born in Virginia, except the 1930 Census which said West Virginia, so I am inclined to believe he was likely born in Virginia, probably in Spotsylvania or Caroline County.

Here's another puzzler: #5 on his Death Certificate says Albert was married when he died. Then, #5a says he was the husband of Alice Roy; however, his wife Alice died 18 years before Albert. #15 says the informant was *Mrs. Albert Roy* and that she did not know who Albert's parents were. What? Something is amiss.

I found confusing documents that suggested someone named Maggie Hackley married Albert Roy, and others had him married to an Alice May Jenkins Allen. What is the truth? Documents suggest that three different women married Albert Roy. But were all three married to the elder Albert born around 1838? Or, was one or more of those women married to his nephew, Albert William Roy, who was born in 1876 in Manassas, but was living with the elder Albert in 1900?

The same confounding questions arose with the many land deeds and probate records involving Albert Roy. Which Albert did what? At long last, I determined that the elder Albert Roy married all three different women—two of whom were named Alice.

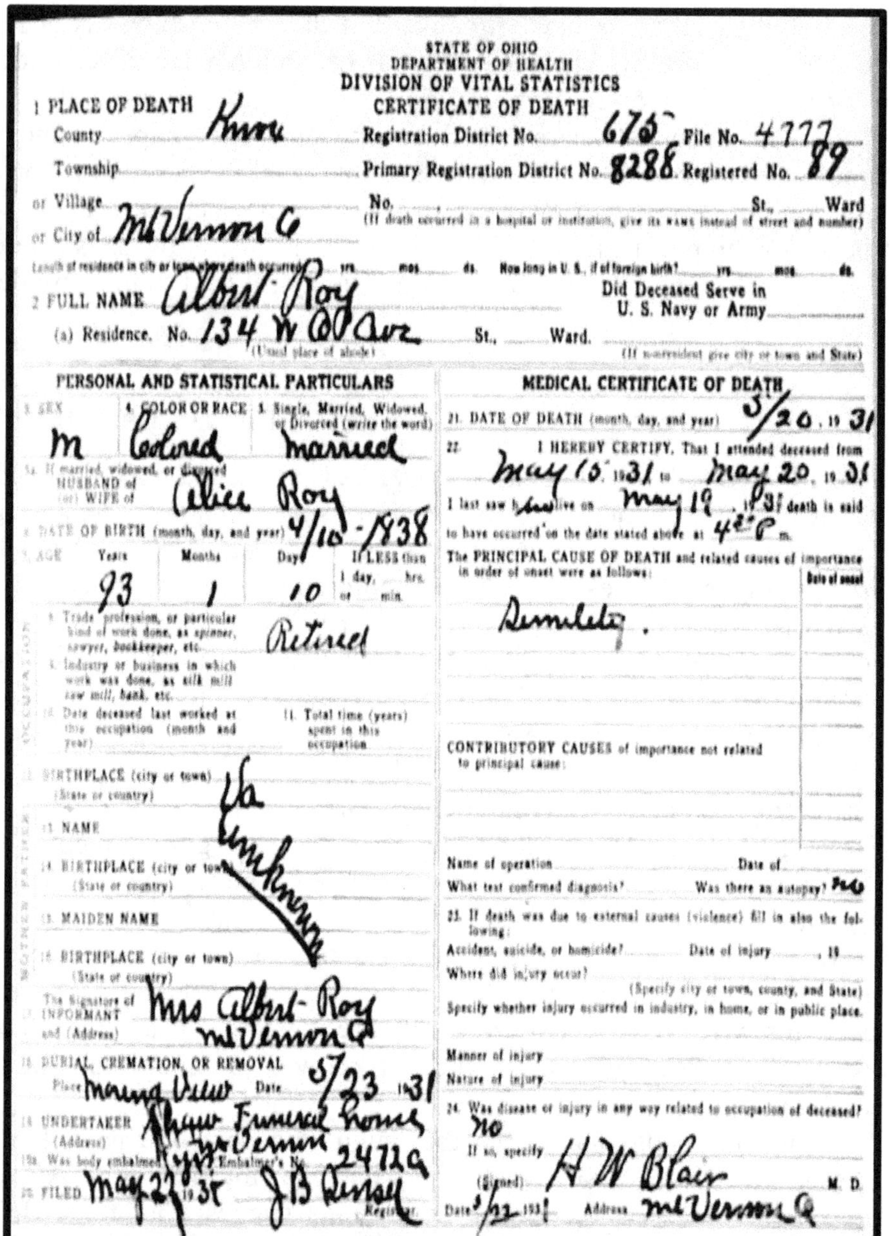
STATE OF OHIO
DEPARTMENT OF HEALTH
DIVISION OF VITAL STATISTICS
CERTIFICATE OF DEATH

1 PLACE OF DEATH
County Knox Registration District No. 675 File No. 4777
Township Primary Registration District No. 8288 Registered No. 89
or Village No. St., Ward
or City of Mt Vernon O (If death occurred in a hospital or institution, give its NAME instead of street and number)
Length of residence in city or town where death occurred yrs. mos. ds. How long in U. S., if of foreign birth? yrs. mos. ds.
2 FULL NAME Albert Roy
Did Deceased Serve in U. S. Navy or Army
(a) Residence. No. 134 W Ch Ave St., Ward. (Usual place of abode) (If nonresident give city or town and State)

PERSONAL AND STATISTICAL PARTICULARS

3 SEX m
4 COLOR OR RACE Colored
5 Single, Married, Widowed, or Divorced (write the word) married
5a If married, widowed, or divorced HUSBAND of (or) WIFE of Alice Roy
6 DATE OF BIRTH (month, day, and year) 4/10-1838
7 AGE Years 93 Months 1 Days 10 If LESS than 1 day, hrs. or min.
8 Trade, profession, or particular kind of work done, as spinner, sawyer, bookkeeper, etc. Retired
9 Industry or business in which work was done, as silk mill, saw mill, bank, etc.
10 Date deceased last worked at this occupation (month and year)
11 Total time (years) spent in this occupation
12 BIRTHPLACE (city or town) (State or country) Va
13 NAME Unknown
14 BIRTHPLACE (city or town) (State or country)
15 MAIDEN NAME
16 BIRTHPLACE (city or town) (State or country)
17 The Signature of INFORMANT and (Address) Mrs Albert Roy Mt Vernon O
18 BURIAL, CREMATION, OR REMOVAL Place Mound View Date 5/23 1931
19 UNDERTAKER (Address) Shaw Funeral Home Mt Vernon
19a Was body embalmed? Embalmer's No. 2472a
20 FILED May 22 1931 J B Kinsey Registrar

MEDICAL CERTIFICATE OF DEATH

21 DATE OF DEATH (month, day, and year) 5/20, 1931
22 I HEREBY CERTIFY, That I attended deceased from May 15 1931 to May 20 1931
I last saw h alive on May 19 1931 death is said to have occurred on the date stated above at 4:20 P m.
The PRINCIPAL CAUSE OF DEATH and related causes of importance in order of onset were as follows: Date of onset
Senility.

CONTRIBUTORY CAUSES of importance not related to principal cause:

Name of operation Date of
What test confirmed diagnosis? Was there an autopsy? no
23 If death was due to external causes (violence) fill in also the following:
Accident, suicide, or homicide? Date of injury , 19
Where did injury occur? (Specify city or town, county, and State)
Specify whether injury occurred in industry, in home, or in public place.
Manner of injury
Nature of injury
24 Was disease or injury in any way related to occupation of deceased? no
If so, specify
(Signed) H W Blair M. D.
Date 5/22 1931 Address Mt Vernon O

***Figure** 47: Albert Roy's Death Certificate, 1931.*

The elder Albert was also probably the one involved with the real estate and probate documents found in Knox County, OH. The younger Albert W. Roy moved to Akron, OH, and died in 1923. Initially, I thought Albert was only married once, to Alice Burris/Burrows for forty-plus years. I was wrong. Here's a synopsis of his wives that clarify some answers to my questions.

The First Alice: A Foundation of Strength and Care

Albert was married to Alice for about 47 years. In 1870, they were living in Manassas, near likely former enslaver Edgar Weir at his Liberia plantation. Also living with them were Alice's *likely* parents, Jacob and Delcenia Burris, a possible cousin named Frankie Ray, and a farm laborer named William. By 1874, childless Albert and Alice became the loving guardians of eight-year-old Ella Roy. Alice, Albert, Ella and Del migrated to Mount Vernonio, living with Columbus Delano in 1880. Alice treated Ella as her own daughter, nurturing and educating her as her own, teaching her skills that would make Ella successful in life.

I believe the 1900 Census undersold Alice's considerable intelligence and capacity. She was far from a passive homemaker. She was Albert's active and capable partner in business and community affairs. Alice had an entrepreneurial spirit, by 1910 working as a landlady, renting rooms in the family's boarding house on West Front Street.

She was a community builder, becoming an active member of the Wayman Chapel African Methodist Episcopal Church. She likely held positions in various segregated social clubs, including the Wayman Chapel choir and the Red Cross Auxiliary. This deep involvement shows she was a social pillar of Mount Vernon's African American community.

Alice stood with Albert in key financial dealings. As an example, Albert and Alice Roy executed a mortgage deed on 24 May 1912, jointly signing to secure a $2,300 with a six percent interest rate. This suggests Alice was an equal financial partner.

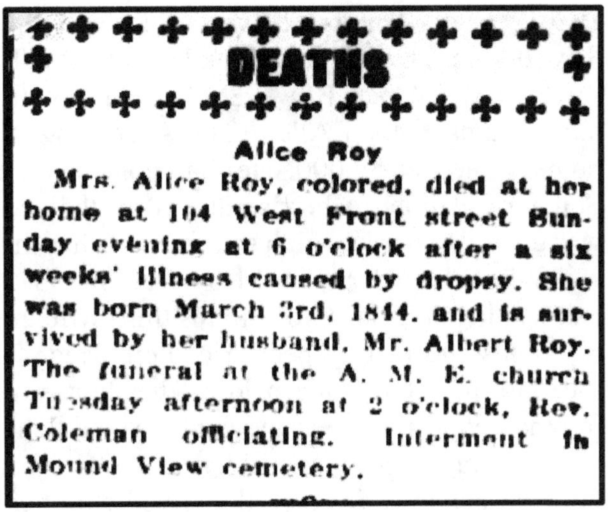

Sadly, Alice passed away in February 1913, following a brief six-week illness from dropsy. (Figure 48) Her funeral was a central community event, held on a Tuesday afternoon at the Wayman AME Church, presided over by Reverend Coleman.

Alice Roy's life was one of quiet but powerful competence, demonstrating a deep devotion to her family, a commitment to her faith, maternal feelings for Ella and an essential partner in Albert's success.

DEATHS

Alice Roy

Mrs. Alice Roy, colored, died at her home at 104 West Front street Sunday evening at 6 o'clock after a six weeks' illness caused by dropsy. She was born March 3rd, 1844, and is survived by her husband, Mr. Albert Roy. The funeral at the A. M. E. church Tuesday afternoon at 2 o'clock, Rev. Coleman officiating. Interment in Mound View cemetery.

***Figure 48**: Alice Roy's Death Notice.*

Albert's Second Wife and the Dowry Dispute

Albert was obviously used to being married, because he remarried in the blink of an eye a few months after his first wife died. On 28 October 1913, Albert married Magdalene (Maggie) Hackley. She was born 15 Aug 1849 in Virginia to Thomas Bell and an unknown mother. I found some interesting DNA connections to those Hackleys in my FAN Club analysis of the 1870 and 1880 Censuses (Appendix D). I found White Hackleys in Spotsylvania County, near the enslaving DeJarnettes, Weirs, Paynes, and Wallers.

It seems like Maggie may have had a dowry because when she died from apoplexy (stroke) in March 1916, there were several contentious land deed battles between Albert and Maggie's executor. The family plodded on.

The Final Marriage: Alice May Roy

Another woman named Alice married her first husband, John Allen, in 1876 in Knox County, OH. They had three children, poetically named Clarence, Florence, and Lawrence. Alice's first husband died in 1912 in Marion, OH. She married Albert Roy in 1919 in Mount Vernon, living in Albert's home at 104 West Ohio Avenue. Grammie Carter's family lived next door to them.

It took a few years to clear up the legal debris from his second wife, but Albert found another willing mate in Alice May Jenkins Allen. They were married by Reverend Lewis on 2 Sep 1919, three years after Maggie died. In 1920, mulatto Albert (82) was living with his mulatto wife, Alice May Allen Roy (60) and two lodgers, John Howard and Truss Smith.

In 1930, Albert Roy (92) was living with his third wife, Alice (70), and *their* grandson John Allen (21). According to the Census, Albert owned his home valued at $2,000. He was able to read and write, but had no radio. Someone claimed Albert's parents' birthplace was in *West* Virginia, but that was the only source which said it was other than Virginia.

When the elder Albert Roy died in 1931, whatever estate he might have had would *likely* have gone to his third wife, not to his niece, Grammie Carter. So, unless he had a specific codicil which I did not find, I was unable to ascertain how Grammie paid off her house mortgage by 1930. Is it possible ironing peoples' clothes and napkins could pay off a $3,000 home?

Anyway, Alice was still living at 104 West Ohio Avenue in 1940. Her 23-year-old nephew, Walter Allen, lived with her while working at a stove store. The home that Albert Roy purchased and lived in before 1900 was valued at $4,000 by 1940. When Alice #2 died in 1942, her estate likely went to her children, not Grammie Carter.

From Exhibit to Legacy: A Vibrant Past Uncovered

"The Community Within" exhibit at the Knox County Historical Society, alongside Ric Sheffield's powerful memoir, *We Got Along*, doesn't just chronicle history—it throws open a window onto the vibrant African American life in Mount Vernon during the pivotal decades of the 1800s and 1900s.

The Roys and Carters weren't just attendees; they were active architects of their community's prosperity! Look at figures like Albert Roy, Samuel Simmons, and Joseph Booker (my formerly enslaved 2xGGF)—they stood tall, presenting H. C. Curry with the past chancellor's badge of the Cooper Knights of Pythias Lodge.

Albert Roy himself was a dynamo, deeply involved in major legal and land dealings and a member of many social clubs right up to his death in 1931. He was a well-respected, involved, and savvy individual who clearly valued his family and community. I long to trace his early life in Virginia, to uncover the roots of his remarkable upstanding character, and perhaps shed more light on the early years of Ella Roy.

The backbone of this community? People like Grammie Carter and her adoptive parents, Albert and Alice. They weren't merely hard workers. They were pillars who took on key roles in the Wayman AME Church and numerous social clubs. Living next door made engagement a seamless part of their daily life!

The Enduring Spirit of Wayman AME Church

I will forever cherish the sight of my mother peering through the windows of her beloved Wayman AME during her last trip to the homeland in 2003. While the building's closure is a disappointment, the plaque that commemorates its significance to the local African American community is a powerful testament to their legacy.

Those pioneers first arrived in Mount Vernon in 1808. They didn't just settle. They opened businesses, worked tirelessly, raised families, helped runaway slaves, and sent their children to integrated schools. Their success is marked by the peak population of 319 in 1880, which was one percent of the total population. Though the numbers have since dwindled, their spirit endures.

When I visited in 2023, the former Wayman AME Church building stood empty, but not forgotten. For over a century, it was the educational, cultural, and spiritual heart of its members. Figure 49s proves the Chapel and grounds are still beautifully maintained—a true source of pride. Grammie Carter and her descendants would certainly be pleased with that enduring respect for Black history in Mount Vernon. The bottom image shows my mother, Mary Carter Marshall, staring through the Chapel doorway as she visited her hometown for the last time in 2003.

Figure 49: Wayman Chapel AME Church. Mary Carter Peers Into Window

CHAPTER 10: Return To Ol' Virginny

Grammie Ella Roy Carter was born in Alexandria, VA, in 1866 and her Uncle Albert Roy's Death Certificate indicated he was born in Virginia around 1838. Because it is often difficult to find historical information about women, I took a deep dive into Albert's past, with the hope of finding more about Ella in the process. This chapter concentrates on Albert's life in Virginia, shedding light on how he became such an accomplished man, working for two of the richest men in Mount Vernon.

Where Was Albert Roy in 1870?

I could not locate Ella Roy's whereabouts anywhere in Virginia in 1870. But the 1870 Census for Manassas, Prince William County (PWC), VA, reported an Albert RAY living with Alice RAY, Frank RAY, Roughton William, Jacob Burrows and Delcenia Burrows (Figure 50). Ten years later, Albert, Alice, Delcenia, and Ella Roy were living at Columbus Delano's LakeHome Manor in Mount Vernon, Knox County, OH.

Name	Albert Ray
Age in 1870	30
Birth Date	abt 1840
Birthplace	Virginia
Dwelling Number	97
Home in 1870	Manassas, Prince William, Virginia
Race	Mulatto
Gender	Male
Post Office	Manassas
Occupation	Farm Laborer
Cannot Read	Yes
Cannot Write	Yes
Male Citizen Over 21	Yes
Inferred Spouse	Alice Ray
Household Members (Name)	**Age**
Albert Ray	**30**
Alice Ray	23
Frank Ray	16
Roughton William	
Jacob Burrows	69
Delcenia Burrows	70

Figure 50: 1870 Manassas, VA, Census

Who Were Albert's Enslaver(s)?

Ella was born free in 1866, her mother had been enslaved, and I suspected her unnamed father was too. I concentrated on finding Albert Roy's enslaver for he might have enslaved Agnes too. Imagine my happiness to find Albert Roy's name listed twice among a list of Former Enslavers in The Freedmen's Bureau's "Census Returns of the Black Population."[74] I know it sounds batty to be overjoyed to find that your relative was enslaved, but more records means more potential evidence of our lineage.

The 1870 Census from Manassas, shown in Figure 50, holds the names I had been searching for, and more …

Mulatto Albert's surname was mistranscribed as Ray, not Roy, which threw me for a loop for a while. Albert (farm laborer, 30) and Alice (keeping house, 23) were inferred as married by 1870 in Manassas, Prince William County. But I was shocked the Census taker said Albert could not read or write. I assumed he was literate because he was a Trustee of the Freedmen's Bureau school in Manassas, so maybe the Census taker made a mistake about Albert's literacy.

Who was 16-year-old Frank Ray who was attending school? I later learned this was actually a female named Frankie or Frances/Francis. I believe her mother was Catherine "Kittie" Roy, born in 1822 in as one of James Campbell Roy's enslaved people in King and Queen County, VA.[75] James Campbell Roy, 1807-1864, had enslaved 20 persons by 1840. Some records indicate his housekeeper "wife" was Mary Ellen Roy (1842-1916), who is sometimes defined as white and sometimes as mulatto. There are records that show Mary Ellen Roy's husband was William E Roy (1830-1885). All I know is that my DNA super-testers match with people who descend from the William E and Mary Ellen Roy ancestral couple. A prime example is their daughter, Mary Jane Roy, who is discussed in Chapter 12 as the wife of Ella's possible father. So, I shall consider Frank/Frankie to be a cousin.

Who was Roughton William, listed as a 20-year-old farm laborer? With such an unusual name, it should be easy to find information about him, right? Nope. I could not find anything beyond what the Census record provided.

Who were Jacob and Delcenia Burrows/Burris? Delcenia's name, along with Albert, Alice, and Ella Roy is on an 1880 Census from Mount Vernon. I assume Delcenia was Alice's mother who, by 1880, was a widow since Jacob did not appear in Ohio. Most records in Mount Vernon generally spelled Delcenia's last name as Burris. I think 70-year-old Delcenia was married to 69-year-old Jacob Burrows (farm laborer). Jacob is another name for me to explore! *Tentatively*, I assume Jacob was Alice's father.

Why weren't Agnes and Ella Roy on any 1870 Census anywhere? WHERE WERE THEY???

One of the first records I found using the Smithsonian Museum Freedmen's Bureau portal was a listing of enslavers and their enslaved. Two Alberts were listed in the 20-to-50 age category. The first Albert Roy (or Ray) had a former owner named Manard (or Masard or Mansad). I could not find any Mansards in Virginia—except for a "mansard" roof and Mansard Press. The other Albert was owned by a Mrs. Spessard (or Spessiard, or Spessara). I found some Spessards in **Petersburg**, Craig County, VA, near where an Albert Roe/Roy was "transported" for work in 1865. The Spessard[76] father was a leader in the Confederacy whose son died tragically during the war. Was one of these records for my Albert Roy born around 1838 in Virginia, and his nephew namesake born in Manassas around 1876?

Albert's Roy Ride to Freedom on a Stolen Horse?

When I started this book project in earnest in 2023, I immediately found thrilling information about a person named Albert Roy in the Freedmen's Bureau records. The documents indicated he and a friend, Henry Newsom, stole two horses from neighbor W.G. Birkett in 1865. A movie raced across my brain as I imagined Albert and Henry galloping to freedom to Fort Monroe, near present-day Hampton, Virginia. Wow! My Albert escaped to the exact location where the first Angolans were brought to "Point Comfort" in 1619 in what is now English-speaking America?

Every nerve in my body tingled with excitement. I wrote a harrowing story about how three enslaved men escaped from a Confederate work camp in Hampton, VA. Then they stealthily made their way to Fort Monroe during the dead of night in 1861. They prayed the Fort's Union commander would help them. Lo and behold, Commander Benjamin F. Butler was the first to claim those runaways as "contrabands of war"—property—who would *not* be returned to their rebel owners.

That momentous act changed everything for African Americans wishing to be free. Thousands walked, ran, swam, or galloped toward every Union workcamp in the nation, but especially to Washington, DC. And it looked like my Albert Roy and his buddy had taken advantage of that avenue to freedom!

I traveled to that very spot in May 2024, reveling that my family was part of the hallowed history of Fort Monroe which included the first Africans. On top of that, Freedmen's Bureau records identified other Roys named Albert in Yorktown, Jamestown, and Williamsburg. My book would be a *blockbuster*, for sure!

I thought I was sniffing up the right tree ... until I realized a transcription typo. The horse stealer, transcribed as Albert Roy, may have actually been someone named Albert *Rip*. That delicious story may not have been for *my* Roy family after all. So, I set aside that compelling book project about Black contraband and buffalo hunters. I vowed to concentrate on following the Genealogical Proof Standard to document as many irrefutable secrets about Grammie Ella Roy Carter's heritage as possible for this book.

Many months passed, then I reviewed those "stole a horse" records again. A Birkett *did* marry into the PWC Weir family and there was a Henry Newsome living nearby in Manassas. So, is the heroic story true? Did my Albert escape to Fort Monroe on horseback after all?

All Roads Led to Manassas

So many records searched. So many false conclusions reached. So many theories dashed to smithereens. So many Albert Roys who *could have been* related to me. So many possible places Albert *could have traveled*. But as I found more and more documents, and spoke with DNA relatives and experts in Virginia, the truth became more evident.

All roads led to Manassas, home of the first and second Battles of Bull Run in the Civil War. And those roads most likely led to the Weir enslaver's Liberia plantation. By 1870, Albert, his wife Alice, her parents, their cousin Frankie, and farm laborer Roughton William were living very close to Edgar Weir, a descendant of the largest slaveholding family in PWC. Genealogists know that many former slaves stayed put after slavery, continuing to work for their former masters. Albert's proximity to Edgar Weir five years after slavery convinced me that he *was* likely owned by Weirs, but I needed more proof.

Expert genealogist and author Linneall Naylor,[77] whose formerly enslaved family was given land near Liberia for their loyalty, believes my Roys were also enslaved by the Weirs. I tightened the strings on my detective hat, searching for additional confirmatory documents.

After slavery, Albert's life had shifted toward community involvement and leadership. Linneall recalls reading something which intimated that Albert was "almost White" and someone who "spoke well." She said he had a prominent role in the community, and he was known for his involvement in the church and his positive contributions to the Manassas community.

In 1869, the 15th Amendment to the US Constitution granted black men the right to vote. You can imagine how proud I was to see Albert Roy and Henry Jackson (See Chapter 12) listed amongst the men deemed "Qualified Voters in Prince William County.

But if life was going so well in Manassas, why did Albert remove himself and his family? Why did they travel 400 miles away to Mount Vernon, to work for former US Secretary of the Interior, Columbus Delano?

During the Reconstruction era (1865-1877), Black people throughout America hoped for a better life. Freedmen's schools were set up with help from the government. These schools taught the formerly enslaved and their children reading, writing, and job skills. Even though there were serious threats of violence from those protesting against education for Black people, these schools were crucial for their future. They found homes and started going to school once it became legal for them to do so.

According to a 20 Nov 1868 letter from W.S. Chase at the Freedmen's Bureau,[78] Albert Roy was serving as a Trustee for the local colored school in Manassas:

Aldie, I visited the point and found the person who had been teaching had given up his school and gone to work some miles away. He had only 7 scholars and could not get more at this season. I sent word to him to communicate to you or myself upon the subject. Mr. A.G. Davis promised he would give , ?, acre of land for a school there. I have not visited but will do so the first week the school at Manassas is in a prospering condition. Miss Tennie Spear, teacher, the colored people are doing a little towards supporting the teacher. The trustees are John Miles, Henry German(?), ALBERT ROY, William Lomax, Sumner Fitts, Hampton Pinn and W.S. Chase.

I am respectfully your Servant, W.S. Chase, A.S.A.Comr.

This designation suggests that Albert was not only literate but also invested in the future of his community, helping to lay the foundations for a new society during Reconstruction.

Many Black families reunited after being split apart during slavery. They put advertisements in newspapers looking for their kin. Maybe that's how Albert stayed in touch with his sister Agnes.

The newly freed folk had to adapt to new freedoms and face many challenges. Even though the war ended slavery, getting to live as free people was not much easier. From 1865 to the early 1900s, they had to find ways to build new lives. But there was resistance from groups like the Ku Klux Klan and "Black Codes"—laws that limited their freedoms and kept them working for White landowners.

Even with these problems, the Black community in Manassas, Virginia, stayed strong. Churches, like the African Methodist Episcopal (AME) Church, played a big role, offering a place to worship, learn, and socialize with family and friends.

Why Was Albert a Witness on a Loyalty Oath?

The Southern Claims Commission let loyal Unionists receive money for property lost during the war, to help support themselves. Many enslavers were bold enough to sign a loyalty oath to get compensation for their land and now-free human property. There is evidence that Albert Roy had friends on both sides of the bitterness-about-slavery-ending aisle.

In 1870, George Trimmer, a builder/farmer worth $13,088, swore an Oath of Loyalty to the Union in a U.S. Southern Claims Commission case. Even though he was a Confederate prisoner of war, as shown in Figure 51, his neighbors like Albert Roy and several others signed as "witnesses to the other facts" of George Trimmer's claim that he did not willingly serve in, or help the cause of the Confederate Army.[79]

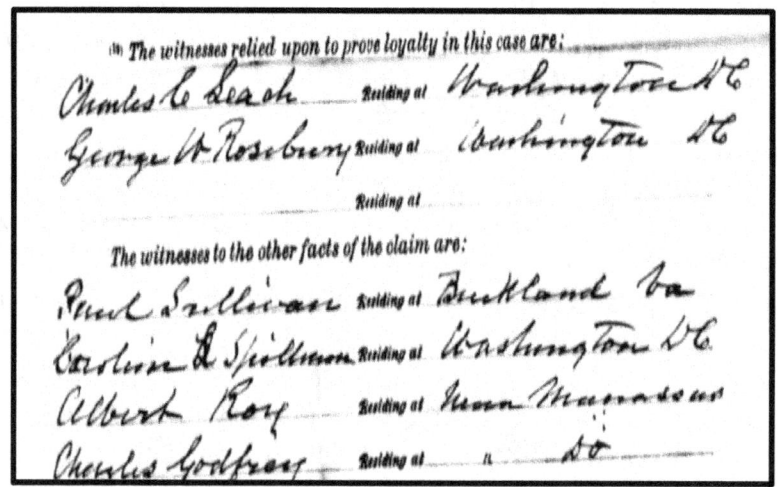

Figure 51: *Albert Witnessed a Loyalty Oath*

Was Albert coerced or paid to sign as a witness, or was he actually Trimmer's friend? How were the other people who signed the Oath associated to Albert Roy? Were they former owners, employers, or friends of his enslaver? Did they help Albert migrate to Ohio?

I used this information to solidify that Albert Roy lived in Manassas as of 1870. I also examined all people on the following partial Loyalty Oath document using rigorous genealogical research and DNA scrutiny.

I found several DNA matches to people whose trees had witness Benjamin Grubbs, so I wondered what part they may have played in my family search. I also noticed that the Charles Godfrey witness lived a few houses from Albert, according to the 1870 Census. So Albert was surrounded by White and Black people who seemed to depend on him for support, work, and maybe even friendship.

The Bottom Line

Albert Roy was a man of many talents. He worked a variety of jobs during his lifetime, some for wealthy, influential bosses like the Braddocks and Delanos. He was a School Trustee in Manassas, multi-property owner in Mount Vernon, restaurant owner, appraiser of wills, and an upstanding member of the Wayman AME Church. He obviously believed in keeping his family safe, having taken Ella, nephew Albert W. Roy, some of Ella's children, and other boarders under his wing in Virginia and Ohio. Albert Roy seemed to be a go-getter who was trusted and liked by all strata of people.

But I still cannot yet figure out why, when and how my Roys left Virginia for Ohio. And I cannot confirm whether Albert helped Grammie Carter pay off her mortgage by 1930, or procure her fine furnishings. However, his stellar track record of service and family protection suggests it is within the realm of probability.

Figure 52: *Was Albert Enslaved by the Weirs at Liberia Plantation?*

CHAPTER 11: Identifying the Roys' Enslavers

The Intricacies of Black Genealogy

Every one of my genealogy projects entices me to embark on a thrilling quest to uncover the well-hidden secret history of my ancestors. I always begin with several primary goals to find documents that prove or disprove theories of parentage. Then I build an online family tree, and interview family members who may already know the focus person I'm writing about.

I collect as many documents as I can, starting with myself, then working backward through the generations. I create a timeline of events on a spreadsheet for each family member encountered. Then comes the hard part ... determining whether my ancestors had been enslaved.

If my ancestor appears on the 1870 Census, but not the 1860 Census, it often means they were enslaved and one must determine who the enslaver was––a feat in itself. I generally perform a community analysis of everyone in the 1870 Census the your ancestors resided, copying and pasting the entire transcribed Census, page by page, into a spreadsheet, so I can sort the data however I wish.

I was fortunate to be able to visit the Weir Plantation in Manassas, Prince William County (PWC), VA, in 2024. The 1870 Census and other documents seem to indicate that Albert Roy was living next to (or in) the Weir Plantation (Figure 52). That started me on a quest to prove or disprove whether some of my Roys were enslaved by the largest plantation owner in PWC.

TIP: If your ancestor lived near a wealthy person and was listed as laborer, it's possible they worked for and may have been enslaved by that rich person. It's time to put on your reading glasses and scour the probate records, inventory lists, tax records, and wills for the wealthy guy to try to find your ancestors' names. Add pertinent documents to your tree and timeline of events.

However, *not* finding your ancestors in the 1860 Census doesn't automatically mean they were enslaved. After emancipation, many African Americans changed their surnames. Some took a surname for the first time, while others replaced names given to them by their former masters. Some even adopted the name of their last owner, a previous owner, or a Black relative.

TIP: *Know that Census takers typically visit houses one by one, street by street, within neighborhoods. If you find your black family listed next to a wealthy White family in the Census, it's possible they worked for them, but that's not a guaranteed fact. That may be a clue that you need to investigate that White person's records for listings of slave names that might be your ancestors. If you're unsure where your family lived in 1870, try searching the Census with different spellings of their surname, as well as in various states where they might have resided.*

On a genealogy trip to Virginia in 2024, I had the good fortune to meet up with Genealogy Queen and author Bernice Bennett. She was kind enough to show me around the Daughters of the American Revolution Research Room. There, I found a Pandora's Box of useful information about Prince William County. One book was called *Some Slaves of Prince William County, Virginia, Partial Will Books 1734-1872*, compiled by Sandra Barlau. (Figure 53) It listed all of my Roy ancestors' names, slave owners, where the file is located in the courthouse. That treasure trove pointed me toward Liberia Plantation.

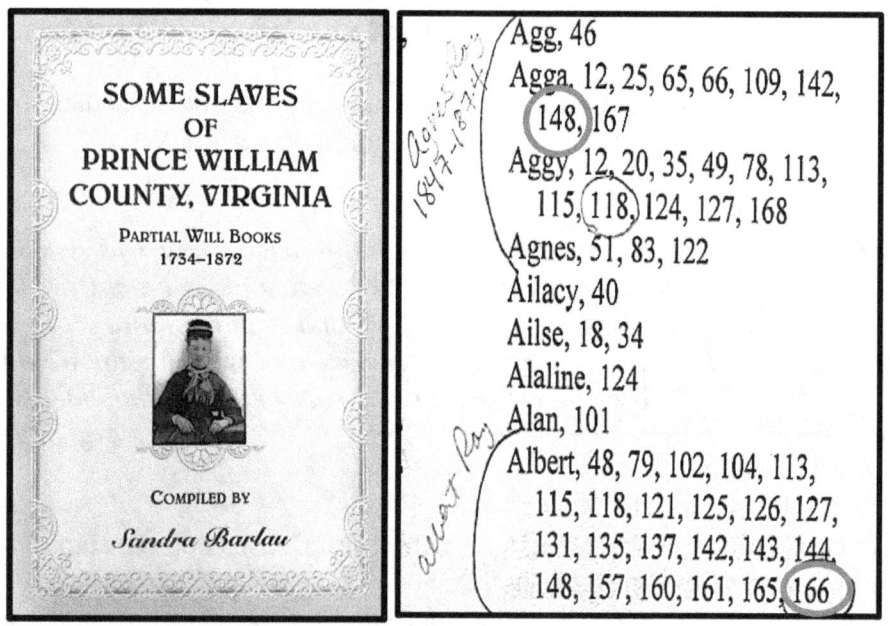

Figure 53: *Agnes & Albert in Some Slaves in PWC Wills, 1723-1872.*

Did the Weirs Enslave Our Roys?

William Weir was the largest slaveholder in Prince William County, VA. The Weirs sold grains and vegetables and raised sheep, horses, cattle, and hogs. A hundred and fifty years ago, William's Liberia plantation was one of the largest and most lucrative farms in western PWC, thanks to 90 unnamed, enslaved workers. (Figure 54)

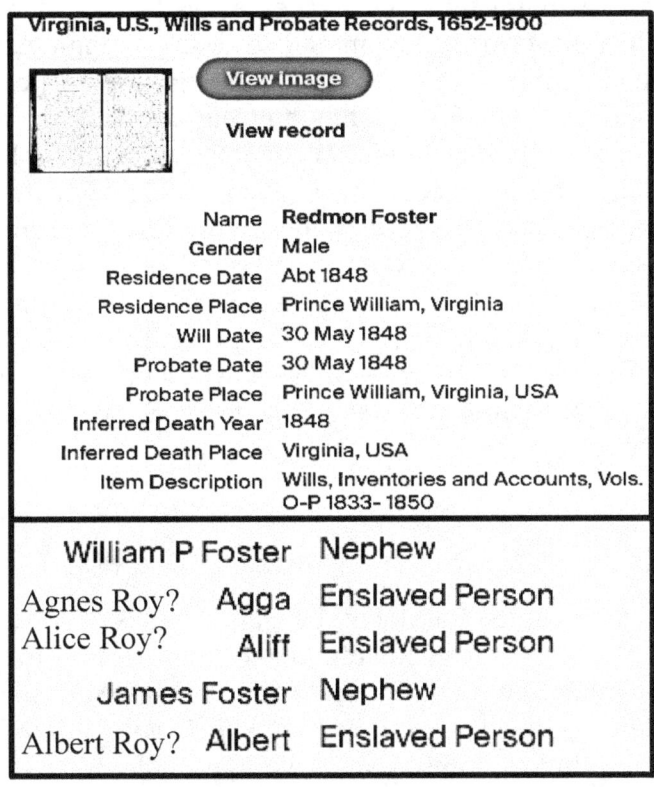

Figure 54: Was Redmon Foster Our Enslaver?

William's house and field workers maintained the Weir's prosperous 1,660-acre farm during the mid-19th century. His house servants included cooks, laundresses, and blacksmiths. Field workers farmed and took care of the work and eatable animals. Gardeners ensured their plantation environs were stunning. Talented carpenters kept the buildings in tip-top shape. Unfortunately, there exists no comprehensive list of all the Weir's slaves by name, or their family connections. The Weir's enslaved Naylor family is usually the only one mentioned in records because they were rewarded with property for their loyalty.

In May 2024, I was treated to a tour of the Liberia Plantation by Rachael Goldberg, a knowledgeable guide from the Manassas Museum. She said the house was commandeered by the Confederates during the first Battle of Bull Run in 1861, then by the Union Army during the second Battle of Bull Run in 1862. Goose bumps prickled on my skin as I stood in rooms that might have hosted President Lincoln and other notable figures who visited before, during, and after the War.

Liberia's history is notable because it served as both a Union and a Confederate base, with graffiti still visible on its walls. I wondered what duties my Roy ancestors performed, imagining possibilities ranging from house or farming servitude during the Civil War, to potential espionage for the Union Army. Perhaps I've watched too many spy movies, but my mind pictured Albert overhearing critical discussions or decoding messages as he and his wife served the military leaders dinner. Yes, I have a vivid imagination.

Why might the Liberia property matter to my lineage search? Proximity. The 1870 Census in Table 9 shows my Roy relatives lived near Edgar Weir. Were Albert and his wife Alice, cousin Frankie, friends (or family?) Jacob and Delcenia, and farm laborer, Roughton William still living at the Liberia plantation? A Freedmen's Bureau record says Ella's mother, Agnes Roy, died in Manassas in 1874. Manassas is not a large town. So, the proximity to Weir enslavers was likely.

Did Redmon Foster Own Albert, Alice and Agnes?

It was a stormy day near the Capitol of the United States of America. Sitting in the Daughters of the American Revolution (DAR) research room, I held my breath while thumbing through Will Book Q, 1851-1858, in the *Some Slaves of Prince William County, Virginia, Partial Will Books 1723-1872* that Sandra Barlau was kind enough to transcribe for world genealogists like me to utilize. I breathed out slowly when I found several of my family names in the Slave Name Index: the "A" names for Agnes, Alice, and Albert are indexed in Figure 52.

I found a compelling record on page 148, but I couldn't scream my excitement in the hallowed DAR room. On 9 Aug 1848, page 39 of the Inventory and Appraisal section of Redmond Foster's probate records, I recognized several family names out of a list of 35 enslaved people. Two were named Agga (nicknames for Agnes), one Aliss (Alice), one Albert and one Matida (Matilda?).

Holy Bejesus! Could this mean that Agnes, Alice, Albert and Matilda were siblings who were once owned by Redmon Foster? Census records confirm their birthdates could have been before 1849.

1870 US Federal Census for Albert Ray, Manassas, Prince William, VA

Surname	Given Name	Age	Birth Year	Gender	Race	Occupation	Real Estate Value	Personal Estate Value	Birthplace
Ray	Albert	30	1840	Male	Mulatto	Farm Laborer			Virginia
Ray	Alice	23	1847	Female	Black	Keeping House			Virginia
Ray	Frank	16	1854	Female	Mulatto	At Home			Virginia
William	Roughton			Male	Black	Farm Laborer			South Carolina
Burrows	Jacob	69	1801	Male	Black	Farm Laborer			Virginia
Burrows	Delcenia	70	1800	Female	Black	Keeping House			Virginia
Diggs	Randolph	59	1811	Male	Black	Blacksmith			Virginia
Diggs	Mary	33	1837	Female	Black	Keeping House			Maryland
Diggs	Andrew	4	1866	Male	Black				District of Columbia
Wacuber	Mary	14	1856	Female	Black				Maryland
Cawthon	Edward	27	1843	Male	White	Farmer	1500	550	England
Cawthon	Frederick	25	1845	Male	White	Farmer	1500		England
Hornbaker	John R	35	1835	Male	White	Miller	16000	2280	New Jersey
Hornbaker	Elizabeth	28	1842	Female	White	Keeping House			New Jersey
Hornbaker	Edwin	11	1859	Male	White	At School			Virginia
Merritt	Oliver P	24	1846	Male	White	At School			Massachusetts
Hornbaker	Levi J	23	1847	Male	White	At School			New Jersey
Hagon	Annie	19	1851	Female	White	Domestic Servant			Virginia
Sheilds	William	23	1847	Male	Black	Farm Laborer			North Carolina
Weir	Edgar V	32	1838	Male	White	Farmer	12000	1275	Virginia
Weir	Eugenia	30	1840	Female	White	Keeping House			Virginia
Weir	Edna	6	1864	Male	White				Virginia
Weir	Harriett	4	1866	Female	White				Virginia

Table 9: 1870 Community Analysis for Manassas, Roys & Weirs.

Who was Redmond Foster, where did he live, and why did he have 35 enslaved people? According to the *PWC Reliquary* journal dated October 2005,[80] Redmon Foster was born on 15 August 1785, in Nokesville, PWC, Virginia. Nokesville is only five miles from Liberia Plantation. Sometimes, proximity is everything. It's a complicated story, but Redmond married Jane L. Hooe REID, with whom the Slave Trader Sheriff Walker Reid Millan is kin. **Fosters,**

Millans, and **Weirs**. Did they gift/trade/sell slaves amongst each other? And who was Richard Atkinson? (Figure 55).

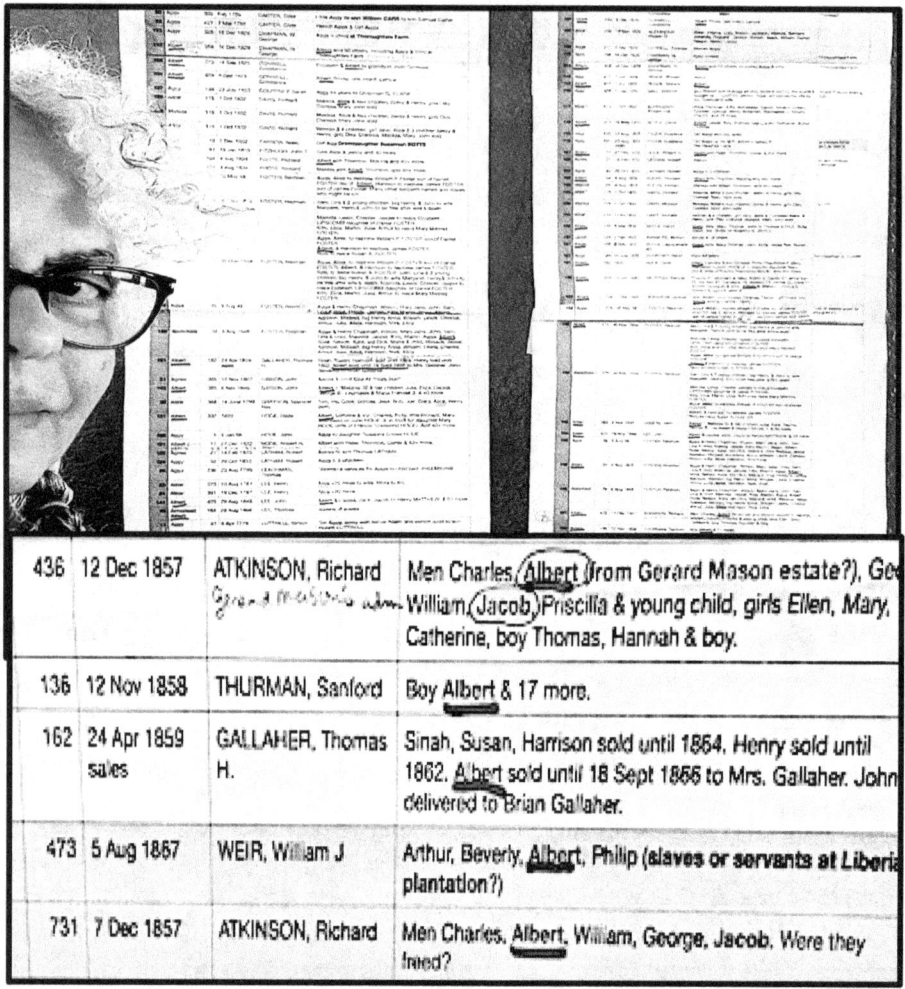

Figure 55: Sleuthing Owners & Owned in PWC.

Did the 1867 Probate Record Prove Anything?

In my research regarding the genealogy of Albert Roy, I found compelling evidence linking him to William J. Weir's estate, particularly through an examination of the probate records and census data from the post-Civil War era.

First, in the book *Some Slaves of Prince William County*, a pivotal record appears on page 473, dated August 5, 1867, which lists William J. Weir in the Estate Accounts section (Figure 54). This record includes the names of

ARTHUR (my grandfather and uncle's name), Beverly, ALBERT (Albert Roy?), and Philip, identified as slaves or servants at Liberia. The mention of these individuals suggests they may have remained on the property after the abolition of slavery, which is significant for understanding Albert's status and potential ongoing relationship with the Weir family.

Second, in the 1870 Census, Albert's family was residing near William's son, Edgar Weir, who continued to live at Liberia. However, my Roy family was not listed in the Weir household census report, indicating a separation from the Weir family despite their proximity.

Third, an entry from December 1857 in the same book records that, "men Charles, ALBERT, William, George, and JACOB were managed by probate lawyer Richard Atkinson following William Weir's death." A man named Jacob was lodging with Albert and Alice Roy in 1870, suggesting a continued connection after they worked for the Weirs.

Given Albert's loyalty to the Weir family, it is plausible that Edgar Weir may have provided him with land to cultivate, similar to the arrangement made for the Naylor family. It's also possible that Albert's sister, Agnes, started working at Liberia (or nearby) after the 1870 Census but before she died a farmer in Manassas in 1874.

Further research is needed to uncover more records that might clarify Albert Roy's circumstances during this period. I must further explore the connections between my formerly enslaved kin and their former owners in this post-Civil War context.

Some of our DNA cousins gave me information about possible Roy, Gaskins, Robinson, and Carter families who lived in Manassas. Local genealogy expert Linneall Naylor, who helped write *Black Communities of Fairfax: A History,* [81] has been of immeasurable support in helping me understand the African-American dynamics in Manassas and neighboring Fairfax County. Our discussions led to hypotheses that my Roys may have been owned by the Weirs. I was delighted to find Roys in the Rose Hill Cemetery, hoping to validate our familial connection on a future trip.

Did I learn anything useful from this laborious probate index exercise? A little bit... or perhaps everything. As shown at the bottom of the on-the-wall chart in Figure 54, I noticed that on 12 Dec 1857, page 436, Inventory and Appraisals, a man named Richard Atkinson had something to do with enslaved men named Charles, Albert, Jacob, George, and William, as well as *Priscilla* and eight other enslaved people. So what? Atkinson was front and center in a *ghoulish affair* in 1850 that involved an enslaved woman named Agness (two s's). I wondered if Albert, Jacob, Priscilla, and Agness were related to me in some way, because they all lived in Prince William County and they all seemed to have Richard Atkinson, Millans, Weirs, and Masons in common.

Did Masons Connect With My 2xGGM?

Maybe nothing. Maybe something gruesome ...

I found an interesting *possible* connection to Gerard Alexander Mason (1793-1849) who lived at the Wood Bridge Plantation in Prince William County, VA. This Gerard had a reputation for being an ugly drunk, a terror to his slaves, and was disagreeable to everyone he did business with. The *Alexandria Gazette* newspaper published grisly stories about several tragedies involving Gerard Mason.[82]

In one of his frenzies, the enslaver reportedly stomped on the back of his personal servant woman. Her back forever broken, she had to crawl on the floor to do her chores, until one day in a drunken fury, he killed her. Mason was tried for her murder, but the jury felt his slaves couldn't be left unsupervised, so Mason was allowed to return to his plantation.

Agness, a strong Black woman known for her candor, was forced to become Gerard's replacement servant. There are various versions of what happened next. One account reported that Mr. Gerard Mason returned home under the influence of liquor. He was offended that Agness had not sharpened his axe and that she wouldn't *turn up her clothes* for him. He threatened to kill her with the ax. She warded off the blow. Wrestling the axe from him resulted in a blow that killed him in his bed. Agness made no effort to escape, telling her mother, Priscilla, what had happened. Another version was that Mason made sexual advances toward Agness as he held her baby over a vat of boiling oil. She reacted by grabbing the axe and hitting him. He fell on his bed, dead.[83]

According to the newspapers, several White neighbors who witnessed Mason's violent acts toward his slaves, came forward to support Agness's self-defense plea. Even so, she was tried, convicted, and hanged in 1850 at the Brentsville Jail in PWC.[84] Her ghost is rumored to haunt the jail to this day. So, of course, I took my family on a field trip to the infamous jail in 2024. The fellow working at the jail gave us a superb historical tour of the building and the adjoining courthouse. Why was I so interested in visiting this location? After Gerard Mason was killed by in 1850, Richard Atkinson, Administrator of Mason's estate from 1850 to 1856, posted a Slave Sale (Figure 56).

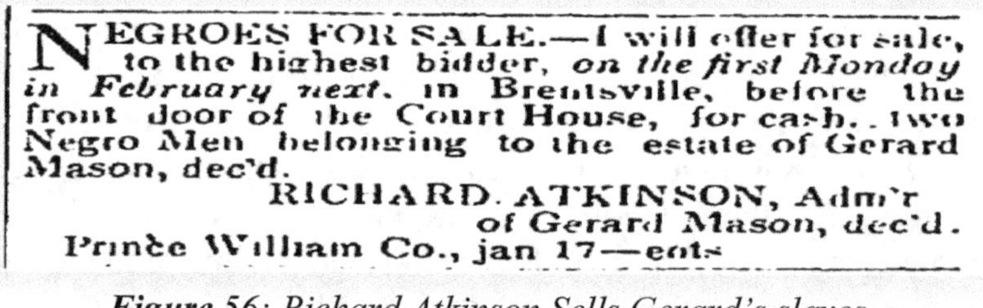

> NEGROES FOR SALE.—I will offer for sale, to the highest bidder, *on the first Monday in February next*, in Brentsville, before the front door of the Court House, for cash, two Negro Men belonging to the estate of Gerard Mason, dec'd.
> RICHARD. ATKINSON, Adm'r
> of Gerard Mason, dec'd.
> Prince William Co., jan 17—eots

Figure 56: *Richard Atkinson Sells Gerard's slaves*

Did Millans and Weirs, who lived close to Gerard Mason's heirs, purchase some of Mason's slaves, via lawyer Atkinson, between 1850 and 1856? Millan was the Administrator of Eleanor A. C. Mason's affairs in 1868.[85] Lawyer Atkinson facilitated many legal transactions for Millans, Weirs, Foster's, and Masons. All those people lived within twenty miles of each other, so I pay attention whenever I see Atkinson's name.

Did Atkinson sell a girl named Agnes born around 1847-48, as well as her unnamed mother born around 1830 to the Millans or Weirs? Did that baby girl, Agnes, become my 2xGGM?

Or, was baby Agnes's mother the hanged Agness that is spelled with two s's? Perhaps we will never know.

What I *did* find were several generations of women named Agnes in the Thomas Whaley Violett family of Fairfax. For example, Agnes Violett Banner Haislip, 1829-1875, in Fairfax County, had a 9- and 42-year-old enslaved female in 1860. So what? Well, Thomas Violette married Elizabeth *Millan*. Were any of Violette's enslaved women named Agnes and gifted to the Millans? I only found one DNA match to my supertesters who had Violettes in their family tree, and few with Millan's in their trees.

On another tac, I studied the Millan's 1850 Slave Schedule in Fairfax County, VA. Walker Millan, 25, was living with his parents, Captain John Millan and Elizabeth Reid Millan. Table 8 reveals John owned ten enslaved people, aged five to 69. It is unknown whether they were one family, or whether any of them was Benjamin Taylor with whom Walker Millan signed a Work Contract in 1866, or if any were a relation to my Agnes Roy. They were nameless property.

After John Millan died in 1858, his estate went largely to his wife, Elizabeth (Table 8). The 1860 Census Slave Schedule shows she owned 14 people. But guess what? She and son Walker Reid Millan were living together. Legally, he owned two females, as shown on the second line of Figure 56. One was 12 (my Agnes?) and the other 30 (Agnes' mother?). I presume the total 16 enslaved people lived together at the Millan's Oakley Plantation.

Those two females in Walker's 1860 coffers would have been 20 and three years old in 1850, but no such slaves were found in the 1850 Census for daddy John Millan. Were those two females were acquired between John's death in 1858 and the 1860 Census?

Once I arranged the chain of events in this way, the answer became clearer. The hanged Agness on the Mason plantation was dead after 1850, so she could not be the 30-year-old woman listed in Millan's 1860 Slave Schedule. Some time after 1850, Walker Millan had as his property a young girl and her likely mother, perhaps from Richard Atkinson or the Weir estate. Were they my future 2xGGM, Agnes, and her unknown mother? I discussed the possibility with genealogists Pat Smith Jenkins and Linneall Naylor, experts on Black history in Fairfax, Loudoun, and Prince William Counties.

Name	John Millan
Residence Date	1850
Residence Place	Fairfax, Virginia, USA
Number of Enslaved People	10
Role	Slave Owner

All Enslaved People (Gender)	Age
Male	69
Female	47
Female	40
Male	15
Male	35
Female	30
Female	16
Male	12
Male	7
Male	5

Name	Elizabeth Millan
Residence Date	1860
Residence Place	Fairfax, Virginia, USA
Number of Enslaved People	14
Role	Slave Owner

Household members

Gender	Age
Male	27
Male	25
Female	17
Female	18
Female	19
Female	20
Female	45
Male	1
Male	25
Male	17
Male	2
Female	3
Female	4
Male	5

Table 8: 1850 and 1860 Census for John and Elizabeth Reid Millan.

Here's my rationale. As already mentioned in Chapter 3, Agnes Roy signed a Work Contract with Walker Reid Millan in Dec 1866, two weeks before Ella was born. He only had two personal slaves, both females. According to the 1860 Census, one girl was 12 (Agnes's age) and the woman was 30 (perhaps Agnes' mother). My Agnes was living in District 6 of Alexandria where Millan was likely working at the former Slave Pen.

All the enslaved people listed under Walker R. Millan in the 1860 Slave Census were "owned" by Millan (Figure 57). However, it appears that Millan only kept 2 of his enslaved people for his own service—a 12-year-old girl and a 30-year-old woman (Agnes and her unnamed mother?). The rest of the enslaved people on this Slave Census appear to have been leased to those listed, and the money went to Millan as profit.[86]

Other deed records from 1858 with Millan's Slave trader partner indicate Millan was supposed to move out of the Slave Pen at 1315 Duke Street in

District 6 in Alexandria. But I wonder if he continued occupying the building. After all, he was voted Sheriff of Fairfax in 1867 and likely needed the jail. Was Agnes (with infant Ella) a servant in that building that oozed such terror when it was the Old Slave Pen? Were those Grammie's unspoken memories?

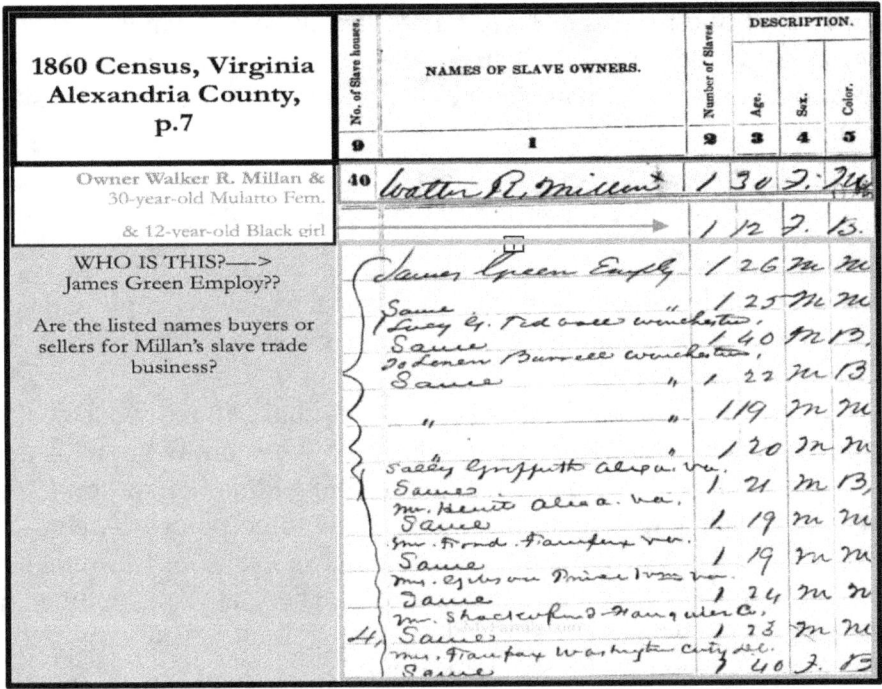

Figure 57: Walker Millan's 1860 Slave Schedule: Agnes & Her Mom?

The 1834 Cohen & Company A Full Directory for Washington City, Georgetown, and Alexandria (Figure 24), placed the reversely-named Armfield & Franklin (as the firm is named in the 1830 US Census) on "Duke near Fayette street'78. Fayette Street is one street east of Payne Street, and for some reason is frequently used in relation to the slave jail at 1315 Duke Street, for example, several times by Kephart, once in a proposed 1853 property division and once in an 1858 letter to Walker R. Millan notifying him that he has sold the property and Walker needs to vacate the premises, and frequently in City tax lists."

Were my suppositions that Agnes was forced to work in the former Slave Pen wrong? There are so many points at which Agnes Roy and Millan's lives intersected, but was she free of him after 1863 when Millan joined the 4th Calvary and fought in the Civil War?

Sheriff Walker Millan's daughter, the widowed Elizabeth *Bessie* Millan Byron, married John P. Mason in 1889, further solidifying the close relationship between the Millans and Masons of Fairfax, VA. Grammie Ella

Roy Carter named one of her daughters Bessie, but that is barely pertinent evidence to prove Grammie is related to the Millans.

I think it probable that Walker Millan was Agnes's enslaver, but I found no deed or inventory documents with Agnes' name that explicitly proved that proclamation. I looked through online will and probate records for Millans to see if I could find listings of slave names that indicated which family member enslaved which slaves, but one must explore records at the Fairfax Courthouse––the records are not available online. I shall attempt to research on site during a future visit.

Did We Find the Enslaver?

Determining who the enslaver was can be as difficult as herding cats. There are so many possibilities and dead ends. Since most enslaved people had no printed last names, it's nearly impossible to find evidence of the correct Alice, or Agnes, or Albert, in my case.

I think it's possible that Alice, Agnes and Albert were enslaved by Redmond Foster before 1848, then sold to the Weir family upon his death.

I also think it's possible that Walker Reid Millan bought the 12- and 30- year old females (Agnes and her mother?) at some point between 1850 and 1860, whether it was from Atkinson's 1850-1856 sales of Mason's slaves, or from William J. Weir's 1857 probate sale. There are any number of other possiblities too, which I may explore in the future. But now, I'd like to concentrate on who Ella Roy's father was.

***Figure** 58: Was Ella Roy's Daddy at Freedmen's Village?*

CHAPTER 12: The Identity of Ella Roy's Father

Freedmen's Bureau records were a godsend to be sure. They uncovered over a dozen revealing documents about Ella's mother, Agnes Roy, and her ancestors living in DC, Manassas, Spotsylvania and Caroline Counties in Virginia. We got a glimpse of what Agnes and Ella's lives were like between 1866 and 1867, when they were protected within the confines of the Freedmen's Village. While I could not pinpoint where her daughter Ella Roy was living between 1867 and 1880, I knew that Agnes died in 1874 in Manassas.

Would I have better luck finding who Ella Roy's father was? Since I had no clue who he was, I kept in the back of my head that he was likely a White man. That seemed the only way to describe why she was so pale all of her life. But that's not necessarily the case.

Figure 58, from the Library of Congress, shows various men living in the Freedmen's Village, along with a woman and child. Could any of those men have been my Ella's father?

I developed five theories of fatherhood on the next pages. Which one do YOU think is correct?

Theory #1: Albert Roy Was Ella's Father

Some of my living relatives believe to this day that Albert Roy was Ella's father. It's understandable. Albert and his wife, Alice, raised Ella as their own precious child in Mount Vernon. Because Grammie Carter never wanted to talk about her past, the truth became a blur after her guardians died. However, I found enough data to answer this Theory #1 question.

It's simple. Agnes's 1874 Death Record said Albert Roy was Agnes' brother. In addition, Grammie Carter's 1962 Obituary also indicated the late Albert and Alice Roy were Ella's Uncle and Aunt.

The bottom line: Since Albert had no known biological children who survived birth with his first wife, Alice Burris, I shall use the 1874 Death Register and Ella's Obituary to prove Albert was *not* Ella's father. Therefore, Theory #1 is false.

Theory #2: Ella's Father Was Surnamed Delano

My mother believed her Grammie Carter's father had to be a White man, because Ella's skin was so pale, and her hair was silkier than it was kinky, like most African Americans.[87] Mom said more than once, "They say Grammie's birth mother died in Virginia, and the Delanos brought her and the other Roys home to Mount Vernon. The 1880 Census confirmed that my Roys were live-in 'servants' for the Delanos. That's all the proof I need to certify that Ella was somehow related to the Delanos." Was Mom's theory true?

"Why would the Delanos take all our Roys into their manor house unless there was a special blood relationship to Grammie?" Mom said. "And it makes so much sense that the Delano family financed Grammie's seemingly affluent lifestyle." Mom's lips pressed together, in an "And that's that!" to end her empassioned soliloquy.

Fast forward to 2025. How might we prove or disprove this Delano theory of parentage? DNA to the rescue … maybe. I built the Delano family tree back to the 1700s. If Columbus was Ella's father—my two-times great-grandfather—we should share DNA with third cousins. According to the *Shared cM Project* chart in Appendix B, third cousins might expect to share an average of 79 centimorgans (cMs), or a range of 0 to 198 cMs. Six of our super-testers had Delano relationship results ranging from an almost insignificant 9 cMs to only 29 cMs. One would expect that at least some of our testers would exhibit much higher cM results for a 2xGGF. Therefore, these results do not convince me that a Delano fathered Ella Roy.

Is there another chance Mom's theory could be *part true*? *Maybe* Columbus left Albert and/or Ella some money when he and his wife died in 1896, even if they weren't blood kin. I found no *proof* of such probate or other monetary dispensation from the Delanos, however, Albert did buy five acres for $1,200 in the *Walker's Addition* of Mount Vernon in 1883. That was likely for lots 213 and 214 at 104 W. Ohio Avenue, three years after living with the Delanos. He bought lot #219 at Gambier and Mechanic Street, and lot #265 at Gambier and Sandusky Streets in 1892, just after the real estate mogul Braddocks moved to Little Rock, Arkansas. So, Albert and wife Alice were wheeling and dealing in real estate acquisitions during the time he worked for the Delanos and Braddocks.

I did ask an analyst at the Library of Congress (LOC) to look through Columbus's personal papers stored at LOC to see if Ella or Albert Roy were mentioned; the clerk found no confirmatory evidence. I personally spent a grueling afternoon at the Ohio State Archives, reading 400 of Delano's personal letters on microfilm. I only found one mention of an African American fellow Delano was recommending be hired as the first Black clerk in the White House.

The bottom line: I could find little compelling evidence that supported Mom's conclusion that Ella Roy Carter was a blood relation to, or received her lovely trinkets directly from the Delano family.

Theory #3: Ella's Father Was Walker Reid Millan

I found oodles of fascinating information about Ella's mulatto mother. Finding proof documents about her father, though, remained a mystery shrouded in disappointment. The overriding theory was that Ella's father had to be a White man, because she looked nearly as pale as a typical White woman.

Could Ella's father have been Walker Reid Millan, the Sheriff of Fairfax, Virginia? Why else did he sign a Work Contract with Agnes Roy "and child" on 15 December 1866, two weeks before Ella was born? Was Ella his child produced during Agnes work history with him, both during and after slavery? Chapter 11 discusses why I think Millan was Ella's enslaver.

Could Walker Millan be biologically related to my family through one of his ancestors?

The 1860 Fairfax Census and Alexandria Slave Schedule indicated Millan owned two females amongst the thirty or so enslaved people that he *may* have *leased* in his Slave Trader business. Could those females be my 12-year-old Agnes Roy and her 30-year-old unnamed mother? Yes.

The 1865 Alexandria Census indicated Agnes Roy was an enslaved resident in 1863. Millan's slave trader business stalled when he galloped away to join the Black Horse Cavalry in 1863 to fight against the Union. Did Millan impregnate Agnes when he returned from the War? Maybe.

Could I prove or disprove this allegation through DNA testing? Maybe. I put a lot of time and effort into researching the online family trees of Millans who match our DNA.

TIP: Use the SEARCH feature of Ancestry.com DNA matching tools and those in MyHeritage.com, 23andme and FamilyTreeDNA.com to find others researching the same surnames and share a common ancestor with you.

Using Ancestry.com DNA Pro Tools, I searched for surnames like ROY (Ella's maiden name), WEIR (largest enslaver in Prince William County), and MILLAN (from the Freedmen's Bureau Work Contract) to see if I could find blood relations with those surnames in their family trees. DNA uncovered one fellow named S. Taylor who shares 17 centimorgans with my Uncle Dale Carter, 14 cMs with my sister Carrie, and 17 cMs with Cousin Julie. Figure 58 shows all matches to the Millan name amongst our DNA super-testers.

S. Taylor lists an ancestor named George Washington Millan who was born in 1820 in Fairfax, VA, living at the Millan family Plantation in Locust

Grove (Figure 59). The amount of relationship is low, though, since that White George Washington Millan was born in 1820 and died in 1876. The further back in history, the weaker the DNA markers. Could our genetic connections to Millans be from George Washington Millan? Maybe.

Of additional interest is our DNA cousin S. Taylor's birthplace: Spotsylvaia, VA. Freedmen's Bureau records hint that many of my Roy ancestors migrated north and west from Spotsylvania and Stafford Counties to DC and Prince William and Fairfax Counties. Unfortunately, I was unable to contact with S. Taylor to learn more about our ancestral connection.

Figures 58 and 59 illustrate how far back the relationship is between my family of super-testers and DNA testers whose family trees show them to be descendants of Millans who lived in Virginia long ago.

DNA Matches (Race)		Julie	JoJo	Kenora	Dale	Kathy	Carrie	Greg	Millan and Other Ancestors
CSherid -	W	13		9					Catherine Millan, B:1655, D:1678 VA Many Chandlers, Sheridan/ReidTrees
Jonathan -	W				13		13		German Millans: Margaret, Hans, Euphy
MaryH -	W				8				Agnes Millan in Ireland.
Melissa -	W						12	12	Spanish Millans; Earles in England
Neil M -	W					10			David Millan from Scotland.
NinaM -	B		15					9	Millan: Geo Wash, Thomas, William, Robinsons in Rappahannock.
Robles -	1%B				14	11			Spanish Millans; Earles in England
Ryan -	B			9					Silverstine Millan 1918, Chester Millan 1915, Catherine Millan 1920, Preston Millan 1922, Sylvest Millan 1886, Stella Millan 1890.
Steven T -	B	17			17		14		Millans: Geo Wash, Geo, Thomas, William, John. Hortons.
TheMorgan -	W							8	Millans: Thomas, Wm, Ann, Lyle
ThomasG -	W							8	Elizabeth Paxton Millan Lyle

Figure 59: DNA Matches to the Millan Family

It's important to remember that people receive about 3500 centimorgans of DNA from *each* parent, so our low numbers in Figure 59 (9 to 29 cMs) indicate our relationships to Millans are low, likely going back to people who lived in the early 1800s or late 1700s. See Appendix B for more information about interpreting DNA results.

I studied online wills, probate records, and deeds for Millans in Fairfax County, back to the 1700s, hoping to connect them to my Agnes Roy, but I was unsuccessful in proving a strong genetic relationship to the Millans, beyond a connection to GeorgeWashington Millan. (Figure 60).

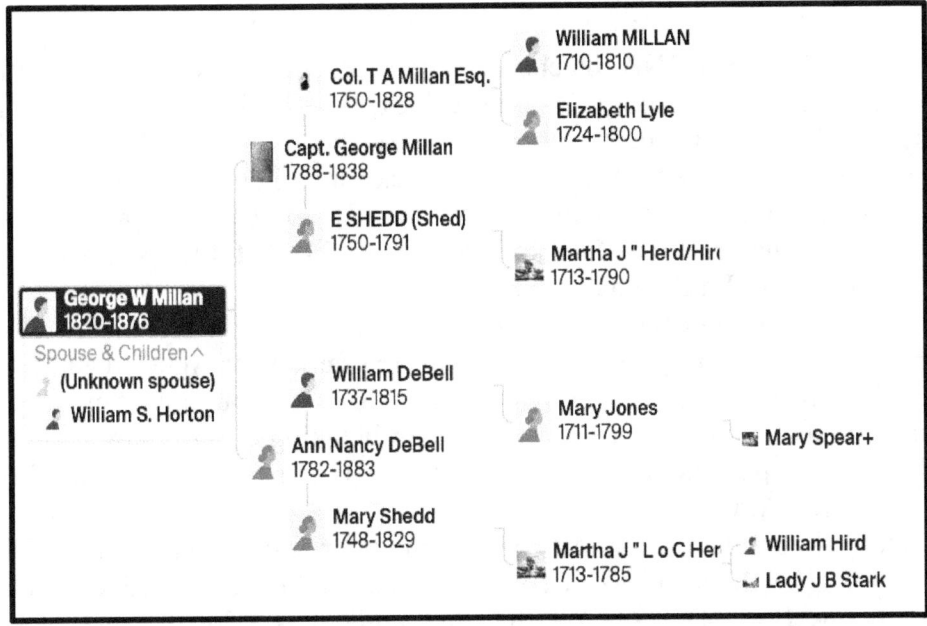

Figure 60: Millan Family Tree & George Washington Millan.

The bottom line: I concluded that the Millans are indeed genetically related to my family, perhaps from a Millan born in the late 1700s or early 1800s. But, it is unlikely that Walker Reid Millan (1824-1891) was Ella's father. The amount of shared DNA was just too low for a two-times great-grandfather.

Theory #4: Ella's Father Was Benjamin Taylor

I noticed that Walker Reid Millan entered into only two Work Contracts, both on 15 Dec 1866. One was with Agnes Roy and child, and the other was with a laborer named Benjamin Taylor. I thought it odd that Benjamin would only be paid a measly $1 per month, compared to Agnes' average $3.50 per month salary. Was he elderly or very young? I assumed Benjamin was a Black man, but I only found documents for White Benjamin Taylors in Virginia.

However, as described in Theory #3, I did find DNA evidence that an S. Taylor descended from Millans from Fairfax, VA. Did he have a relative named Benjamin Taylor who was enslaved by the Millans? I could not find any credible information about Benjamin Taylor. The bottom line: I could not determine whether Benjamin Taylor was related to Ella Roy. More research is neccessary.

Theory #5: William Henry Jackson Was Ella's Dad

For years, I had seen DNA matches who had Jacksons in their trees, but I had no clue which of my family lines those Jacksons matched ... until now. The useful Ancestry ThruLines tool in Figure 61 shows that our DNA matches found eleven people with William Henry Jackson in their trees. Yes!

Our DNA matches' trees indicate William H. Jackson, born around 1850, married a woman named Mary Jane Roy in 1874; that's the same year my Agnes Roy died. Was that a coincidence?

Why did William Henry Jackson—who may have fathered my Ella—marry 19-year-old Mary Jane Roy in 1874, the same year Agnes died? Hmm. Had William Henry been living with Agnes and Ella throughout Agnes's fatal bout with tuberculosis? Was the Jackson family taking care of baby Ella while both her young parents tilled the fields in Manassas, Freedmen's Village farms, or Fauquier, VA, where William Jackson was born?

Did William decide to marry Mary Jane after Agnes died in 1874? Were Agnes and Mary Jane sisters or cousins who shared the same grandparents? I don't know. But I DO KNOW that my family has a lot of Ancestry.com *ThruLines* DNA matches in common with Mary Jane Roy's family. They also have William Henry Jackson, and his father Henry Jackson, in their trees. That proves we are related to the Jacksons *somehow*, but how?

NOTE: Ancestry.com's ThruLines tool is only as good as the accuracy of other members' trees. You must conduct a thorough analysis of proof documents before treating ThruLines estimates as gospel. But ThruLines is an excellent tool to give you HINTS about blood relatives who might be related to you.

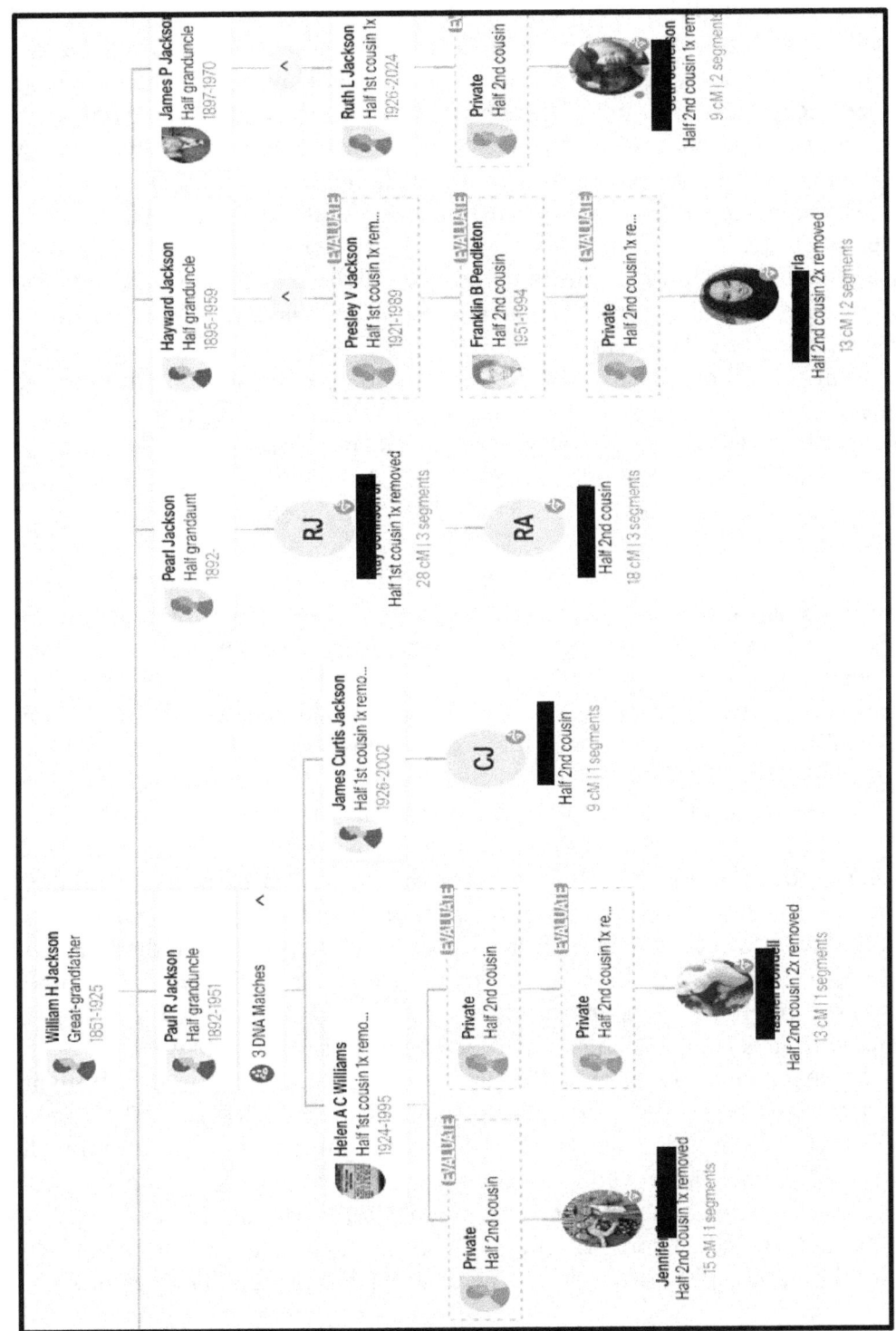

Figure 61: Does "Thru-Lines" Cinch a Jackson Fatherhood?

Did Ella's unnamed father have Jackson roots in Alexandria, DC, or the adjacent Fairfax, Prince William, Loudoun, or Fauquier Counties? I had already found solid Roy DNA matches from genealogists named Marilu and Linneal in the Manassas area. But another woman, Kaylee, had the *trifecta* in her tree: Roys, Carters, and a William Henry Jackson from the same areas as I was researching. Do those third and fourth cousins who have William Henry Jackson in their trees prove he was Ella's Dad, my 2xGGF? Possibly.

The easiest parentage theory is that teenage William Henry Jackson was a little *too friendly* with Agnes Roy during a frosty day late in March 1866, near District 6 in Alexandria. Nine months later, two days after Christmas, out popped Ella Roy. But what documented proof do I have that William Henry Jackson could be Ella's daddy?

I found a Work Contract dated 6 Dec 1865 between W.S. Howser and someone named William Jackson and three others, as shown in the partial contract in Figure 62. William would receive $6 per month for a year, working as a farmer. But the other folks mentioned in that contract would receive $12 each per month. Why the difference? Was William much younger or older than the others?

There were slightly different birthdates among the people who have a William Henry Jackson in their trees; some say he was born in 1849 and others say it was 1850 or 1851. In any case, he was likely younger than 18. Perhaps that's why he was paid less. "If" that's the reason, then it lends more credence to my theory that Ella's Dad was that teenager. William was in DC, within miles of where Agnes Roy was living, four months before she was impregnated with her daughter Ella.

Agnes and Ella lived at the East Capitol Hill Barracks between late 1866 and 1867. At some point, they moved to Manassas, then Agnes became a farmer before she died in 1874. Perhaps she wanted to be near her brother, Albert, who worked as a farmer at (or near) the Weirs' Liberia plantation. If that theory is correct, did infant Ella Roy stay with her mother in the fields, or was she watched by her Aunt Alice Roy? Or, was baby Ella living with other Roys who migrated from Spotsylvania and Caroline Counties? Or, was Ella living with Jacksons? I needed more documents to stick the answer.

My excitement level shot through the roof when I noticed a William Jackson in the 1870 Agricultural Schedule for Manassas. (Figure 63) Was he my 2xGGF? Reading about his farm gave me a glimpse into his lifestyle. He owned 20 acres of improved land and 60 acres of woodland, for a cash value of $500. He owned one horse and one milch cow, valued at $65. He produced 100 bushels of Indian corn, 12 of oats, 10 of Irish potatoes, and 50 pounds of butter during the 1870 year. The value of animals sent for slaughter was $50 and the estimated value of all farm production was $154. This description gave me vision of his lifestyle.

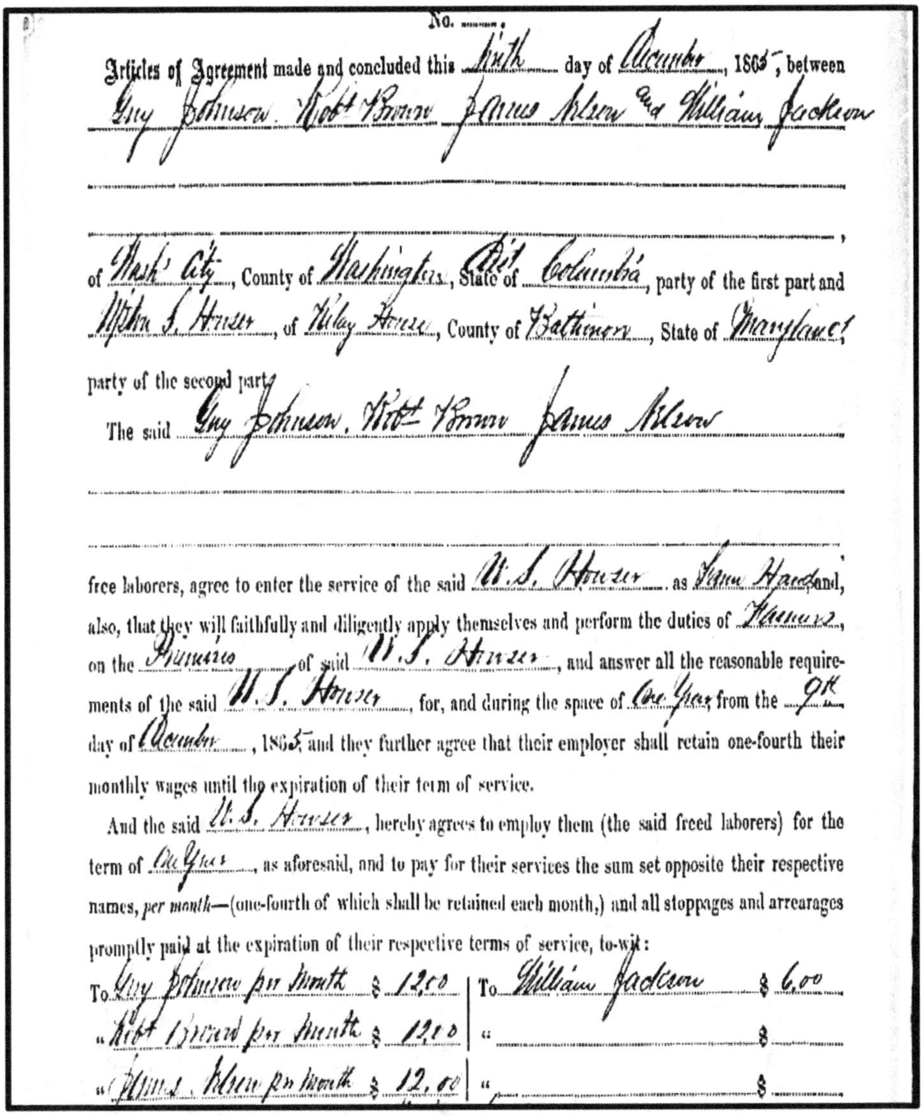

No. ......

Articles of Agreement made and concluded this Ninth day of December, 1865, between Guy Johnson, Robt Brown, James Nelson and William Jackson

of Wash' City, County of Washington, Dist. Columbia, party of the first part and Wm. S. Houser, of Riley House, County of Baltimore, State of Maryland, party of the second part.

The said Guy Johnson, Robt Brown, James Nelson

free laborers, agree to enter the service of the said W. S. Houser as Farm Hands, and, also, that they will faithfully and diligently apply themselves and perform the duties of Farmers, on the Premises of said W. S. Houser, and answer all the reasonable requirements of the said W. S. Houser, for, and during the space of One Year from the 9th day of December, 1865, and they further agree that their employer shall retain one-fourth their monthly wages until the expiration of their term of service.

And the said W. S. Houser, hereby agrees to employ them (the said freed laborers) for the term of One Year, as aforesaid, and to pay for their services the sum set opposite their respective names, *per month*—(one-fourth of which shall be retained each month,) and all stoppages and arrearages promptly paid at the expiration of their respective terms of service, to-wit:

To Guy Johnson per month	$ 12.00	To William Jackson	$ 6.00
" Robt Brown per month	$ 12.00	"	$
" James Nelson per month	$ 12.00	"	$

***Figure** 62: December 1865 Work Contract with William Jackson.*

1870 Agricultural Census Schedule

Schedule 3 – Productions of Agriculture in _Manassas_ in the County of _PWC_ in the Post Office _____ in the State of _VA_

Name of Agent, Owner or Manager	Acres of Land			Present Cash Value		Total amount of wages paid during the year including value of board	Live Stock June 1, 1870							Produce during the year ending June 1, 1870								
	Improved	Woodland	Other unimproved	Of Farm	Of Farming Implements and Machinery		Horses	Mules and Asses	Milch Cows	Working Oxen	Other Cattle	Sheep	Swine	Value of all live stock	Wheat Spring	Wheat Winter	Rye	Indian Corn	Oats	Barley	Buckwheat	Rice	Tobacco
	No	No	No	Dolls	Dolls	Dolls	No	No	No	No	No	No	No	Dolls	Bush	Bush	Bush	Bush	Bush	Bush	Bush	Lbs	Lbs
	2	3	4	5	6	7	8	9	10	11	12	13	14	15	16	17	18	19	20	21	22	23	24
1 Jackson, Wm	20	60		500	5		1		1					65				100	12				

	Cotton	Wool	Peas and Beans	Potatoes		Orchard Products	Wine	Produce of Market Gardens	Dairy Products			Hay	Seed		Hops	Hemp	Flax	Flaxseed	Silk cocoons	Sugar		Molasses	Bees		Forest products	Value of Home Manufactures	Value of animals slaughtered or sold to slaughter	Estimated Value of all farm production including betterments and addition to stock
				Irish	Sweet				Butter	Cheese	Milk sold		Clover	Grass						Maple	Cane		Wax	Honey				
	Bales (150 lbs.)	Lbs	Bush	Bush	Bush	Dolls	Gallons	Dolls	Lbs	Lbs	Gallons	Tons	Bush	Bush	Lbs	Tons	Lbs	Bush	Lbs	Lbs	Hhds (1,000 lbs)	Gallons	Lbs	Lbs	Dolls	Dolls	Dolls	Dolls
	25	26	27	28	29	30	31	32	33	34	35	36	37	38	39	40	41	42	43	44	45	46	47	48	49	50	51	52
1				10		50																					50	154

Figure 63: *1870 Agricultural Census in Manassas: William Jackson*

I couldn't determine how close this William Jackson lived to Albert because Albert did not appear in any PWC township in the Agricultural Schedule. That meant Albert didn't own or manage any land. So, I looked in the regular Census to find out how close Albert and William Jackson lived to each other. Maybe I'd find Agnes and baby Ella living with the Jacksons.

Albert was listed on page 15. Listed on page 23 was a Black farm laborer named Willie Jackson (75), housewife Wilky (65) and Richmond Jackson (21) family. Those were the wrong Jacksons, but surprise, surprise! They were living next to White MALANS whose total estate was worth $2,000. Should their Malan name be spelled Millan?

Their family consisted of John (49), Frances (35), Margaret (11), Lucy (8), Josephine (5), John (2)and LeRoy (5/12). I keep searching. Were they related to Slave Trader Walker Reid Millan?

Was the William Jackson on Census page 28 the family I sought? The head of the household was 43-year-old William, a Mulatto farm laborer whose real estate was worth $500 and his personal estate was $100. His wife was Susan and his daughters were Ellen, Susannah, and Lattie. His son was a 15-year-old named William. Wait a minute. The William Henry Jackson I thought was Ella's dad was 15 in 1865 and living in Alexandria or DC. This young William in Manassas was 15 in 1870, born in 1855, so this kid was too young to be her daddy. Heavy sigh.

However… what about his daddy named William? In 1865, his father would have been about 38 years old, so he *could* be Ella's father. Manassas isn't far from Alexandria and DC where Agnes was living in the spring of 1866 when Ella was conceived. Was this Manassas William Jackson living or visiting in DC or Alexandria in 1866 when Ella was conceived? It's possible, but I need documents to prove or disprove that assertion.

The bottom line: William H. Jackson, born between 1849 and 1851, is definitely related to us. However, the centimorgans of relationship (9cM to 58cM) are too low to certify that William H. was my 2xGGF. While he is not the slam-dunk daddy that I crave, he's the closest link I found.

Theory 6: Did Henry Jackson Bed Agnes Roy?

It's possible that 15-year-old William Henry Jackson had a tryst with 19-year-old Agnes Roy in March 1866. But is it more likely that his father, Henry Jackson, did the *deed*?

Freedmen's Bureau records to the rescue yet again. I found a July 1865 contract in Alexandria City for a $225 plot of land, three blocks from the infamous Slave Pen where Walker Millan conducted his Slave Trader business before the Civil War (Figure 64). The land was a few blocks from where Agnes Roy was living in 1865. Did the legal transaction between Alexander Jackson and a Henry Jackson involve William Henry Jackson's daddy? Was Henry's proximity to Agnes compelling proof that he could have impregnated Agnes Roy in March 1866, three months after the following contract was issued?

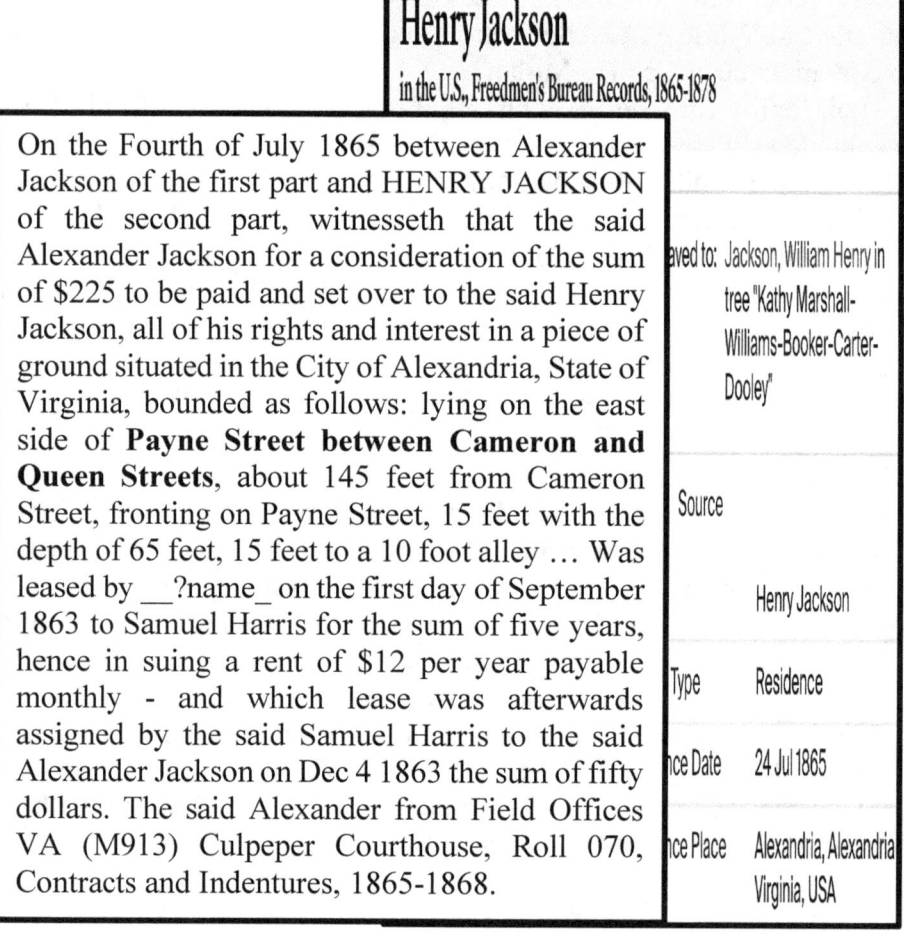

Figure 64: Deed with Henry Jackson in Alexandria in 1865.

Is Henry My First USCT?

Several of our DNA matches' trees indicated that Henry Jackson (1834-1888) was William Henry Jackson's father. Others had an 1823 birthdate, but they all agreed that Henry Jackson died in 1888. Some of the Henry Jackson records I found were for a White man, which absolutely could be correct, but most of our DNA matches had a Black Henry Jackson in their trees.

A golden ticket[88] flashed on my computer screen as I searched for documents that proved whether William Henry Jackson was my 2xGGF and Henry Jackson my 3xGGF. I almost cried when I learned Henry Jackson served in the United States Colored Troops (USCT). In all my five decades of chasing down Black ancestors, he is the first USCT relation I may have found.

The USCT was created during the American Civil War after President Lincoln signed the Emancipation Proclamation in 1863. That was during a dire time when it looked like the Union was going to lose the war to the Confederacy. If that had happened, slavery might still be the law of the land.

Comprising over 180,000 African American soldiers, the USCT played a crucial role in Union victories, earning respect for their bravery and resilience. Those regiments not only significantly contributed to the war effort but also marked a vital step toward the recognition of African Americans' rights and their fight for freedom and equality. The service records of those individuals were finally being made available from the National Archives to online research repositories such as FOLD3.com, FamilySearch.org, and Ancestry.com.

US Civil War records affirmed Private Henry A. Jackson served in the 1st regiment, US Colored Infantry, Company H (Figure 65 and Figure 66).

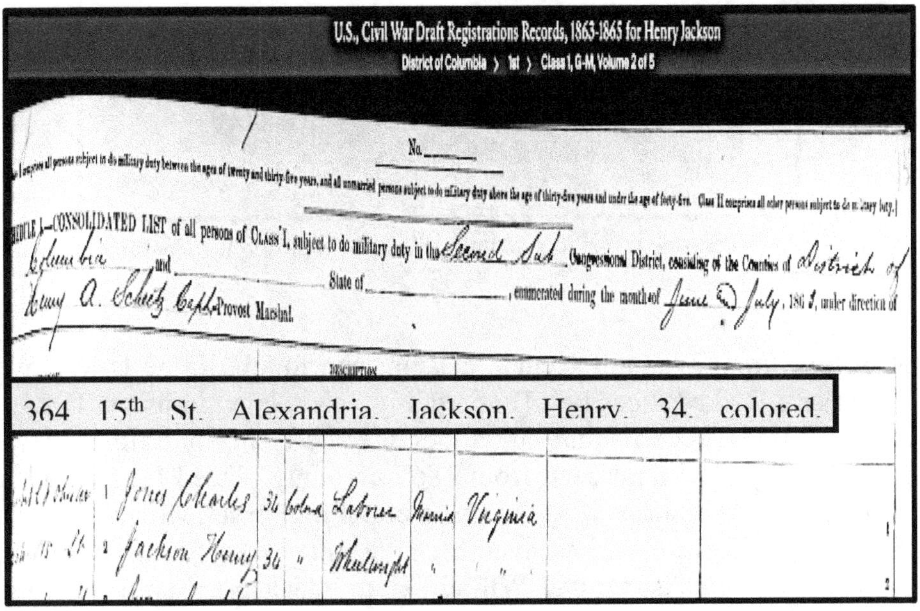
U.S., Civil War Draft Registrations Records, 1863-1865 for Henry Jackson
District of Columbia › 1st › Class 1, G-M, Volume 2 of 5
364 15th St. Alexandria. Jackson. Henry. 34. colored.

***Figure** 65: U.S. Civil War Draft Registration Records.*

His service is noted in plaque A-3 in the African American Civil War Memorial in Alexandria, which I visited in May 2024. The 1853-1911 Virginia Death Register indicates Henry Jackson was born in *1823* and died 7 Mar 1888 in Loudoun, VA from heart disease. He was a farmer married to *Little* Jackson. Some records said Henry married *Lydia Ann*, some say *Letta* or *Little*. Truthfully, the inferred 1829 birth date in his military records isn't *that* different than the official death record of 1834. Truthfully, JACKSON is one of the most common surnames for Black folk, followed by the fairly common given names of William and Henry. Was the following USCT record for my 3xGGF Henry Jackson? I would LOVE that, believe me, but I'll have to do more research to prove or disprove that allegation.

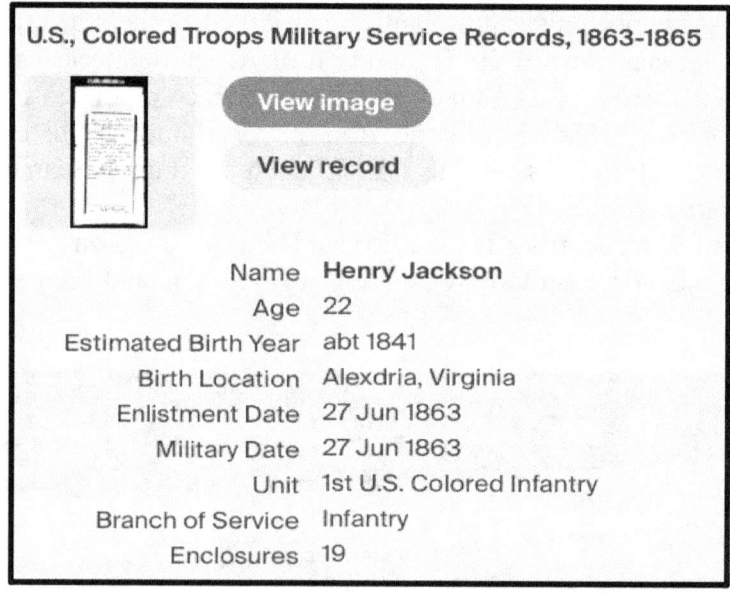

Figure 66: *USCT Service Record for Henry Jackson.*

The bottom line: Was this Henry Jackson who fought in the USCT my Ella Roy Carter's Daddy? Possibly. He certainly was related to us via DNA, but I found no primary records that directly connected Henry or William Henry to my Agnes Roy. The land deed from 1865 certainly placed Henry Jackson in District 6 of Alexandria, VA. That's compelling. But there were so many different birthdates on various records, and there were SO MANY William Jacksons, Henry Jacksons, and William Henry Jacksons in Virginia and DC that it's hard to know whether any of them were my direct ancestor. I'll continue to research this exciting topic until I am sure of the answer.

CHAPTER 13: Echoes of a Woman's Tale

NOTE: This is a chapter of speculative nonfiction, imagining several consecutive days of Ella's life as a 14-year-old girl living in the Delano's LakeHome property in 1880. Documentary evidence of Ella's teenage years is sparse, except for the 1880 Census in Mount Vernon, and her marriage certificate in 1884. The six vignettes in this chapter glimpse a picture of Ella Roy's early life, before and after her mother died in 1874.

Part I: Waking to the Nightmare

Colorful yellow and orange butterflies flit among the pink blossoms of the Eastern Redbud trees next to the apple orchard. It is a beautiful summer morning at the LakeHome property. The sun rises in the east, shining on the duck pond within view of my third-floor bedroom window. I love waking up to the sound of squawking ducks flapping their wings and splashing water at one another.

My tiny sleeping nook is in the third-floor servants' wing. My sleeping space is separated from my adopted parents, Uncle Albert and Aunt Alice, by an eight-foot wall. Each room has white-painted dresser drawers, a desk, a wooden chair, and in my room just one single bed. The window trim is white. Every wall on that floor is painted a light gray above five feet to the ceiling. But a woven, diamond-shaped wallpaper of pastel light silver and cream covers the lower portions of each room. Although there are no doors to our bedrooms, we still have a measure of privacy. I position my large dresser in such a way that it hides my changing area and chamber pot.

The dresser contains my nightshift, a few undergarments, socks, and hair combing supplies. My daily work uniform consists of a stiff, black cotton shift, white apron, and white cap to cover my frizzy auburn curls. I hang my uniform and my church dresses on pegs in the bright hallway. My black work shoes rest next to my church shoes underneath the dresses.

Nothing else fits in my little space which is about eight feet wide and twelve feet deep.

I love having my little bed in front of the tall, arched window so I can watch the night sky before entering dreamland. I always wake at the crack of dawn hearing Alice moving around. All of us workers on the third floor get up at the same time, get dressed, empty our chamber pots into the second floor bathroom, and help each other prepare for a new day.

This morning, I struggle to wake. It's another of my scary nightmares. Something about a huge man trying to grab me in the darkness—the same nightmare as always. "Come here, Ella Roy!" The devious man reaches for my arms, my chest, my behind. Who knows what he intends to do, but my soul knows he isn't up to anything good. Uncle Albert runs into my room, strokes my moist curls, and tries to calm me down from the all-too-familiar nightmare.

Once I have my wits about me, I sit up and ask, "You are my uncle, aren't you? I mean, you and my mother have the same parents, right?"

Albert cocks his head to the side, his lips pursed in concentration. "I wish I could respond plain and true, my girl, but your simple question is tough to answer simply. We colored folks have no choice, except to be Black and die." A gruff, forced laugh fights the sour bile that burbles up from his stomach. He explains, "To be Black and die is an odd expression our people often used because we had few choices in life prior to 1865 when we were *owned* ..." Ella joined in the tired, oft-spoken verse:

She recites, "Just like a dog, to fetch whatever our masters wanted whenever they wanted it. Like a plow, to work the soil from sunup to sundown, in the rain, in the cold, without pay. Like cows, to give enslaver's pale babies *our* mother's milk."

But this time, Albert holds up his hand for her to be quiet. He adds a new phrase she hasn't heard before. "Like enslavers who make black and white sow babies by ..."

Alice runs in and puts a finger to her lips, forcing Albert to stop talking. "Come on you two, we're late getting breakfast." The conversation was over ... for the moment.

Part II: Forbidden Fruit

Later in the day, when Alice and Ella have a chance to rest in the gazebo by the pond, they continue the conversation from that morning.

"I'm sorry I had to interrupt Albert's speech from this morning. I guessed where the conversation was headed. *I'm pretty sure that my woman's approach will be more appropriate to transition ten-year-old Ella from childhood to womanhood, rather than Albert's gruffer male viewpoint.*

I put an arm around my niece, whom I have raised for much of her young life. "Honey, you are old enough now to learn how children are created, especially ones who look light, bright, and darn near White, like you."

Ella starts fidgeting, tapping her feet, braiding and unbraiding her frizzy auburn hair as she watches ducks flapping in the water. Maybe she doesn't want to know the truth. Maybe she wants to stay a little girl, coddled and cuddled at this beautiful LakeHome property. But no, she inhales, gathering her nerve, lifting her head. "Okay, I'm ready. Tell me what I need to know."

All morning, I prepared how to deliver the talk, but I am nervous now that the time has come.

"Picture this, Ella: From the crack of dawn till the sun dips below the horizon, six days a week, you toil under the scorching sun or in a hot house. Your reward is a meager shack, crammed with maybe eight other people. Your weary bones rest on a straw-filled sack on the floor. Or, if you are lucky, a bed off the ground. A single wool blanket is your only covering, unless you find old scraps of fabric to sew together into quilts for the bed and to cover the walls to keep out cold winter winds.

"A pound of salted pork and a peck of cornmeal become your sustenance for the entire week. A cruel lottery determines who gets a full share and who only gets a half. Sometimes, the men sneak into the woods to kill game for the family, but the penalty for getting caught fishing or hunting is severe: whipping, solitary confinement, or hanging by the neck are common punishments."

Ella shudders and wraps her arms around her thin body.

"Children haul wood and water for the field workers outside, their tiny bodies fueling the plantation's engine. Laundresses scrub clothes with homemade soap, their hands raw, the heat of flat irons their only respite during the chill of winter. Blacksmiths, their muscles straining, forge and mend tools, which are the lifeblood of the plantation.

"In the fields, under an unforgiving sun, field slaves sow and reap, their backs bend, but their spirits are unbroken. Corn, beans, potatoes, tobacco—the fruits of their labor, are all unpaid. They gather eggs, milk cows, shear sheep. Their days are a relentless cycle of toil.

"Reading? That is forbidden fruit, a dangerous weapon in the eyes of their masters. So, it is illegal to teach enslaved people how to read and write. They wouldn't want to have enslaved people writing their own Freedom Papers whenever they wish, would they?"

"ALICE!" Mrs. Delano calls from the house. We jump up and race toward the house. The story will have to wait.

Part III: Prayer, Powder and the Pot

That night, after the Roys are safely in their quarters, Alice comes into Ella's bedroom. "Have you said your prayers yet?" Ella jumps off her bed, kneels down with her hands on the mattress. "Now I lay me down the sleep, I pray the Lord my soul to keep …"

Alice asks, "Do you want me to continue my earlier story?" Ella nods, her eyes hungry for the important information that Alice has to tell her.

"Let's start with church. Our people are very spiritual, wouldn't you say?" Ella nods. "We're lucky our Wayman AME Church is within walking distance. The teachings are to keep us safe in the Lord's blanket. But sometimes the White masters didn't let us know the whole word of the Lord. I heard from friends from other plantations that smart slave masters only exposed their workers to certain parts of the Bible."

Ella looks confused. "What do you mean?"

Alice said, "Well, sometimes they only taught us the Bible passages that warned us to work hard, and never run away from our masters, *if* we want to get into Heaven. This was the harsh reality of an enslaved person's existence. Your Uncle Albert and I lived next to Edgar Weir, son of the richest slave owner in Prince William County. His family owned the Liberia Plantation, a sprawling historic estate in the town of Manassas, Virginia. That's where two of the early battles of the Civil War were fought near Bull Run.

Ella's eyes stared at Alice, wanting to know more. "Did you see the fighting? Bloody bodies?"

"Of course, child, it was all around us. So noisy, so scary. We didn't know what to do, except our normal chores, when we could. I heard that 3,000 Union soldiers and 2,000 Confederate fighters died during the first Battle of Bull Run which the slavery-loving Confederates won. But thousands more Union soldiers died than Confederates during the second big battle but the Union won. Within one day of the fighting, it smelled like death everywhere. Eighty to ninety colored souls were bound by chains to keep the Weir family's operation thriving in the mid-1800s. This is what I remember growing up in Manassas."

Ella studies me but says nothing. Maybe she's thinking about how luxurious her life is here at LakeHome. She certainly is luckier than I was at about the same age.

"House slaves did the same type of work we do here for the Delanos. Some call those who cook and clean *the privileged few*. House Negroes' lives were thought to be easier than the field hands who endured the plantation's physical labor outside. Cooks whipped up meals in a separate kitchen building."

Ella asked, "Why is that? Wouldn't the food get cold if it was made in another building?"

I answered, "You are so smart to ask that question. But the reason they did it that way was in case there was a fire in the kitchen, it wouldn't spread to the main house. Enslaved servers would rush the prepared food from the outdoor kitchen through the Whistling Walk, to a small nook next to the dining room."

"What's a Whistling Walk?" Ella asks.

"It was like an outdoor hallway, usually with no roof, where servers would whistle as they carried the prepared food in large heavy pots and pans from the kitchen into the main house. If they were whistling, the owners believed they couldn't be sampling the meals, right?" Ella shrugged her shoulders.

"So, imagine in the dead of winter, the servers had to rush from the house through a snowy Whistling Walk, pick up heavy containers of food, rush back through the Walk while whistling to the Big House. Then the waiters would arrange the food onto fancy plates and platters to take into the dining room, to serve to the family and guests. Imagine how many trips had to be made for each meal, no matter the weather!"

"Some owners allowed the enslaved kitchen and waiter staff to eat the owners' leftovers. Other owners watched the servants with hawk-like eyes, ensuring they did not taste any of the master's food. They preferred giving any leftovers to the pigs."

Ella scrunched up her face at the cruelty of some masters. "Wouldn't they want to keep their workers strong by feeding them well?" Ella asked.

"Oh, my dear girl. Doesn't that make perfect sense?"

Alice yawned then said, "I think that's where we should end the story tonight. I'm mighty tired."

Part IV: The Indoor Servant's Edge

The following night, after Ella climbs into her bed, she wonders why Alice is telling her these stories. It's so unlike her to be so open about the past. But it sure is interesting to here how she grew up in that place ... Manassas, I think she called it. I wonder what story she'll tell tonight ...

"Ella?" Alice quietly comes into my bedroom to see if I'm asleep. There is a full moon outside, so a lot of light comes into my room.

"Aunt Alice, are you going to continue the story from yesterday?"

"Sure, if you want me to."

"Of course."

Alice sits at the edge of Ella's bed, facing the window. "We were talking about the fantastic and rotten things about being an indoor house servant compared to someone who works outside in the fields. On the surface, enslaved house servants had more opportunities to eat better food and to work in a drier, cleaner environment. They had uniforms and sometimes received hand-me-down clothes from the owners. Inside staff smelled cleaner than field hands and were entrusted with taking care of the master's children. That often included nursing their babies."

Ella puts up her hand. "Wait! So, in slavery days, they made our colored women nurse and take care of their babies. I don't understand. If we weren't human enough to eat with them, or go to church in the same seats with them, or learn to read and write with them, why would they entrust their babies to drink our milk?" Ella asked, her brow furrowed, questioning.

She is so perceptive! "You make a perfectly reasonable observation, my dear girl. That's exactly how it was—and still is—to a large degree. You may not be a slave now, but you are a house servant, always separate from our bosses. Would you ever think of eating a sandwich with George in the dining room?"

Ella thought for a moment. "Well, sure. He probably wouldn't mind. We're buddies, after all. Why would that be a problem?"

I look at her innocence with mixed emotions. *I guess it's good she feels comfortable with the employer's energetic grandson. But she is, first and foremost, an employee. And I don't even want to think about her becoming more womanly, day by day, with that rambunctious rather attractive boy around ...*

"Ella, many of our race believed inside work was better than toiling outside in the fields. Inside servants had the potential to get more information, have more social status, more of everything than farm hands. It's true that we must stand, invisible, for long periods of time in the dining room as the master's family eats. But, if we are smart, we can pretend to be stupid while we learn about local and national news, gossip, and other secrets about the community. This information might improve our knowledge of the world. House servants have more access to books which can help us understand how to read and write. Servants know how to speak well, dress presentably, and act civilly. Our servant ancestors passed down those skills, which helped us secure these plum jobs here at LakeHome. The Delanos trust us with their house, their children's lives, and their secrets, if we listen well enough. Uncle Albert learns about finances and real estate by listening to the Delano's conversations. He may share that information with other people at the church so we all become smarter about the world.

"All is not perfect with this scenario, my dear. There was, and still is, a devilish consequence to being an inside worker, but I want to talk about that next time."

"But, but, how can I sleep? Now, I'm going to be imagining all sorts of bad things."

Part V: Making a Baby Horse

All day long, Ella watched me as I did my chores. It was creepy, actually. She now has a thirst to know what the consequences are being a live-in house servant. Tonight is the night we've been dreading. I asked Albert for his opinion on the best way to proceed and he promised to help me.

Ella's eyes widen as Albert accompanies me for tonight's bedtime story. Sitting on her bed, she crosses her arms in front of her chest and says, "Wow, this must be really important if both of you are here to tell tonnight's bedtime story. So, tell me, why is being an inside servant sometimes a bad thing?"

Albert pulls up the chair and I sit on the bed with Ella.

I suck in my breath, then begin, my eyes search her face for comprehension. "It was—and still is—much easier for the master or employer, or their sons, or their male friends to come up behind a female servant and …" I pause.

"And what?" Ella's eyes widen as she tries to imagine what the horrible secret is that her adopted parents have kept her from knowing for so long.

Albert pipes up. His deep voice low, "Any man could have his way with any female slave or employee, but it's much easier to do with a house servant, who is often alone doing her household chores in the kitchen, the basement, or the …" I stop, allowing that to sink in. But Ella's face remains blank, naive, not understanding.

Albert tries another tactic. "Ella, you've been to the horse barn, haven't you?"

She says, "Sure. Sometimes I take lunch to the workers out there."

Albert says, "Yes, of course. But do you ever *watch* the horses in the barn, or when they romp outside in the fenced-in yard?"

"Of course, Uncle Albert. They're so beautiful. I told Mr. D. I'd like to ride the big black one sometime."

The blood drains from Albert's face at her innocent statement, but I clear my throat and continue. "Have you ever seen a male horse seem to *ride* a female horse from her backside?"

Ella started laughing. "Yes, it was the funniest thing I ever saw. I couldn't figure out how he got his big self on her back like that. And why he'd want to do that in the first place? It looked awkward and uncomfortable to me."

I ask, "Do you know what they were *actually* doing?"

"Playing tag?

Albert says, "No, my dear. They were making a baby horse."

Ella looks shocked, tilting her head and frowning like he's joking. "What do you mean, making a baby horse?"

Albert speaks up, using a formal teacher's voice. "Well, Ella … you see … a male horse, just like a male human being, has an *organ*—a part of his body that kind of looks like a sausage. He inserts that organ into a special opening between a female's legs. Then the organ releases a liquid-like substance into the female. If that female is old enough to have her monthly bleeding"—he turns to look at Ella for a moment—"the liquid from that male organ could make a baby grow inside the female horse."

I add, "For people, the process of making a baby is similar. Nine months later, a human baby is born, but it's eleven months for a baby horse."

The light bulb finally seems to flicker as Ella's mouth opens wide. She's seen the red stains on my sheets when she washes them. She looks at me, then out the window, then at Albert, then back at me, silent, processing what we just told her.

I continue, "So, Ella, enslaved women working inside the Big House at the plantation were often forced by their master, and/or his male family members, and/or their male friends, to *submit* to their male organ. Nine months later, the female might pop out a bright-skinned child who looks like you and me, a mixture of black and white. The lighter the skin color, the more likely generations of White men have had their way with our Negro female ancestors. For decades upon decades, that's exactly how the planter class grew their crop of Negroes, instead of having to buy them."

Ella looks confused. "What do you mean, 'grew their crop of Negroes', Aunt Alice?"

"Just like I said, darlin'. Men used their organ to make more babies for free, and the children of slave mothers were born forever enslaved."

Ella's mouth drops open, as she looks from Albert to me.

"But that's not the worst of it," I say.

Ella mumbles, "I'm not sure how much more of this story I can take."

"OK, this is the last of it. The *harvesting* of brown babies became the master's property, like a horse, that could be sold to anyone at any time for the right price. That's one of the many reasons it's hard for us to know who our blood kin is. If we have light skin like ours, it means our Daddy could be the master or any other man. We just don't know, darlin' girl."

Part VI: The Shattered Peace

Ella is silent. Her head drops toward her chest. Perhaps she's crying or trying to process what all this means to her quest to find her parents. In a low voice, she raises her head. Her eyes flash. "Who is my father?"

I grab her hands in mine. "I'm so sorry, Ella, but we really don't know for sure. It could have been one of the Weir boys at their Liberia plantation in Manassas. Or, it could have been a friend who came to one of their dinner parties. It could have been an overseer who whipped the field hands into shape and whose house was near the slave quarters. It could have been a boy named Jackson who lived in Alexandria. It could have been a politician who lived in Washington DC before you were born … Or, it could have been this White fellow named Walker Millan who was the Sheriff of Fairfax County not too far from here. Nobody knows for sure. Any man, White or Black could have come up behind your mother while she was working, while she was sleeping, while she was bathing, while she was gardening, while she was walking to the store, or while she was sitting on a bench for a moment of rest. She would have to submit to his organ, or be beaten, whipped, sold, or even killed."

Tears stream down Ella's face as she grits her teeth and asks in a determined voice, "Then who is my mother?"

I put my arm around one of Ella's shoulders and Albert scoots around to the other side, patting her back. Albert whispers, "Your mother's name was Agnes, Agnes Roy. She was my ten-years-younger half-sister."

"Was?" Ella whispers.

I reply, "Yes, she died in 1874 from consumption in Manassas, Virginia. She was only 27 years old, unmarried, and working as a farmer at the time of her death. Thankfully, she had mentioned Albert's name to someone, and the authorities tracked us down. As Agnes's next of kin, we gladly became your guardian parents. We tried to have a baby for so many years, but it was not God's plan. Albert and I could never make a baby that lived past birth."

Ella pressed her head against my chest.

Albert croons, "Darlin'girl, we have been beyond-the-moon thrilled to have you in our lives. We only want to protect you from hurt."

Ella's fists tighten in her lap and her voice becomes firm. "**I only knew her as Mama.** Why wouldn't you at least tell me her name? Why did you keep her memory from me?" Tears roll down Ella's face, but she vigorously swipes them away with her hand, perhaps not wanting to appear vulnerable.

Albert says, "We're not exactly sure about everything your mother had to go through during her short life. Like the story we told you, a lot of times enslavers sold or gifted a family member away. We suspect Agnes was in the clutches of Walker Reid Millan, Sheriff of Fairfax County. For a time, he worked in that horrible Slave Pen and Jail in Alexandria, right before the Civil War started. The Slave Traders there captured, beat, and sold thousands of men, women, and children from their families. Many ended up far away in a State called Louisiana.

"You were born in December 1866, but we found out that Millan signed a Work Contract listing your mother's name *and child* which I think was referring to you. The contract forced Agnes to do housework for Millan until May 1867. But we don't know if Agnes ever worked for him. If she did, maybe it was at his family's house. But it's possible she was working in that terrible Slave Pen where so many people died a terrible death, or endured an exceedingly difficult life. How many ghosts are trapped in that building? It's possible that Millan was Agnes's former slave master who wanted her back in his clutches after the Civil War. You were probably with your mother during those first years. I don't know. She and I didn't grow up together, but our Roy family in Manassas and other places like Spotsylvania County, tried to find her. We didn't even know about you until someone came to my door asking if I knew Agnes Roy."

I say, "Since we didn't know where your mother was, we thought it would be easier for you to think of us as your parents. Honestly, we only wanted to make your life a little easier, dear child. We don't know how or when your mother got to Alexandria. We don't know what her life was like, or where you were living during your first few years. Agnes dropped from our lives long ago. Sold? Stolen? Loaned? Killed? We didn't know where she was for years."

"But why, why, **WHY?**" The girl-woman's voice booms louder and louder with each word. Albert puts his index finger to his lips, beckoning her to keep her voice low, but to no avail.

The normally quiet and respectful Ella yells in a fury, "So, after all these years of me agonizing about my mother ... after all the nightmares about men grabbing at me, why wouldn't you just tell me the truth?" Her fists ball like a prize fighter waiting to knock her opponent's head off.

"Shush, shush," we plead. We don't want the Delanos to investigate why Ella is screaming. We don't want to be fired from this plum working assignment. Ella sobs quietly. Albert and I hug her, hoping to make her feel safe and loved. I sigh. The truth has shattered the fragile peace of our home, a wound that will bleed across generations.

CHAPTER 14: The Search for Robert Carter's Roots

Warm memories of my mother's cozy house washed over me during a hot summer afternoon in Sacramento, California, in 2006. She lived in an active senior community which had tennis courts, a pool, jacuzzi, and a small putting green. Mom rode her bicycle along wide streets, meeting friends in the local community center where residents could play card games, work on a communal puzzle, take dance and art lessons, or just gab with neighbors.

During her last full year of sharing her grace with the world, we huddled together in her sunny kitchen trying to unfurl her family's past. I placed a batch of fresh peanut butter cookies and glasses of iced tea on her round dining table which held her computer and our research documents.

My mother had been an athletic tomboy who excelled at basketball, roller skating, and tennis as a child. She kept her body strong throughout her entire life, directing her competitive skills toward tennis, golf, and bridge. After seven years of health, her cancer returned with gusto in 2003. Her fitness ebbed dramatically over the next three years, loosing the use of one arm, then needing a walker, then a wheelchair, but her brain remained sharp as a proverbial tack.

One Saturday, as we poured over genealogy printouts from the nearby library, Mom looked down at her dainty hands. "After all this time, you'd think I wouldn't care, but I have two Bucket List items I'd dearly love to achieve before I die."

I cringed, conscious of Mom's *terminal* prognosis before I asked, "What two things, Mom?" in as bright a voice as I could muster.

She looked up, as if pleading to the Almighty in the heavens. "First, I want to live to eighty. Eight more glorious years of life on this Good Earth. Please, Lord." Her black eyes flashed at me, her resolve clear.

"Second, I yearn to learn what happened to my wayward father, Arthur Taft Carter." I reached over to hug my brave mother, wanting more than anything to help her dreams come true.

"Mom, what do you know about your grandfather, Robert Carter?"

"Daughter Dear, you may not believe this but I don't know anything about my father, let alone *his* daddy. Nobody said a word about Grandpa Robert, at least not in my recollection. I've never seen pictures of either man, but I imagine my father looked like an amalgamation of my three handsome brothers."

Fast forward to 2025. I used artificial intelligence to guesstimate what my maternal grandfather, Arthur Taft Carter, may have looked like (Figure 67). I uploaded photos of Uncle Dale (one of my super-testers), Uncle George, Uncle Sonny/Arthur to Google Gemini and ChatGPT. I can certainly see family traits in the generated image of Arthur and an AI rendition of what my Great-grandfather Arthur Carter may have looked like. (Figure 63):

Dale Edward (1938-alive) George William (1936-2003) Arthur Lewis (1933-2006) Arthur Taft??? (1908-1995)

Robert and Ella Roy Carter's children:

Ben Andrew (1892-1919) Bessie Ruth (1902-1995) Richard (1906-1995) Arthur pix? (1909-1995)

Figure 67: Artificial intelligence image of Grandpa Arthur Carter Sr.

For some reason, I was unable to get AI to do the same thing for generating an amalgamation for Great-grandfather Robert Carter from his sons Richard, Benjamin, and an AI version of my grandfather, Arthur Carter (above). Maybe if I find out more about Robert's background, I'll find his parents and other information to fill in his puzzle pieces.

Who Were Robert's Parents?

According to the Knox County, OH, Probate Court, Robt (Robert) Carter was licensed to marry Ella Roy on 4 December 1884. Sadly, the form didn't contain the names of their parents. (Figure 68)

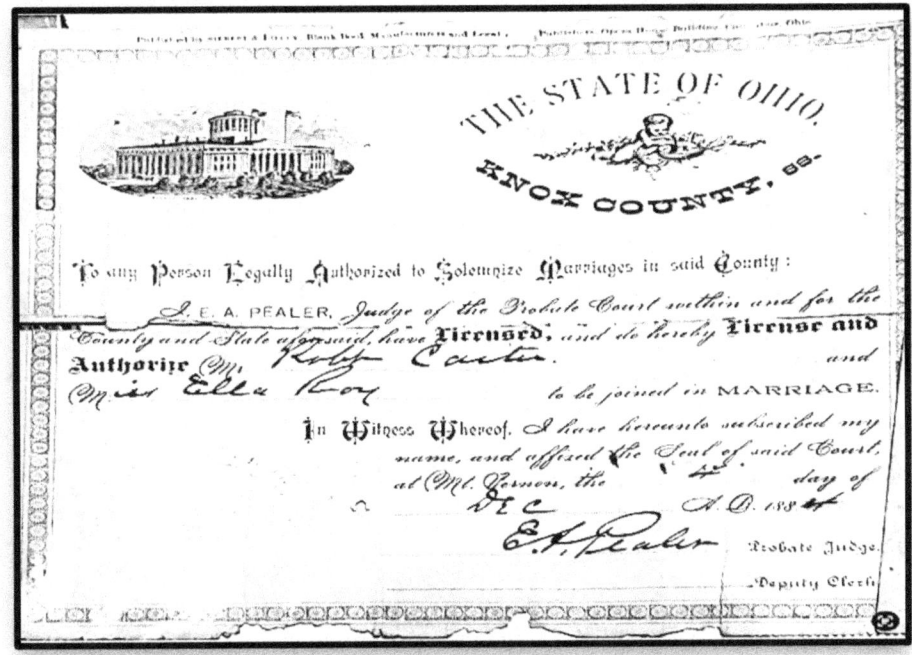

Figure 68: Robert & Ella's Marriage License, 4 Dec 1884

We know that teenage Ella Roy was working as a servant for Columbus Delano in 1880 at his LakeHome mansion on Martinsburg Road. But what was Robert Carter doing during that time period? How long had he been living in Mount Vernon? How and when did Robert get to Mount Vernon if he was born in DC, according to his 1909 Death Certificate. Were his parents also born in DC? What type of work occupied Robert's days and who was his family? Did he and Ella meet at the Wayman Chapel AME church about one mile from the Delanos' house?

Robert's 1909 Death Certificate indicated he was born in Washington, DC on 29 November 1859 (Figure 69). Did he really die exactly 50 years later in the Bangs Infirmary (also called the Poorhouse) in Knox County, OH? If so, why does the certificate say he was 50 years, 9 months and 14 days old? Were there errors on that document?)

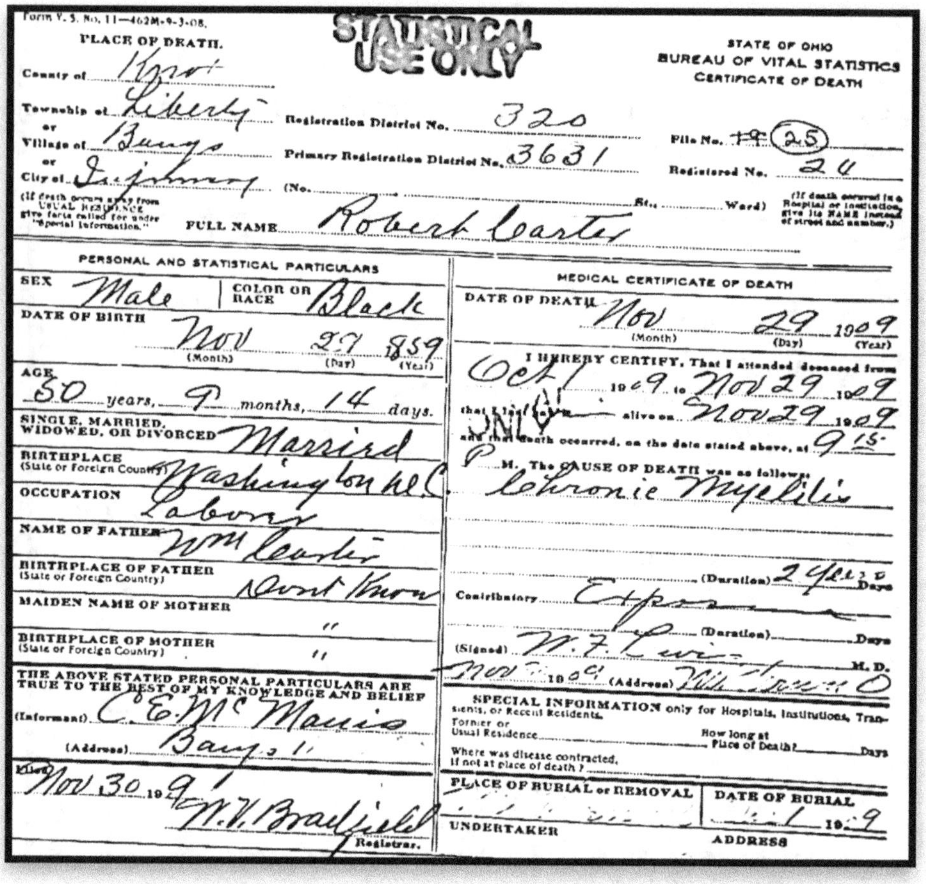

Form V. S. No. 11—462M-9-3-08.

STATISTICAL USE ONLY

PLACE OF DEATH.

STATE OF OHIO
BUREAU OF VITAL STATISTICS
CERTIFICATE OF DEATH

County of Knox
Township of Liberty
or Village of Bangs
or City of Infirmary
(If death occurs away from USUAL RESIDENCE give facts called for under "Special Information.")

Registration District No. 320
Primary Registration District No. 3631
(No. ... St., ... Ward)
File No. (25)
Registered No. 24
(If death occurred in a Hospital or Institution, give its NAME instead of street and number.)

FULL NAME Robert Carter

PERSONAL AND STATISTICAL PARTICULARS

SEX Male | COLOR OR RACE Black

DATE OF BIRTH Nov (Month) 27 (Day) 1859 (Year)

AGE 50 years, 9 months, 14 days.

SINGLE, MARRIED, WIDOWED, OR DIVORCED Married

BIRTHPLACE (State or Foreign Country) Washington D.C.

OCCUPATION Laborer

NAME OF FATHER Wm Carter

BIRTHPLACE OF FATHER (State or Foreign Country) Dont Know

MAIDEN NAME OF MOTHER "

BIRTHPLACE OF MOTHER (State or Foreign Country) "

THE ABOVE STATED PERSONAL PARTICULARS ARE TRUE TO THE BEST OF MY KNOWLEDGE AND BELIEF

(Informant) C.E. McManis

(Address) Bangs, O.

Filed Nov 30, 1909 W.V. Bradfield, Registrar.

MEDICAL CERTIFICATE OF DEATH

DATE OF DEATH Nov (Month) 29 (Day) 1909 (Year)

I HEREBY CERTIFY, That I attended deceased from Oct 1, 1909, to Nov 29, 1909

that I last saw h... alive on Nov 29, 1909

and that death occurred, on the date stated above, at 9:15 P.M. The CAUSE OF DEATH was as follows:

Chronic Myelitis

(Duration) 2 years ... Days

Contributory Exposure

(Duration) ... Days

(Signed) M.F. Curi... M.D.

Nov ... 1909 (Address) ...

SPECIAL INFORMATION only for Hospitals, Institutions, Transients, or Recent Residents.

Former or Usual Residence ... How long at Place of Death? ... Days

Where was disease contracted, if not at place of death?

PLACE OF BURIAL or REMOVAL | DATE OF BURIAL ... 1909

UNDERTAKER | ADDRESS

Figure 69: Robert Carter's Death Certificate, Bangs, OH, 1909.

I imagined the chill of late November settling over the infirmary for poor folks with medical and mental disorders. That's where my 2xGGF Robert Carter breathed his last breath. For two years, he battled chronic myelitis, a debilitating inflammation of the spinal cord that slowly robbed him of his strength. But why was *exposure* listed as another factor in his death? Was it caused by working around dangerous metals and gases during his lifetime? Perhaps the nature of Robert's occupation was physically taxing, contributing to the exhaustion noted by the attending physician.

The most exciting reveal was learning "**Wm (William) Carter**" was Robert's father. But "which" William Carter was correct? It's such a common name, especially in Virginia. William's birthplace was listed as "Don't Know," as were Robert's mother's name and birthplace. Heavy sigh. Did the informant, C.E. McManis, actually know my great-grandfather's family history or did he guess at Robert's father's name? I question the accuracy of Robert's age information, but it's one of the few documents I have, so I've got to work with it.

I decided to start from the end of Robert's life, then work backward. Meaning, I checked to see if there was a Wm Carter living in or near Mount Vernon, about five miles from where Robert died in Bangs, OH.

Hurrah! The 1876-77 City Directory described a *laborer* named William Carter residing at North Catherine Street. Living with him were four unnamed adult males, three adult females, three male children, and two female children. Was my 16-year-old Robert among those male children in that Directory? (Figure 70)

In the 1876-77 White's MV Directory:	Adults		Minors	
Could this William Carter be Robert Carter's father?	M	F	M	F
Carter, William, laborer, res n Catharine street.	4	3	3	2

Figure 70: 1876-77 Mount Vernon (OH) City Directory for Carters.

The 1880 Census listed Wm., his wife, Lydia, and their children: Wm. (11), Jos. (9), Ellen (4), and Sarah (14). They were all White (Figure 71).

Knox > Clinton > 145					
149	Carter	Wm.	White Male	65	Abt 1815
149	Carter	Lydia	White Female	45	Abt 1835
149	Carter	Wm.	White Male	11	Abt 1869
149	Carter	Jos.	White Male	9	Abt 1871
149	Carter	Ellen	White Female	4	Abt 1876
149	Carter	Sarah	White Female	14	Abt 1866

Figure 71: 1880 Knox, OH, Census for Carters

Robert Carter was not listed with those White Carters. Is this exercise a dead-end? Even if Robert was not blood kin, but was working and living with that Carter family, he should be listed with them in the Census. But he was not there. Where was my Robert Carter living in 1880?

After more searching, I found a Robert Carter in the 1884/85 Mount Vernon, City Directory. Nine Carters lived in Mount Vernon, five of whom lived on Harkness Road (Figure 72).

Figure 72: 1884-85 Mount Vernon City Directory for Carters.

My great-grandfather, Robert Carter, was living at 405 E. Gambier Street in 1884-85 (Figure 73), in the grand home of Charley Cooper who, with his brother Elias, established an iron foundry in 1833. They poured castings for hog troughs, plows, stoves, and maple syrup kettles. Over the decades, they grew their business into a lucrative iron powerhouse, making compressors for railroads and manufacturing companies. "Coopers" (later called Cooper-Bessemer) hired my family as machinists and laborers, as described in my *The Ancestors Are Smiling!* book. I wondered whether Robert Carter was a body servant, chauffeur, cook, farmer, rancher, or office clerk?

Figure 73: Where Robert Carter worked/lived in 1884/85.

At each step of the investigation process, I used Ancestry's "Member Connect" tool to see who else had these same Carters in their online family trees. Why? Because it's easy to determine if those connections are also blood relatives ... and they might have evidentiary documents that would improve the veracity of my lineage theories.

Even though my Robert was not living with those White Carters, I created their family tree to learn where their ancestors came from and whether they had been enslavers.

I noticed the William Carter family was living close to Columbus Delano's 300-acre property (Figure 74). If Robert Carter *was* part of William's family and Ella Roy was living with the Delanos nearby, is that how Robert and Ella met? Were the Mount Vernon Carters related to my Robert Carter? And guess who else was living near the Delanos at the outskirts of town? Jacksons! Were those Jacksons related to my family?

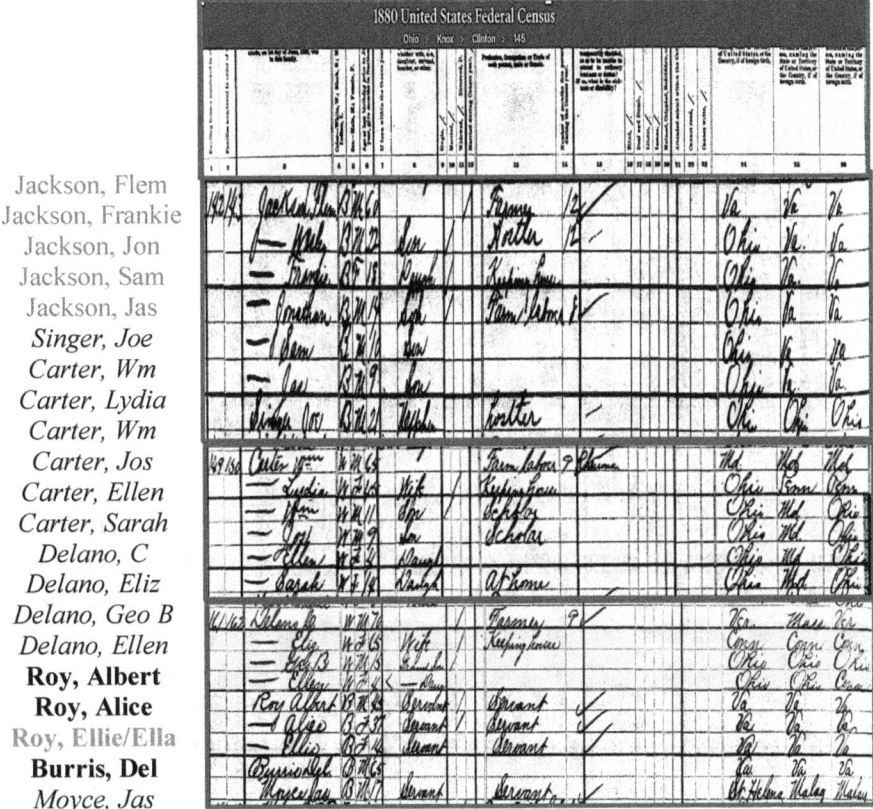

Figure 74: Carters and Jacksons Lived Near Delanos.

DNA to the Rescue?

Could DNA help determine whether the William Carter family is related to mine? I added him as my Robert Carter's Daddy in my theoretical family tree, then ran Ancestry's ThruLines tool. **How fabulous!** I found six DNA matches to me and William Carter's ancestors. Maybe, just maybe, this William Carter *is* my missing link after all.

Darn! I found two major problems with this Carter line of inquiry. First, the 23andme.com DNA testing company says my mother's brother, Dale Carter, has a paternal Y-DNA haplogroup of B-M109. Men carrying B-M109 spread far and wide, below the Sahara desert from Cameroon to Tanzania, and in the east from Egypt to South Africa. Therefore, our B-M109 haplogroup is African. Since men carry the same Y-DNA markers from father to son, I must conclude that our Carter men are Black.[89] Those Mount Vernon Carters are White, so they cannot be our blood kin.

Second, those six DNA matches descended from Logsdons who *married into* the Carters, not the Carters themselves. And those Logsdons are all Caucasian. So the "My Great-grandfather came from Mount Vernon Carters" theory does not pan out. Back to the drawing board.

Was My Robert Carter Born in DC or Virginia?

Robert's 1909 Death Certificate said he was born in Washington, DC, so I began searching for Census records there for a "Robert Carter born between 1856 and 1862 in DC." The left block in Figure 75 indicates that Lizzie *Payne* (30) was living with Sarah *Carter* (40) and 16-year-old Robert Carter in DC in 1870. In 1860, "Paynes" married into my Carter family and lived in Mount Vernon, so this lead might have legs. Now to find a William Carter.

The middle block from 1880 in DC shows a mulatto Robert Carter (22) working as a waiter in DC. His unnamed father and mother were born in Virginia. It indicates Robert was married in 1880, four years before he married Ella Roy in Mount Vernon. It's possible this Robert divorced his first wife, or that she died, before marrying Ella in 1884. This scenario *might* explain why Robert migrated away from DC to start a new life in Ohio. I searched that Census for a nearby father named William Carter. No luck.

Was Robert Carter was born in DC? Well, I looked for him in Manassas, too, since I knew our Roys were living there in 1870. Hallelujah! As the right block in Figure 75 shows, I found a Black William (53) *and* a Black Robert (13) Carter living together, close to Albert and Alice Roy. Robert's birth year, 1857, is close to what his Death Certificate reported. Hmm, Carters and Jetts?

1870 in DC

Name	Robert Carter
Age in 1870	16
Birth Date	abt 1854
Birthplace	Virginia
Dwelling Number	2038
Home in 1870	Washington Ward 5, lumbia
Race	Black
Gender	Male
Post Office	Washington
Occupation	Works Brick Yard
Cannot Read	Yes
Cannot Write	Yes

embers

Name	Age
Sarah Carter	40
Lizzie Payne	30
Robert Carter	16

1880 in DC

Name	Robert Carter
Age	22
Birth Date	Abt 1858
Birthplace	Virginia
Home in 1880	Washington, Washington, District of Columbia, District of Columbia, USA
Street	K-Street NW
House Number	1907
Dwelling Number	149
Race	Mulatto
Gender	Male
Relation to Head of House	Self (Head)
Marital Status	Married
Spouse's Name	Betsey L. Carter
Father's Birthplace	Virginia
Mother's Birthplace	Virginia
Occupation	Waiter

1870 in Manassas, PWC, VA

Name	Robert Carter
Age in 1870	13
Birth Date	abt 1857
Birthplace	Virginia
Dwelling Number	37
Home in 1870	Manassas, Prince William
Race	Black
Gender	Male
Post Office	Manassas
Occupation	At School
Attended School	Yes
Cannot Read	Yes
Cannot Write	Yes
Inferred Father	William Carter

embers

Name	Age
William Carter	53
Robert Carter	13
Lucy Jett	43
Phillip Jett	16
Richard Jett	10
Randolph Jett	8
Georgianna Jett	5
Elizabeth Jett	2/12

Lewis Jett, Black, 20, was living near Richard Weir in 1870.

***Figure 75:** Searching for Robert Carter in 1870 and 1880 DC Census.*

Are Jetts Part of My Carter Ancestry?

Who were those Jetts listed in the Carter household in the 1870 Manassas Census? Could Lucy Jett be my Robert Carter's mother, and William Carter his father? I plugged the Jett surname into DNA matching programs, then ThruLines, to see if I could pinpoint who my blood family was. I did not find any Jett DNA matches in Manassas, or other parts of Virginia, among any of my super-testers from the 1800s, but there were some matches to Jetts from the 1700s.

I created a spreadsheet which tracks the DNA matches for four of our super-testers (me, Uncle Dale Carter, and cousins Kenora and JoAnn). It contains the number of centimorgans of relationship. None of the matches where greater than 23cMs, indicating they are perhaps fourth cousins who share a three-times great-grandparent with us.[90] I also color-coded all of those helpful groupings using Ancestry.com PRO tools to clarify how DNA matches might intersect our family in various ways, including Jetts who lived in Virginia during the 1800s.

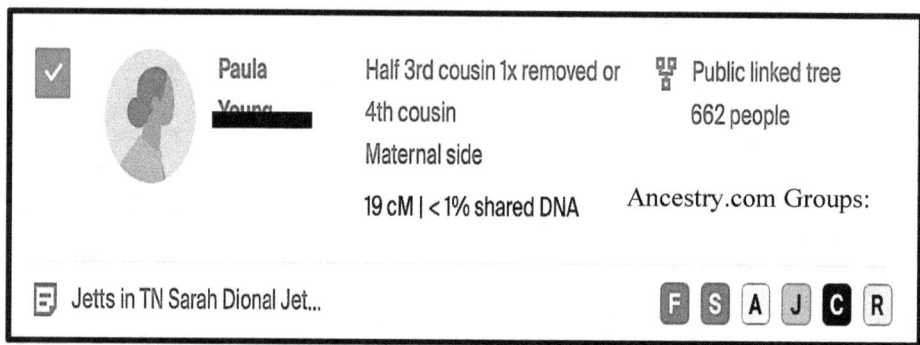

Figure 76: Looking for Relatives with Jetts.

Paula's tree from Figure 76 has Jetts (Group J), as well as documents for relatives in Fairfax County (F), and Spotsylvania County (S), the surname Ames (A), surname Jett (J), Caroline County (C) and Rays (R). But she didn't have Carters in her tree. However, there were no clear connections to our super-testers, save a few Jetts who had lived in Stafford County, which is near Spotsylvania and Caroline Counties. That's the origin of many Roys who migrated to DC and Prince William County during the 1860s. While more investigation could be done on those few Jett DNA matches, I decided to try another tactic.

Were My Carters Free Persons of Color?

By 1860, some experts believe 90 percent of all Africans in America had been enslaved at some point in their lives. But that means 10 percent were born free and an unknown percentage of blacks achieved freedom at some point in their lives. So, I took a positive approach: maybe my Carter great-great-grandparents were free people of color in DC. President Abraham Lincoln signed the "District of Columbia Emancipation Act" into law on April 16, 1862. It ended slavery in DC and freed 3,000 enslaved people living in the Capitol. The act provided up to $300 per enslaver to compensate owners for the loss of their free laborers.

Many freedmen and freedwomen had another plan for their lives. During the intensity of Civil War fighting, they rushed to the Capitol and Union Army posts by the thousands, becoming "contraband"—property of war—which kept them from being returned to their enslavers. This unexpected influx of brown- and black-skinned humanity severely taxed Union housing and food resources. Those freedom seekers volunteered their labors to help win the war and rebuild the United States of America.

Were Robert Carter's family free people of color? Like my other family members, I scoured Freedmen's Bureau and Census records, and City Directories for information about Robert Carter's family who were living in Washington, DC as of 1859 when he was born, according to Robert's Death Certificate. "Robert" and "Carter" are both *very* common names, thanks to the largest slave owner in Virginia sporting those names. On August 1, 1791, enslaver Robert Carter III took the legal steps to gradually manumit more than 500 of his enslaved workers. That was the largest individual emancipation before 1860. Many who were freed kept the surname Carter and/or named their children Robert, perhaps to honor their former owner who freed them. Does that mean my Carters were never enslaved? No.

In Ward 5 of Washington, DC, in 1870, a 16-year-old teenager named Robert Carter was working in the brickyard. He lived with Sarah Carter and Lizzie Payne (Figure 77). Things are starting to heat up.

We have Carters who married Paynes (Figure 77). But wait! In the 1850 and 1860 Census, I found free Black Carters who *could* have been my kin. Ward 5 was bordered by the Anacostia River on the east, Benning Road on the south, New Jersey Avenue on the west, and Riggs Road on the north. Two railroad lines traversed the area. Most of the men on this 1870 Census page were working in the brickyard with teenaged Robert (Figure 78). Nine families—32 people—lived in four buildings. I couldn't imagine such lose quarters.

1850 Census Fairfax,

Name	Julia Carter
Gender	Female
Race	Mulatto
Residence Age	23
Birth Date	abt 1827
Birthplace	Virginia
Residence Date	1850
Home in 1850	Fairfax, Virginia, USA
Cannot Read, Write	Yes
Line Number	17
Dwelling Number	144
Family Number	144

Household members

Name	Age
Joseph Carter	51
Cornelia Carter	51
Letty Carter	25
Julia Carter	23
Joseph Carter	17
Albert Carter	15
Mary Carter	6
James Quander	2

1860 Census DC

Name	Julia Carter
Age	35
Birth Year	abt 1825
Gender	Female
Race	Colored (Black)
Birth Place	Virginia
Home in 1860	Washington Ward 7, Washington, District of Columbia
Post Office	Washington
Dwelling Number	1367
Family Number	1477
Occupation	Washer
Personal Estate Value	15
Cannot Read, Write	Y
Inferred Child	Arthur Carter; Richard Carter

Household members

Name	Age
Julia Carter	35
Arthur Carter	18
Richard Carter	10
George Carter	12
Sophia J Clements	30
Charles Carter	6
Robert Carter	4
Edward Carter	9/12
Mary Haines	12
Mary Haines	50

1880 Census DC

Name	Benjamin Carter
Age	63
Birth Date	Abt 1817
Birthplace	Virginia
Home in 1880	Washington, Washington, District of Columbia, District of Columbia, USA
Street	Seventeenth Street SE
House Number	144
Dwelling Number	82
Race	Black
Gender	Male
Relation to Head of House	Self (Head)
Marital Status	Married
Spouse's Name	Julia Carter
Father's Birthplace	Virginia
Mother's Birthplace	Virginia
Occupation	Laborer
Months Not Employed	12
Sick	Rheumatism
Maimed, Crippled, or Bedridden	Y
Cannot Read	Y
Cannot Write	Y
Neighbors	View others on page

Household members

Name	Age
Benjamin Carter	63
Julia Carter	53
Samuel Carter	26
Sarah Carter	18

Figure 77: Looking for Traces of Robert Carter in DC.

My first theory was that Robert and Ella named their children after their relatives, e.g., William, Alice, George, Roy, Robert, Charles, Bessie, Ralph, Richard Albert, and Arthur Carter. Head-of-household Julia Carter had many of our given family names and surnames in 1860.

Name	Robert Carter
Age	4
Birth Year	abt 1856
Gender	Male
Race	Colored (Black)
Birth Place	District of Columbia
Home in 1860	Washington Ward 7, Washington, District of Columbia
Post Office	Washington
Dwelling Number	1367
Family Number	1477

Household Members (Name)		Age
Julia Carter	B Washing $15	35
Arthur Carter	B Brick	18
Richard Carter	M Laborer	10
George Carter	M	12
Sophia J Clements	?	30
Charles Carter	B	6
Robert Carter	B	**4**
Edward Carter	M	9/12
Mary Haines	B	12
Mary Haines	B Mid-wife	50

Figure 78: Robert Carter in Ward 7, DC, 1870

Julia Carter was born in 1825, so I looked for her name in the 1850 Census, finding her parents were Joseph Carter and wife named Cornelia.

Could Freedmen's Bureau records save the day again?

My heart skipped a beat when I found a seven-year-old Robert Carter with six other Carters, five Rays, and four Jacksons next to each other on the same page. They all arrived at the Freedmen's Village on 8 Jun 1867. How likely is it that they migrated together from Caroline and Spotsylvania Counties to freedom in DC? Did their children intermarry then migrate to other states, like Ohio? Are the puzzle pieces finally coming together?

I needed more conclusive evidence.

The Bottom Line: My leading theory of Great-Grandfather Robert Carter's parents were Julia Carter from DC as his mother, and a still-to-be-found father named William Carter. I'm hoping my grandchildren will resume the hunt if I don't beat them to it.

CHAPTER 15: The Carter Family's Bondage

Alex Haley's *Roots* TV miniseries catapulted a worldwide interest in genealogy in 1977. Even though I joined the crowd, writing letters to my relatives in Ohio asking about my maternal and paternal family lines, I made little progress finding ancestors who lived before 1880.

Imagine my renewed detective vigor when thousands of Freedmen's Bureau records became available to the masses online. Imagine the scream that issued from my lips when I learned DeJarnette and Roe enslavers from Spotsylvania and Caroline Counties had the names of our maternal Roys in their family probate records. More surprising was finding out the DeJarnettes were neighbors and buddies with the Waller enslavers who treated *Roots'* Kunta Kinte so savagely (Chapter 8).

So what? Since Black Carters appear on many of the genealogy documents for my Roys, is it is possible that Carters traveled with our Roys and Jacksons?

Robert Carter was born before the Civil War began, in 1859, in the District of Columbia, according to his 1909 Death Certificate. His father was listed as "Wm.," but his mother was unknown. I searched for Robert and his family in DC for over a year. There were *many* Carters named Robert and William in DC, per the 1870 and 1880 Census, but I could not prove any of those relationships to be my family.

Enter the Freedmen's Bureau records repository to the rescue. I had so much good luck finding Ella Roy's mother, Agnes, that I tried the same techniques for Robert Carter's lineage. Using the Smithsonian Bureau portal, hope filling my heart, I typed "Robert Carter from the District of Columbia" (Figure 79).

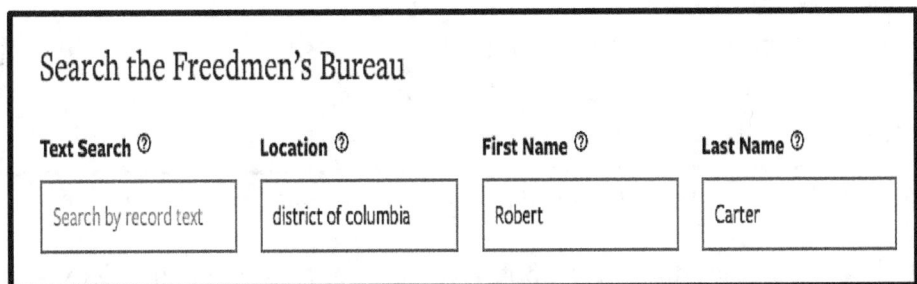

Figure 79: Freedmen's Bureau Access Portal.

The first Freedmen's Bureau result knocked me off my feet. Page 102, from the Records of the Field Offices for the District of Columbia, Register of People Arriving at Freedmen's Village, Volume (84), indicated that Robert Carter was seven years old, as of June 8, 1866 (meaning a spot-on 1859 birth year). Robert and seven other CARTERS—and three JACKSONS and five RAYS/ROYS—on the same page—arrived in DC from Caroline County, VA. (Table 10).

DC Arrival Freed Folk Age From Caroline Status				
June 8th √	Moses Carter	12	Caroline Co Va.	single
June 8th √	Sarah Carter	33	Caroline Co Va.	Married
June 8th √	Sarah G. Carter	2	Caroline Co Va.	Single
June 8th √	Becca Carter	10	Caroline Co Va.	Single
June 8th √	Cordelia Carter	5	Caroline Co Va.	Single
June 8th √	Robert Carter	7	Caroline Co Va.	single
June 8th √	Archie Carter	41	Caroline Co Va.	Married
June 8th √	Samuel Ray	2	Caroline Co Va.	Single
June 8th √	Lucy Ray	13	Caroline Co Va.	Single
June 8th √	Moses Ray	10	Caroline Co Va.	Single
June 8th √	Ned Ray	7	Caroline Co Va.	Single
June 8th √	Wm. Ray	9	Caroline Co Va.	Single
June 8th √	Lena Brooks	80	Caroline Co Va.	Widow
June 8th √	Hannah Carter	20	Caroline Co Va.	Widow
June 8th √	Margaret Davis	10	Caroline Co Va.	Single
June 8th √	Ann Jackson	22	Caroline Co Va.	Widow
June 8th √	Isibella Jackson	16	Caroline Co Va.	Single
June 8th √	Betsy Jackson	64	Caroline Co Va.	Married
June 8th √	Jane Jackson	5	Caroline Co Va.	Single

Table 10: Carters, Roys & Jacksons Travel from Caroline Co., 1867.

Caroline County is adjacent to Spotsylvania County where Agnes Roy's family came from. Did the Carters, Jacksons and Roys know each other before they ended up in the Freedmen's Village in 1865-66? And near where my son moved his family! I immediately began looking for people who had Carters born in *Caroline* County in their trees. Did you hear my shriek when Judith

Carter's (1769-1827) father was John and ... Judith's mother was listed as Hannah Beverly CHEW, born in 1736 in *Spotsylvania* and died there in 1821? Why is this so significant?

While searching for our Roys, I found an 1827 marriage certificate between Peter Roy and Agnes CHEW in the Freedmen's Bureau Records (Figure 80). They migrated from Caroline County to DC as of 8 June 1867, when their marriage was documented. I think they are my third or fourth great grandparents who ended up in the District of Columbia.

Several of my DNA matches show a Peter Roy and wife named Matilda from Caroline County and who migrated to Manassas in Prince William County. Did my Carters also come from Caroline and Spotsylvania Counties, and walking or riding horses to freedom in DC?

Second marriage 1767-68 of John Carter II was to Hannah Chew b. Spotsylvania Co. d. there 1821 (see Beverley Family)

Children of John Carter II and Hannah Chew

1. Mary Beverley Carter m. Richard Stevens.
2. Margaret Chew Carter b. 1-14-1771, m. Zachariah Taliaferro (p. 294)
3. Judith Carter b. 1773, m. Joseph Sutton.
4. Lucy Carter b. 1775. m. Burton Taliaferro.
5. Robert Carter b. 1777 d. unm. prior to 1827.
6. Elizabeth Matilda Carter b. 1780, d. prior 1827, unm.

IV. Margaret Chew Carter (p. 294)(Thomas Carter 1, John Carter I 2, John Carter II 3) b. 1-14-1771 Virginia, d. 5-19-1822 at her home "Mt. Jolly" near Pendleton, S.C., m. 7-31-1802 at her father's home in Virginia to Zachariah Taliaferro Jr. an old bachelor, lawyer of South Carolina. He was b. Caroline Co., Va. 4-28-1759. d. South Carolina 4-17-1831. He was a son of Zachariah Taliaferro, Sr., and a soldier in the Revolution. After the War he studied law and settled near Pendleton, S. C. See the Taliaferro Family.

Figure 80: Enslaver John Carter Marries Hannah Chew

Figure *81: Springfield, Clark County, Ohio, 1900*

CHAPTER 16: The Journey to Springfield

America thrived from 1879 to 1882, driven by a boom in railroad construction that offered vast economic opportunities. Yet this prosperity throttled down abruptly in 1882, as railroad expansion slowed and iron and steel industries suffered from mismanagement and rate wars. This downturn closed factories and mines, leaving a million workers jobless. Many, including our Roy and Carter families, abandoned their homes in Mount Vernon, seeking better prospects elsewhere.

It was a wintery Sunday afternoon in 1884, a few days after Thanksgiving. Robert Carter and Ella Roy ambled along the frosty, redbrick sidewalk, hand in hand, their hearts warmed by a love that ignored the snowflakes that kissed their faces. They'd just left Wayman African Methodist Episcopal Church on West Ohio Avenue, near the raging Kokosing River. The townsfolk had just begun embracing the festive Christmas season, affixing fragrant pine boughs to the storefronts and wrapping red ribbons around the shiny black lampposts.

Robert's deep voice filled with tenderness as he proclaimed, "Honey, you know I love you more than anyone, don't you?" He readjusted his bowler hat after a gust of wind nearly blew it off. A calf-length overcoat protected his black suit. He looked like a distinguished gentleman indeed.

Ella's fingers gently clasped his. She wore a beige wool coat and a matching hat, with brown leather shoes protecting her tiny feet from the cold.

Robert gazed into his girlfriend's hazel-gray eyes that filled him with such admiration and longing. "I knew I loved you when I first saw you in that breathtaking dress on the Public Square. You remember, when Mr. Delano was making that speech about his time in Washington, next to the Civil War Monument? You stood beside him in that tight, buttoned bodice with those silky ribbons flowing around your hips. You looked like a warrior holding a mighty sword across your body." His voice carrying an emotional nostalgia, he readjusted his hat as he savored the vision of the petite, auburn-haired woman standing next to him.

Ella's pale cheeks blushed as she looked up at the handsome man beside her. His golden-brown skin, full lips, and lush eyelashes caused her heart to flutter with the shared recollection. However, she had felt powerless on stage with Mr. Delano, like she was on an auction block to be prodded and poked by the cheering onlookers. Trying to forget the past, Ella held Robert's hand tightly as they navigated the snowy path together, their love a beacon of light in the dim, gray air.

"You know how hard I work for Charley Cooper at his mansion, driving him to various locations and doing whatever tasks he and his family request.

But I heard from the grapevine that his ironworks business is struggling. I'm concerned he might let me go any day now. I want to act first, for us." He pointed his gloved finger at Ella, then at himself, as they strolled along.

Ella nodded, wondering where the conversation was headed.

"But, honey, no matter how hard I try to make more money, it's simply not enough, and this economic downturn does not appear to be lifting. Coopers and the Glass Factory have already laid off many of our friends. We colored are always the first to go, you know, and it's not getting any better. I've been thinking about moving."

"Moving where, Robert?" Ella looked concerned.

"Springfield, westward in Clark County. My friends say plenty of businesses are hiring." (Figure 81)

Ella looked horrified, maybe thinking about her life without Robert at her side. She uttered, "Springfield, near Dayton? That's so far away, Robert. How can that be good for *us*?" Ella teared, the depth of her emotions welling, as they continued strolling through the festive streets. Reaching Public Square at the heart of downtown, they stood before a giant blue spruce tree adorned with Christmas ribbons and bows.

Ella shivered, hoping she knew what was coming next.

Her beau stopped in his tracks and looked down at his lady fair. "Girl, you know I could never leave you behind," Robert said, his voice catching in his throat.

Robert faced Ella and took both of her small hands in his. "I would be honored, Miss Ella Roy, if you would accompany me for the rest of my life. Will you grant me the privilege of being your husband?"

His warm breath floated up in the air, as Robert's hand slipped to the inside breast pocket of his overcoat. He pulled out a small black velvet box. As he opened it, the gleam of a delicate gold band caught Ella's eye, and she gasped with delight.

"Just so you know, I already sought your Uncle Albert's blessing," Robert continued, his voice husky, yet romantic and reassuring.

A flicker of worry crossed Ella's face, but it vanished as Robert added, "He gave his wholehearted permission. Now, my sweet, it is all up to you. Would you do me the honor of becoming my bride before this year ends?"

Trembling, Ella lifted her left hand and Robert gently placed the engagement ring on her fourth finger. Their lips met in a soft kiss that deepened as he drew her close, their hearts beating as one. Around them, onlookers erupted in cheers, witnessing the romantic marriage proposal unfolding before their eyes.

Soon after, at the cozy Wayman AME Church Chapel, a joyful noise was heard up and down the frosty street on the 27th of December in 1884 when

Robert and Ella said "I do." He placed a small diamond ring on her finger (thanks to a monetary gift from his generous employer, Charlie Cooper). Robert lifted the short white veil, then kissed his bride for the first time. Cheers erupted, and the choir sang like angels. Parishioners lined up to give their blessings and well wishes. There was a touch of sadness in the air, though, because everyone knew the young couple would soon leave Mount Vernon for Springfield, OH. But today, for that moment in time, joy was in abundance.

Uncle Albert respected Robert's strong work ethic. The two men often had serious conversations, along with other Black movers and shakers, about work and social opportunities in Mount Vernon and beyond. Albert had worked for Columbus Delano for several years, even running a store for him. He also absorbed business tips and tricks from another boss, real estate tycoon John Sellers Braddock, learning how to buy and sell properties and grow his own businesses. It paid to have friends in high places. When Delano's daughter, Ellen, married John Ames, they moved to Springfield, OH, for a few years. Maybe Robert and Ella traveled with the Ameses and worked for them for a while, until they found other jobs.

Robert and Ella Leave Mount Vernon, OH

"Honey, it's time to move on." Robert told his wife soon after they married in December 1884. "A new year should bring a new life for us in Springfield."

The new bride, now Mrs. Ella Carter, was raised in the traditional way: to let the man make life-altering decisions, without question. Usually quiet and non-confrontational, Ella did her best to *get along by going along.*

"About how long do you think it will take to get there on the train?" Ella asked, as she combed her lustrous silky auburn hair before braiding it and affixing it to the top of her head with black bobby pins.

Her husband said, "If we could hop on Delano's Springfield Railroad line there will be a lot of stops along the way, but we'd be there by noon if we leave early in the morning. We'll pack our clothes, shoes, and maybe some snacks for the trip, wearing our heavy coats on the train. It'll be an exciting adventure, don't you think, Honey?"

Ella nodded and forced a smile, but inside she felt queasy at the thought of being so far away from Uncle Albert and Aunt Alice, the only family she had known for most of her life. Her husband was gung-ho and ready to go, though, so she put on a brave face and began thinking about what she would pack.

Between 1885 and 1906, Springfield, Ohio was a manufacturing hub known as "The Champion City" because the Champion Farm Equipment brand experienced significant growth and activity. Growth continued with the rise of other industries, solidifying Springfield's reputation as a manufacturing center,[91] embodying the American dream, where hard work could create a new future. In 1900, known for its industries and diverse population, German, Irish, and Italian immigrants enriched the city's culture, along with a small population of African Americans.

Robert and Ella would eventually live in seven different homes in Springfield between about 1889 to 1906, when they moved back to Mount Vernon, OH.

Table 11 and Figure 82 trace the trajectory of the newly-wed's lives as they navigate the industrial era in Springfield, OH.

\multicolumn{5}{c}{Robert and Ella Carter Family in Springfield and Mount Vernon, OH}
House Head	Spouse	Date	Residence	Other Family in House
Robert	Ella	1889 (1885-1888?)	431 E. High St.	William (1885-1885), Alice (1887-1887)
Robert	Ella	1890	98 Central Ave	George (1890-1890)
Robert	Ella	1892	56 N. Foster	Bennie (1892)
Robert	Ella	1894	278 S Mechanic	Bennie, Roy (1894)
Robert	Ella	1896	McCreight Av near Fountain	Bennie, Roy, Robert (1896-1904)
Robert	Ella	1889	McCreight Av near Fountain?	Bennie, Roy, Robert
Robert	Ella	1901	106 E. North (or Spencer)	Charles (1899-1899), Bennie, Roy, Robert, Bessie (1901)
Robert	Ella	1902	106 E. North (or Spencer)	Bennie, Roy, Robert, Bessie
Robert	Ella	1903	106 E. North (or Spencer)	Bennie, Roy, Robert, Bessie, Ralph (1903)
Robert	Ella	1904	106 E. North (or Spencer)	Bennie, Roy, Robert, Bessie, Ralph
Robert	Ella	1905	16 S Yellow Springs	Bennie, Roy, Robert, Bessie, Ralph
Ella	Springfield	1906	Mount Vernon, OH	Bennie, Roy, Robert, Bessie, Ralph, Richard (1906)
Ella	Springfield	1908	Mount Vernon, OH	Bennie, Roy, Bessie, Ralph, Richard, Arthur (1908)

Table 11: Robert & Ella Carter's Residences 1889-1906: City Directories.

Factories produced chemicals, drills, brass items, and furnaces. They needed workers. For Black Americans looking for better lives, Springfield was a hopeful place. Trains not only brought goods but also people looking for a fresh start. And start they did, eventually creating eleven children over about eleven years.

Industries Near Where Carters Lived in Springfield, Ohio, 1890-1905	
1890—98 Central/Centre (img 24 of 62) Near: Central School Hurley Iron and Brass Foundry Norman, J. M., Machine Shop United States Baking Co Streets: 98 S Centre/Central, S [57-119] Factory, S [41-110] High, W [59-155] Jefferson, W [56-134] Mechanic, S [42-98] Washington, W [60-149]	1892 & 1900-1904—106 E. North/Spense (img 37 of 62) Near: Kelly, O. S., Co.s Boiler Works North St. A. Meth. Episc. Church North St. Public School Springfield Brewery Vorce & Blee, Brewery Streets: Columbia, E [42-158] 56 N Foster, N [45-65] Limestone, N [50-140] 106 E, North, E [32-157] Spring, N [40-115]
1894—278 S Mechanic (img 21 of 62) Near: Davenport, E., Box Factory Second Baptist Church Wiley Meth. Church, Colored Streets: Centre, S [199-297] Clarke [50-145] Factory, S [173-268] Fair [100-151] 278: Mechanic, S [200-269] Pleasant, W [61-151]	1896—N S McCreight near Fountain (img 25 of 62) Near: Gas Works Kelly, O. S., Co.s Warehouse Springfield Gas Works Bridge over LaGonda/Buck River Streets: Fisher [100-125] Fountain Ave., N [100-155] Frey Limestone, N [83-155] North, E [2-30] North, W [2-50] Rockaway Near McCreight by Fountain Av
1905—16 S Yellow Springs 16 S Yellow Springs (img 10 of 62), Near: St. Pauls M. E. Church Streets: High, W [257-328] Light, S [2-36] Light, S [37-96] Main, W [247-323] Race, S [1-96] 16 S Yellow Springs, S [1-109]	

Figure 82: Industries Near Where Robert & Ella Live in Springfield

How interesting. The Carter newlyweds left Mount Vernon to start a new life, but guess who showed up in their new home? Columbus Delano's daughter, Elizabeth, also known as Mrs. John Ames, caused some kind of ruckus in Springfield on 23 June 1887. The scuttlebutt was that she earned a $5 fine for profanity as she was passing through Springfield on her Dad's train. The local newspaper mentioned the embarrassing incident.

Years ago, I assumed Elizabeth Delano was living in Springfield for a couple of years. I even mused that Robert and Ella worked for her when they first arrived there after marrying. But I found no evidence that Elizabeth resided for any amount of time in Springfield. She seemed to prefer the more cultured life in DC and Maryland, until her death in 1904, eight years after her parents died.

The 1890 U.S. Census had burned, but Springfield's City Directories came to the rescue for 1875, 1889, 1890, 1892, 1893, 1894, 1896, and 1900 through 1909. I built a large spreadsheet that recorded every Carter surname, residence, occupation, and family information from 1875 to 1906. Figure 83 lists Carters living in Springfield in 1889; those preceded by an asterisk are Black folk.

I also accessed *Sanborn Fire Insurance Maps* to note where Robert and Ella's family lived from 1889 to 1906. I mapped their approximate whereabouts on a map that, unfortunately, is too large for inclusion in this book.

Could I find Carters with the first name of William (my Robert's father's name)? Could I find Robert and Ella's children's names, like: William, Charley (Chas.), George, Richard, and Robert. Did I finally find our Carter kin? Did Robert and Ella move to Springfield because Robert's father, William, was already living there with other family members?

I wondered how many of the names in Figure 83 were relatives to our Carters in Springfield in 1889, while Robert was a coachman living at 431 East High Street?

My family could have been living there as early as 1885 when their first child, William, was stillborn. Baby Alice, likely named after Ella's Aunt Alice, was born in 1887 but was not still alive as of the 1900 Census.

I printed out all the *Springfield City Directories* from 1885 to 1905. That's over 300 records added to a color-coded spreadsheet, so I could sort the data as I pleased.

The 1889 Directory was especially interesting. Several of the Carters were living at Richard Carter's farm on the east end of June Street were named *Charles*, Isaac, Lemuel and *Richard* Jr. Could the elder Richard be my great-grandfather Robert's Uncle, and could the other Carters living at Richard's farm be my Robert's cousins? Could the *Wm* J. Carter on the bottom line be Robert's father?

Roy was born in the house at 278 South Mechanic in 1894, near the Davenport Box Factory and the Wiley Methodist Church. Robert Jr. bounded into the world in 1896, but poor little Charley may have been stillborn in 1899 while they lived at South McCreight near Fountain Avenue, near the Springfield Gas Works. Was he named after one of the *Chas.* in Figure 83?

George W. (William?) was born in 1890 and may have died shortly thereafter, when the family was living at 98 Central Avenue. Was he named after the coachman in Springfield?[92]

```
  | Carter Abbie, domestic, 18 S. Center
* | Carter Augustus, watchman, res 59 S. Sycamore
* | Carter Chas. C. hod carrier, res s s Pleasant near Old Dayton
  |     Road
* | Carter Chas. R. laborer, res 221 W. Southern Av
  | Carter Edward, driver, res 164 Clark
  | Carter Eliza, widow of Harry, res 164 Clark
  | Carter Emma, res, 18 Summer,
  | Carter G. R. telegraph operator, W. U. Tel.  Co. res Eagle City
* | Carter Geo. coachman, 190 S. Market
* | Carter Henry, laborer, res 18 Summer
  | Carter Isaac, laborer, res Richard Carter's
  | Carter Jas. laborer, res 164 Clark
  | Carter Mrs. Jas. B. widow, res 371 N. Limestone
  | Carter Lizzie, res rear 38 W. Jefferson
  | Carter Mrs. M. Jane, res Martha Jones', E. High st
  | Carter Nellie, res 18 Summer
  | Carter Noah W. laborer, res Burnett Road, E. Springfield
* | Carter Richard, laborer, res off e s N. Limestone nr Corp. Line
* | Carter Richard, jr. laborer, res Richard Carter's
* | Carter Robert, coachman, 431 E. High
  | Carter Warren N. traveling salesman, res s e c Liberty and Center
* | Carter Wm. laborer, res 102 Winter
```

Figure *83: Carters in Springfield, OH, in 1889*

Grammie's days were likely filled with the endless tasks of keeping a home and raising so many young children while Robert worked various day laborer jobs. There were electric street cars, but Black people were not always accepted on public conveyances, so they may have had to walk long distances to work and school. Perhaps the family moved each time Robert got a new job in a different part of town.

Y-DNA evidence affirmed that our Carter paternal line came from Africa. So, I was only interested in Black Carters, but the Directories did not provide race information, nor where the residents were born or their ages. I needed Census records to provide more data. Starting with 1900, Ella was mentioned a couple of times as Robert's wife, but she was never mentioned as a separate entity. That clued me that she likely did not work outside the home. Ella's obituary said she birthed eleven children from 1885 to 1908, so she probably didn't have the time or energy for anything but child rearing.

By the summer of 1900, my Carter family was renting a home at 106 East North or 106 Spence Street. (The City Directory address differs from that in the Census.) Ella had birthed seven children by then, but only three were alive in 1900: Benjamin was eight, Roy six, and Robert was three years old. It's hard to imagine the mental and physical stress Grammie Carter braved, especially losing so many babies. Winters are freezing in Ohio, though, and their snuggling created four additional children between 1900 and 1908: Bessie, Richard, Robert and Arthur. (Figure 67)

Baby girl Bessie came screaming into the world in 1901, when they resided at the 106 East North house near the Boiler Works, Springfield Brewery, and North Street Public School. Our Carter family lived in that house from 1900 to 1904. Bessie was determined to live a long full life, spreading joy and taking care of her family, until she was 91 years of age. Some of her progeny are still alive, including Kenora and JoAnn, and their children, and other cousins who provided DNA samples.

Ralph was born in the East North house in 1903. By 17, he was working as a "Furnace-Out-Boy" for a milk bottle factory and living on West Vine Street in Mount Vernon. Something significant must have happened because by 1930, Ralph was an inmate in the Columbus State Hospital for the Insane until his death in 1979. My maternal first cousins, Jeff Carter and Coley Thomas, were born with a mental illness. Therefore, schizophrenia or other mental illnesses may run in our family. As adults, my cousins lived in halfway houses that helped them survive.

I was surprised to learn Ella and her kids were back in Mount Vernon, by 1905, according to the City Directory. Did the family split up, or did Robert send them to safety when lynchings became a problem in Springfield between 1904 and 1906?[93]

Richard Albert Carter was born in 1906 in Mount Vernon. He married Edna Louise Byrd in 1923, and they had sons named Richard Douglas "Dickie" (1931-1964) and Robert E. "Bobby" Carter (1932-2010). Their sons were some of my mother's favorite playmates. (Figure 84) As of 1950, Richard worked full-time for RockBit Manufacturing and his wife, Edna Byrd—another family that intermarried with my kin—was a housekeeper in a private home. Like several family members, Richard was a smoker and drinker, but he loved to have a good time enjoying life, and ultimately lived to the ripe age of 89. The last child, Arthur, my grandfather, was born in 1908 in Mount Vernon, one year before his father, Robert, died in the Knox County Infirmary in Bangs Township.

Sigh. None of these interesting revelations about Robert and Ella's children satisfied my hunger to find out who Robert's parents were or whether they were enslaved. So, what's next? I now have a bare bones understanding of where the family was in Springfield for a dozen or so years, and a probable reason why they left Mount Vernon in the mid-to-late 1880s, but who were Robert's parents?

I began a concerted effort to create family trees for all the Black Carters I found in Springfield, starting with the ones born in Virginia. I did a deep dive into records for the following people: Augustus, George H., Louisa, Richard,

Figure 84: Robert and Richard Carter, 1942.

and William J. in Springfield. Sadly, I found little conclusive evidence that tied them to my Robert Carter's family. I branched out and started looking for surnames like Payne, Fields, and Hackleys who were friends, associates and neighbors of our Carters in Virginia and Washington, DC. Sure enough, a Thomas Payne family was on page 39 in the 1900 Springfield Census, while my Carters were on page 41.

Who Were Robert Carter's Parents?

Your guess is almost as good as mine. I scoured every avenue I could think of to find documents that **proved** unequivocally who Robert's parents were and who they weren't. I am left with the following questions to ponder for the future research:

1. Was Robert's 1909 Death Certificate correct that he was born in 1859 in DC? I think it is possible, yes. However, it is equally possible that he was born elsewhere, like Caroline or Spotsylvania County like my Roys, Carters,

Jacksons, and thousands of others who migrated to DC in the early-to-mid 1860s.

2. **Was Robert's father named William Carter**, or some other name? I believe this is probably true because his 1909 Death Certificate says so, Robert and Ella named their first child William Carter, and many of our Carters named their sons William, either as a first or middle name (like my Uncle George William Carter). But I still need to find documents that specify the correct William Carter's birth information and his enslaver.

3. In a future study, I will investigate whether the Wm J. Carter (and son Augustus), and Richard Carter (and sons Charles, Isaac, Lemuel and Richard Jr.), found living in Springfield, are connected in any way to my Robert Carter.

4. **Who was Robert's mother?** I don't think the Lucy Jett living with William and Robert Carter in Prince William County in 1870 was my Robert's mother. Her children named Jett in the 1870 Census were older than Robert, indicating they all may have had the same Jett father. If the Wm J. Carter in Springfield is Robert's dad, then maybe his unnamed wife was my Robert's mother.

My preponderant theory is that my great-great-grandmother was Julia Carter. As Figure 77 shows, she lived with people named Arthur, George, Robert, Charles, Edward, and Mary—all my family names. The birth year and birth place for Julia's son, Robert, is close to what I'm searching for. Of course, that'[s not enough to prove anything, but it's a good start. I'm hoping my grandchildren will resume the hunt for the truth if I don't beat them to it.

CHAPTER 17: The Trials of Widowhood

My hard-working husband, Robert Carter, is now laid up in the Bangs Asylum (Figure 85). Many call it the Poorhouse. Yes, it's an elegant building known for its stately appearance and manicured lawns, but I cringe at the unholy screams emanating from the open windows whenever I visit.

Figure 85: Robert Carter's last years in Bangs Asylum, OH.

On Sunday, 28 November 1909, the day preceding Robert's 50th birthday, my kids and I traveled by horse-drawn buggy to visit him. Our eldest son, Bennie (17), drove the carriage while my daughter Bessie (8) transported a special birthday cake for her daddy on her lap. I held infant Arthur in my arms, while Richard (4) and Ralph (6) sat in the back of the cart.

The weather was unseasonably warm for late November, with maple and buckeye trees along Columbus Road showcasing their vibrant red, yellow, and orange foliage. I sniffled. How could the landscape be so delightful, in contrast to the inner horrors of the building that kept my husband captive. During the brief five-mile journey to Bangs, the kids and I wondered whether Robert would recognize us, be able to speak, or sit upright.

My husband spent a few years at Bangs due to chronic myelitis, which the doctors described as an inflammation of the spinal cord. With each visit, my once handsome Robert looked thinner, spoke less, and struggled to sit up. His hair was thinner and grayer, his eyes cloudier, his dark skin ashy. He was dissolving before our eyes. We tried to stay upbeat for him, singing "Happy Birthday" and telling him about the kids' school achievements. But the constant screaming from the other patients unnerved us all. We said our goodbyes, kissed his unshaven cheek, and left him alone after only an hour's visit. Everyone was quiet on the trip home.

That night, after putting the children to bed, I considered our future. Uncle Albert helped us move into his 201 North Norton Street property following our quick departure from Springfield. I left there with the kids in about 1905, when lynchings became a scary problem. Shortly afterward, Robert became a patient at Bangs.

I managed the household responsibilities while the kids went to school. Technically, I was still married and our children had a father, but that was in name only. Robert was no longer present in their daily lives. I hoped he would recover and resume his leadership role in our family. Rearing young children by yourself is no fun, especially when you have three rambunctious boys and needed a job to put food on the table.

Sadly, my prayers went unfulfilled. On 29 Nov 1909, Robert's 50th birthday, it rained for the first time in weeks. The following day, a messenger arrived with the news that Robert had taken his last breath after our visit. I felt devastated that we weren't with him during his last moments, but was glad we could love on him for that hour. Bangs staff buried my Robert on 1 Dec 1909 in Mount Vernon's Mound View Cemetery.

A few weeks after my husband's passing, I received his death certificate. The informant, CE McManus, provided somewhat incorrect details on the official documents. They didn't include my name or his parents' information. His age was wrong, despite the birth and death dates right on the document. Had they contacted me, those errors could have been avoided.

Now what?

I have no husband, no money, no job, no savings, and I can't pay the rent. I pray morning, noon, and night for guidance, and I ask my church family to put in a good word *up there* for us. But I can't see my way out of this predicament.

Hmm, who could be knocking at my door at this hour of the morning?

I throw on a flowered housedress, wipe my teary eyes, smooth back my whitening hair, and answer the door. It's Uncle Albert. I call him Papa. He wears his signature gray suit. His black muttonchop sideburns are fluffier than ever. He senses my mood and I confide my concerns.

In his serious business voice, he says, "Now, Ella, you know I would never let your family starve in the streets. You and your children are most welcome to live in one of my properties on West Front Street, but you'll have to share a space with Mary Tippins, the current roomer. You'll be safe, next door to the church, and close to me and the Sharpes, the Mayles, and the Sites." One-year-old Arthur claps his chubby hands, breaking the tension, prompting us to laugh. Relief washes over me like a warm shower.

Albert holds up his index finger. "And … I heard about a government program regarding destitute children. You might qualify for monetary aid."

I smile. "Well, that certainly describes my destitute babies!"

But Uncle Albert's face looks stern. "But in exchange for the housing, I need you to do something for me … I need someone to keep my restaurant clean. How does that sound? A fair trade?"

I rush to the man who has been like a father to me for most of my life. He threw me a life vest, and I grabbed onto his offer with all my might, hugging him close. It takes a few months of red tape, but I eventually qualified to receive $10 per month for my children for the entire 1911 year. What a blessing, indeed!

The first three years of the 1910 decade went fairly smoothly, with the older kids in school, government money, and Papa Albert's restaurant running successfully. But in early 1913, Aunt Alice fell ill for six weeks, from dropsy. Then the unthinkable. She died. She had been a full-time mother to me, teaching me to cook, sew, clean house, and handle my *female* issues. I couldn't imagine my life without her positive influence. But time stops for nobody.

Frankly, I was upset that Uncle Albert only waited six months before marrying a younger woman named Magdalene Eleanor "Maggie" Bell Hackley. Perhaps he missed being married after forty-some-odd years. Maggie was well-to-do, but I don't think Papa Albert married her for her money. I willed myself to be happy that he found someone else to love. He could no longer keep up the restaurant, so he found a job as a janitor in 1915. Then, he helped me find another home, on West Vine Street.

Maggie passed away in March 1916, which led to significant legal squabbling between Papa and her relatives.

In 1919, Albert married a third time, to Alice May Allen. They were still living at 104 West Ohio Avenue with two lodgers, and the Sites were still living next door. Then, we moved to a smaller house at 134 West Ohio Avenue.

The Depression hit the country hard in 1929. But the hardest moment in my life came in 1931 when Albert Roy, my 93-year-old rock, died from dementia, leaving his third wife and her grandson to carry on. It doesn't seem like Alice knew much about Albert's past, though. For she provided incorrect information for his Death Certificate, saying Uncle Albert was first married at the age of 62 (wrong) and that his parents were born in West Virginia (wrong). All other records indicate he and his parents were born in Virginia, likely in eastern Virginia.

Papa's house was worth $2,000 at his death, but he left no will or probate records, so his third wife, named Alice, had to manage his affairs on her own. Life went on, my children became adults, and they had children who visited me from time to time.

CHAPTER 18: Mom, We Have Problem …

Grammie's Youngest Son Has News

There's so much rain today. Glad to be stuck indoors, sipping my orange pekoe tea. The colder-than-average weather reports in the newspaper say this February has been one of the wettest on record. Thankfully, my favorite flowered housedress takes away some of the gloom, as does the calming warmth of the tea. I can hardly wait for my beloved camellias to bloom in a couple of months. The back door opens, then slams shut.

"Mom?" My youngest child, Arthur, calls my name.

"I'm in the dining room, Arthur dear."

He comes in like a wet whirlwind, removing his sopping coat and hat, and hanging them on a peg in the pantry. I notice that his blue auto mechanic shirt and muddy black pants need washing, and his five-o'clock shadow needs a quick shave.

Arthur takes the seat across from me. He seems nervous, with both hands gripping the table. Something is wrong. He stutters, "Ma-Mom, we have a little problem …"

Does he need money again? Did he rob a bank? Get fired? What has my handsome son gotten himself into this time? His pomaded, wavy black hair and thick eyebrows remind me of those Italian mafiosos on the newsreels at the movies. A million possibilities run through my mind, none of them good. "Honey, what's the matter?"

Arthur looks down at the table. Then he mumbles something about a girl. (Figure 86)

"Speak up, son, you know these old ears can't hear so well anymore."

"Do you remember that lovely young lady I told you about? Mr. Williams' daughter? The one who sings in the church choir and has that snazzy flapper hairstyle? She has the cutest smile when she looks up at me." Arthur stares at his hands, wishing they would fly him anywhere but here. "Well, I've been seeing Pearlie on the weekends for a while now. She works in some old lady's house in Dayton. Sorry, no offense, Mom."

Figure *86: Pearl Williams, 1926.*

Hmm, so that's where he goes on weekends. I fan my 63-year-old hand as if to say, "Go on with your story, Boy!"

"Pearl's staying at a boarding house near her job, and um, sometimes we go out to dinner and a movie. You know, getting to know each other. And, well, you know what happens, right?" His piercing sienna brown eyes beg me to understand without him saying more.

"I don't like where this is heading, Arthur. What happened?" My tone is serious.

Just then, my beefy son, Richard, the former football star, slams open the door and enters the kitchen, unlit cigarette hanging out of his mouth, as usual. "You tell Mom you knocked that girl up, yet?"

Uh-oh. My arms cross protectively in front of my chest, safeguarding myself for the now not-so-secret news.

Arthur jumps up and stutters. "We-well, you see, Mo-Mom." He shuffles his feet side to side and his hands start whirling in the air, speaking for themselves. "You know how things go after a date, right? You might exchange a kiss or two, then a tight hug, and then things get heated and, well …"

"Yes, Lawd!" Richard exclaims, snapping his fingers.

I sigh, shaking my head, eyes closed, hands gripping my shoulders tighter, getting myself ready to hear the awful truth that will change all our lives.

Arthur says, "Well, Mom, we were in my car after a funny Charlie Chaplin movie. Oh my God, how we laughed and laughed."

I stomp my feet and slap the table. "And?" I scowl.

He said, "Well, things just happened. And yesterday, she told me she might be pregnant."

Oof! I feel like someone kicked me in the stomach. Poor Pearl. I know she's a straight-laced, good girl, but she got charmed by a charmer. That's my son's best and worst attribute: charming innocent people to give him what he wants.

Gritting my teeth, "So what are you planning to do, Arthur?"

He hangs his head in silence.

"Who are we kidding? There's only one thing you *can* do, son." My lips are moving normally, but my brain is cranking a mile a minute, trying to figure out how to get my darling but delinquent son out of the current mess that he created.

I admit to having spoiled my boys rotten. After my husband died in 1909, we were poorer than church mice, receiving one dollar a month per child from the government to live on. My kind Uncle Albert helped us stay afloat, while I cleaned his restaurant. I also take in ironing jobs, scrimping and saving to pay off the mortgage on this fine house.

My son, Roy, keeps my lawn mowed, but Arthur rarely has a job, and when he does, he doesn't offer to help pay my bills or do the chores. They eat my food, smoke those nasty cigarettes outside, and bring over their loud friends. They won't go to church, except to drive me and my granddaughters sometimes. They don't do a darn thing to better our Negro community. And now, we have an unplanned pregnancy on the way. I can't let my church friends know. He's got to fix this problem, now.

"Have you already asked the girl to marry you?"

Arthur's head shoots up. "Heck no!" Then he catches himself. "I mean, not yet."

Richard is laughing so hard he almost falls over the chair he's leaning against.

"You've got to do the right thing, son. We can't have that kind of scandal in this family. Has she told her parents yet?"

"I don't think so," he said slowly. "Her father's cool, though. Sherm Williams is a musician, so I'm sure he understands how these things can happen. But Pearlie is afraid of what her mother's going to say or do. Mrs. Myrtle Booker Williams is a piece of work! She's a pious, mean ol' lady, and Pearlie's afraid her mother will disown her."

"What you have done before marriage, you shouldn't have done. That's why you've got to marry her right away. That's why we must talk with her parents as soon as possible. Do you understand me, boy?"

"Yes, ma'am," Arthur mumbles.

There are so many tasks we must complete before the girl starts showing: talking with her parents, forcing a marriage proposal, visiting the justice of the peace in Dayton, sending out wedding announcements …

Arthur looks at the floor, shuffling his feet, trying to act contrite, with brother Richard cackling like a hyena. Arthur punches him in the gut, which swiftly stops the giggles.

"Don't you love the girl?" I ask.

"Well, she's beautiful and sweet, sure, but maybe a little too reserved for me. And she's always got her nose in a book." He shuddered. "Honestly, Mom, I don't see myself *ever* being married. There's too many fish in the sea to catch just one. I'm only 21, after all." His brother claps him on the shoulder in solidarity.

"Well, you should have thought about that before you put Pearl in a compromised position. Now you're stuck. She's stuck. We're all stuck in this mess. Contact Pearl right away and tell her you'll be taking me to visit her parents tomorrow, so you can ask for their permission to marry her. Understood?" He nods.

He may be a foot taller than me, but I give him the stink eye, daring him to argue. That boy is not totally stupid. He knows that having a two-parent family is the only moral, Christian thing to do.

Little did I know that the *deed* was done *months before* this day of reckoning. On the 7th of March, 1929, Arthur T. Carter and Pearl L. Williams signed an Affidavit for Marriage at the Probate Court in Montgomery County,

OH. Arthur listed himself as a porter living in Mount Vernon, and Pearl a domestic house cleaner in Dayton. There was no wedding.

Two months later, on the 5th of May, their baby girl, Norma Deane Carter, was born. I invited the new family to live in my house on West Vine Street, since Pearl could no longer work and take care of a baby alone in Dayton. And, her parents shunned her for a while, disappointed in her judgment.

Now that Art, Pearl, and baby Norma have moved in with me, I can see for myself the glaring differences in Arthur and Pearl's personalities. My son is always joking around and cavorting at night with his buddies. Pearl is quiet and seems respectful, but her face shows disgust that my three adult sons, Art, Roy, and Richard are still living with me, rent-free. My daughter-in-law never challenges me out loud, but it's obvious she disapproves of my leniency. Truth be told, even my capable daughter, Bessie Carter Payne, who lives next door, agrees with Pearl's sentiment. But they are such dear boys ...

The biggest difficulty is that my sometimes haughty daughter-in-law does not accept my suggestions regarding Baby Norma's care, even though I have birthed 11 children. I want to swaddle Norma one way, but Pearl prefers how her mother handles clothing, diapers, feeding, etc.

My son keeps tomcatting around instead of supporting his family like a responsible man. Oh, Robert, what should I do about our wayward son? I smell danger. The atmosphere in my house feels strained, like a powder keg ready to blow.

The threesome lived with me the first half of 1930, but Pearl decided they should move into her parents' two-story row house near Cooper's steel manufacturing plant. Myrtle started watching the baby while my daughter-in-law worked as a domestic in a neighbor's house during the day. That arrangement only lasted a few months, then Art moved back home with me.

Even though the relationship between Pearl and Arthur was nearly extinct, she still loved him. They obviously *got together* occasionally. Hence, Sarah Lavata Carter was born in October 1930; she carried their longtime family Williams/Myers middle name of Lavata. Nine months after bringing Pearl a bouquet of pretty flowers on Valentines Day, baby Ronald was born, and died, in October 1931. Five of my babies died young, so I know how Pearl must have felt, but she wouldn't accept consolation or advice from me.

Arthur began commuting out of town a few days a week, allegedly seeking work. On a snowy day late in March, he came back for a quick visit. Arthur "Sonny" Lewis Carter was born nine months later in January 1933. After that, my son was gone most of the time, coming back just long enough to make another baby. The townspeople people snickered, saying Pearl only had to *look* at Art before she got pregnant again, and again. On Easter Sunday in 1934, their fifth child, Mary Ellen [this author's mother], came into the world. Then,

George William arrived in 1936, Elizabeth "Betty" Ann in 1937, followed by Dale Edward Carter in 1938. They had seven "stair-step" children[94] raised with significant support from Pearl's parents (Figure 87).

Figure 87: Pearl Carter (left) & her stair-step kids, c. 1940.

I felt a little guilty about the situation, but what could I do? Yes, maybe I could have insisted that Art and Roy rent their own place instead of living with me. But having a man around at night is a comfort. And I love cooking for my boys.

The animosity between Pearl and me bloomed when I learned she forbade her children—my grandchildren—from visiting me by themselves. But those darlings continued to visit me *by accident*. I love this picture of my stairstep grandchildren, starting with Pearl on the left, then Norma born in 1929, Sara, Sonny, Mary, George, Betty, and Dale-in-diapers, the last-born in 1938.

Probing Grandpa Arthur's Secrets

My mother only remembers seeing her father once in 1939. The Father of the Year gave her a nickel on her fifth birthday, then seemed to disappear from the Earth. In her final years, Mom searched for the father who had seven children he abandoned.

In 2023, I seriously took up the mantle in this Black ancestor detective project, but I learned few juicy bits about my grandfather. I vowed to find him, even though Mom's been gone for 20 years.

I studied Census records, City Directories, military documents, divorce decrees, forty pages of incarceration records, and his Death Certificate. They painted a picture of a hedonistic, fun-loving, attractive person who may have used his looks and charm to float through life. Arthur had jobs as a newspaper carrier and car washer, but often he was unemployed, living off his mother, Ella Roy Carter, and other family when he wasn't in Dayton, Toledo, or Cleveland for short stints.

Born 2 May 1908 in Mount Vernon, Grandpa Arthur dropped out of school after the seventh grade to work as a newspaper delivery boy. Then had various low-level jobs in car shops. On 7 Mar 1929, he married Pearl Lavata Williams in Dayton, OH. Their first of eight children, Norma Deane Carter, was born 5 May 1929. The threesome lived for six months with Ella, then withGrandma Pearl William's family in 1930, when Arthur was washing cars for a living. Soon, Arthur moved back to his mother's house, visiting Pearl often enough to make eight babies in nine years from 1929 to 1938.

In 1940, Arthur registered for the Draft at age 32. The military described him as five feet ten inches tall and 165 pounds, dark complexion, brown eyes, and black hair (Figure 88). His registration card said he lived with Ella Carter, even though he came and went as he pleased. Before Thanksgiving that same year, Grandpa Arthur changed the trajectory of his life. He *borrowed* a friend's car to look for work. The car owner reported to the Sheriff that Arthur took the car without permission (AKA stealing). You can imagine what came next.

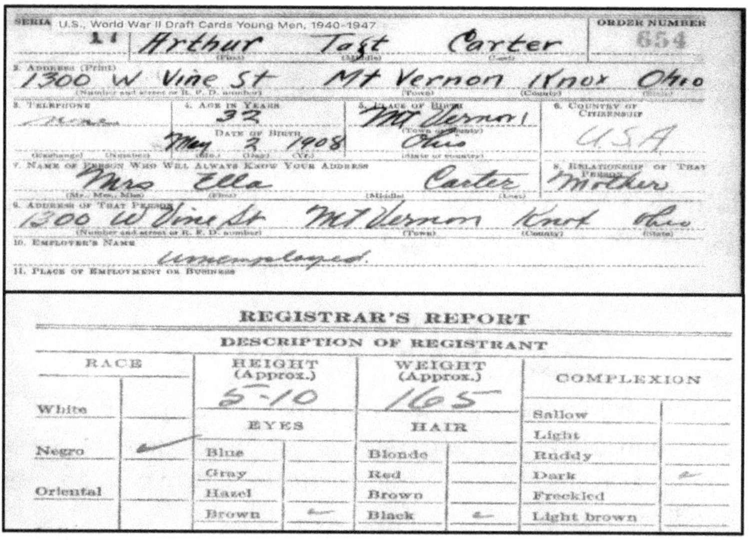
SERIAL U.S., World War II Draft Cards Young Men, 1940-1947 ORDER NUMBER 654

1. Arthur Taft Carter (First) (Middle) (Last)

2. Address (Print) 1300 W Vine St Mt Vernon Knox Ohio (Number and street or R. F. D. number) (Town) (County) (State)

3. Telephone None (Exchange) (Number)

4. Age in Years 32 Date of Birth May 2 1908 (Mo.) (Day) (Yr.)

5. Place of Birth Mt Vernon (Town or county) Ohio (State or country)

6. Country of Citizenship USA

7. Name of Person Who Will Always Know Your Address Mrs Ella Carter (Mr., Mrs., Miss) (First) (Middle) (Last)

8. Relationship of That Person Mother

9. Address of That Person 1300 W Vine St Mt Vernon Knox Ohio (Number and street or R. F. D. number) (Town) (County) (State)

10. Employer's Name unemployed.

11. Place of Employment or Business

REGISTRAR'S REPORT

DESCRIPTION OF REGISTRANT

RACE		HEIGHT (Approx.)		WEIGHT (Approx.)		COMPLEXION	
		5-10		165			
White		EYES		HAIR		Sallow	
						Light	
Negro	✓	Blue		Blonde		Ruddy	
		Gray		Red		Dark	✓
Oriental		Hazel		Brown		Freckled	
		Brown	✓	Black	✓	Light brown	

***Figure** 88: Arthur Carter's WWII Draft Registration, 1940.*

Grandpa Arthur found himself in jail for several months. Then, he was incarcerated in February 1941 and sent to the Ohio State Penitentiary in Columbus, OH. Grandma Pearl's parents had enough. They forced her to file for divorce, finalized in January 1942 on the grounds of gross neglect. Grandma asked for full custody of their seven children, as well as *other equitable relief* (monetary support). Grandma received a few dollars every month to pay rent on their 101 Walnut Street House.

In 2025, I requested the Mount Vernon Sheriff's office to email me a copy of the enforcement documents. Forty pages later, I pieced together that Arthur was transferred from the Mount Vernon jail to the Ohio State Penitentiary in Columbus. But for how long? A yellow Post-it note from Mom's files indicates her brother, Sonny (Arthur), said their dad wasn't released until 1956. There was another revelation on that note: Grandmother Pearl Williams Carter *finally* told Grandpa to never again come around.

Arthur's social security card (Figure 89), issued before 1951 listed his last residence as Pittsburgh, Pennsylvania.

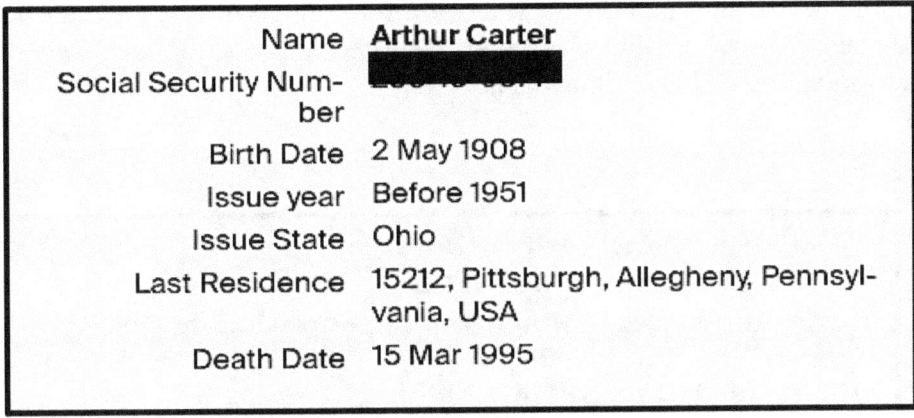

Figure 89: Arthur Carter's SSN Card.

On the hunt for more information, I found the funniest document. A woman named Martha A. Carter, living in Columbus, OH, divorced my Grandpa Arthur Carter due to gross neglect! (Figure 90) I imagined my Grandma Pearl laughing until she cried learning she wasn't the only one he'd scammed.

Ohio Divorce Index, 1962-1963, 1967-1971, 1973-2007	
View record	
Name	Arthur T Carter
Decree Date	7 Jan 1971
Decree Place	Franklin, Ohio, USA
Residence	Columbus, Franklin
Grounds for Divorce	Gross Neglect of Duty
To Whom Decree Granted	Husband
Marriage Duration (Years)	07
Number of Minor Children	1
Spouse	Martha A Carter
Certificate Number	8934
Volume Number	2316

Figure 90: Arthur Carter Divorce Decree, Columbus, OH, 1971

Grandfather Arthur died on 15 Mar 1995 in Pittsburgh, PA, zip code 15212. The cause? A myocardial infarction. I suspect he would have liked such a fancy-sounding ending (Figure 91).

Name	**Arthur Carter**
Birth Date	2 May 1908
Birth Place	Mount Vernon, Knox County, Ohio, United States of America
Death Date	15 Mar 1995
Death Place	Pittsburgh, Allegheny County, Pennsylvania, United States of America
Cemetery	Saint Stanislaus and Saint Anthony Cemetery
Burial or Cremation Place	Shaler Township, Allegheny County, Pennsylvania, United States of America
Has Bio?	N
Father	Robert Carter
Mother	Ella Carter

Figure 91: Records of Arthur Carter's life after MV, 1908-1995.

CHAPTER 19: Grammie's Children

I rushed to lift the freshly baked oatmeal cookies off the tray so they would start cooling for my hot date ... with my grandchildren. Son Arthur's kids would often drop by my house after school in the late 1940s, whooping and hollering as they approached. Oh! Here they come. I can hear them singing long before seeing them:

"Oh, do you know the muffin man, the muffin man, the muffin man? Oh, do you know the muffin man who lives on Drury Lane?"

"Grammie Carter! Hello. Did you miss us?" The kids ask sweetly, seeking my hug.

"I sure did. Tell me about your day at school."

"Well," Usually quiet Mary speaks first. "We got an assignment to interview one of our elders to see what life was like back in the old days." She smoothed her black-and-white-checked dress, her thick black braids crossing atop her head, like mine, waiting for me to speak.

My face blanches whiter than usual. I don't like talking about my past, so I change her assignment just a smidgeon. "How about I tell you about your daddy and his siblings when they were young?"

"Yes! Yes!" The boys scream in unison, and Mary nods her approval.

"OK, let's start with my most famous child: Benjamin Carter. Bennie was born in in Springfield, OH, a couple of hours from here. How old would he be today in 1948, if he was born in 1892?" The kids' brains try to figure it out without paper and pencil. Random numbers fill the air: 30? 45? 56?

I interrupt, "Who said 56?"

Eleven-year-old Betty, in a gingham blue-and-white-checked dress and black shoes, raises her hand. I said, "Good job. You get an extra cookie!" She grabbed it from the plate I held, before I could change my mond.

"Now back to my story. Bennie loved cars. Fast cars. Blue cars. Small cars."

"Me too!" yells Arthur Lewis—who everybody calls Sonny.

I continue, "Bennie was a hard worker. By 17, he was an off-bracer at the Glass factory. He lived with my Uncle Albert for several years after your grandfather, Robert Carter, died. Oh, my Bennie was so handsome. He had chiseled facial features, a cleft chin, short black hair, and piercing, dark brown eyes. He was almost six feet tall and slender, spoke well, was polite, and made more than a few women swoon with his signature Bowler hats. During the last year of World War I, Bennie signed up with the Eighth Infantry in the National

Guard. He breezed through military training at the Columbus, OH, Barracks. In April 1918, Private Carter sailed to France as part of the American Forces.

George, who always wore plaid shirts and jeans said, "Did Bennie kill bad guys?" All the boys made rat-ta-tat noises and pretended to be shooting guns.

Tears welled up and I spoke slowly. "Maybe ... My Bennie earned a Purple Heart for his service. Do you know what that means?" Blank stares.

Stout, take-charge Sarah, in a green dress, wore a camellia flower in a single thick braid. She replied, "He made the *ultimate* sacrifice." The other kids frowned.

"Yes, Sarah. My Bennie was killed in action on 1 Sep 1918. When I received notification of his death, I collapsed to the floor." Betty jumped up and stroked my arm with such gentleness that I held her tight, while the boys quietly continued munching their cookies. I reenergized my voice. "But this is why your Uncle Bennie is famous. Our Mount Vernon community honored his sacrifice by renaming the local American Legion Post as the Ben Carter Auxiliary 349. It's always tough when a parent survives their child. However, Bennie's legacy endures, reminding everyone that he was a courageous Negro man who gave his life while serving this country."

"I grieved my son's death to be sure, but life went on. I still had five children at home: Bessie, Roy, Ralph, Richard, and your Daddy, Arthur. Uncle Albert helped me find a house on West Vine Street, near Riverside Park."

Wide-eyed little Dale stuttered, "D-do you m-mean th-this house, r-right h-here?"

"I sure do. For the first several years, I could only afford to rent this beautiful home, but with a lot of effort and help from others, I was able to purchase it by 1930."

Timid, 14-year-old Mary asked, "But how did you get the money to pay off this beautiful house? No offense, Grammie, but it doesn't seem like you *ever* work, well, besides making us cookies and delicious Sunday dinners and helping at the church. Did you have a fairy godmother who gave you the money?"

I burst out laughing. Kids say the darndest things, don't they? "That is an honest question, Mary. Well, I used to clean Uncle Albert's restaurant, and I worked in White peoples' houses, just like your mother. But I actually make a decent sum of money by ironing napkins and tablecloths for the towns' professionals." I cup my hand on one side of my mouth and whisper to the girls, "And maybe I got a little help from Uncle Albert."

On another visit from my grandkids, I told them a story that made their eyes open wide. "My only living daughter, Bessie Ruth Carter, married Kenneth Payne about 30 years ago. They were living on Ann Street, by Wooster Avenue, about 30 blocks from here. They wanted to live closer to me so I could help babysit their daughter, Ruth Ella. But that was too far for me to walk every day, so Uncle Albert came to the rescue! Again. He paid for their house to be moved from across town to next door."

Beefy Sonny combed his thick fingers through his wavy Black hair, then pointed next door. "Grammie, do you mean that house was moved from across town? How? It didn't have wings, did it?"

I chuckled, shaking my head. "It was incredible! Workers used levers, jacks, and steel beams to lift a two-story house from its foundation. They placed it on logs and greased beams like a track, then horses pulled it with a capstan and pulley. The house traveled smoothly and arrived relatively intact next door." Everyone looked at Bessie's house in a new light, amazed at its journey.

"You know, I have enjoyed watching all you little darlings grow up as the decades fly by. It's comforting to know my family lives next door, in case I need help.

George said, "Who else would you bake cookies for?" Then he chomped on his third peanut butter cookie.

"That's true. My Bessie is a good girl and has become a strong Christian woman. I just love how calm she is, no matter what happens. And she always dresses so stylishly, with her pretty pearls around her neck. She's one in a million, for sure. I couldn't be prouder of the tight-knit family she has raised."

Ken and Bessie own their home too, like many Negroes in this town. He's an excellent car mechanic, probably because he's had to work since he was a boy. Bessie stayed in school through the 8th grade, then got married at 16, then started her family right away. Their daughter, Beatrice—you kids know her as Beattie—lived with her parents and worked as a housecleaner. Ruth Ella was the first in her family to graduate from high school, in 1936, followed by Beattie in 1938. I was so proud of both girls.

"What about your other kids?" Sarah asked in her usual bossy voice, as she practiced her balance by standing on one foot.

"Roy was born in 1894. He's an outgoing fellow who left school after the 7th grade. He's always been shorter than the other boys, with a little beer belly and dark complected like his daddy. He worked many short term jobs during his lifetime, like being a spinner in the glass factory, and he's sold cars—all my boys are crazy about cars." The boys shouted, "Me too!" *Maybe I shouldn't tell this next bit, but it's the truth.* "While working at the Erie Bowling Alley in Cleveland, Roy got in some kind of trouble at the hotel where he slept, and was put in jail for a while. Then, he spent some time in Toledo doing Lord knows what. After registering for the War effort in 1942, he ended up in Chicago working for the Willens Printing Company. But, he always came back to my house as his safe haven between jobs." George yawned.

"Now, I've got a sad story to tell." All ears perked up. "My poor Ralphie. Born in 1903, we soon learned there was something wrong with his brain. He had trouble learning in school." The boys pointed at one another and giggled, suggesting they weren't the best students either. "Or maybe Ralph just couldn't sit still." I watched at Dale and George wrestling on the grass for a moment. "My Ralphie sometimes had fits of anger that nobody could calm, and he kept getting fired from jobs because of his temper. So, with considerable regret, I had to put him into the Columbus State Hospital for the Insane, and that's where he remains to this day." The girls shudder and the boys finally look somber.

Mary speaks up. "We need an uplifting story now, Grammie. What about our dad? What's his life story? We know almost nothing about him."

Oops! Did I make a mistake in volunteering to talk about all my children with them? Too late now, old girl.

I clear my throat, trying to think of the best way to tell the tale of their irresponsible father whom I love with all my heart. "My youngest, Arthur Taft Carter, was born 2 May 1908, the same year as your mother, Pearl." The girls' ears perked up. "Art got a job as a newspaper boy when he was about 11. Unfortunately, he didn't like teachers telling him what to do."

The eldest boy, Sonny, a golf caddy who looked like an Italian linebacker with his wavy black hair and solidly built body, snickered, "You got that right, I hated school too," then he turned a perfect cartwheel on the grass.

"Your dad abandoned school after the seventh grade and my kind-hearted son-in-law, Kenneth, gave him a job in his car repair shop. Later, Art found jobs in Dayton, staying with some of Bessie's kids. And I think that's where Arthur connected with your mom after she graduated from high school. Like most Negro girls, Pearl was cleaning somebody's house during the day and sleeping in a girls' boarding house at night. Your Dad and Pearl met and started dating, got married, then quickly began having children. They lived with me for half a year in 1930, then both moved in with Pearl's parents on North Norton Street. Your dad got a job washing cars for awhile, then he moved back home with me while Pearl and Baby Norma stayed with her parents."

Sarah said, "I remember Mommie saying Daddy had loud words with Grandma Williams. Grandma said he was lazy and needed to pay her for feeding his kids. Then Grandma Williams kicked him out of the house."

I nodded. "Yes, your Daddy was what they call 'a rolling stone, wherever he left his hat was his home.' He flitted from one job to another, in and out of town, sometimes living with me, sometimes living who knows where.

Obviously, he visited your mother at least once a year, creating you seven stair-step children in seven years."

Mary looked so sad, her dark eyes studying the sidewalk. "Grammie," she said, barely audibly, "I only remember meeting my Daddy Dearest once. It was at your house on my fifth birthday and he gave me a nickel. He never comes by to see us, but I keep getting more brothers and sisters. I don't even know what he looks like anymore."

My heart went out to her, to all those children that my son made but never supported. I put my arm around Mary's blossoming teenage body. "Yes, of course I remember that day in 1939 when we celebrated your birthday, right here at my house." I smoothed down her frizzy bangs with my hand and tried to smile. *No wonder Pearl was mad at me. I should have insisted that Art support his family, or kick him out of my house.*

I looked into Mary's eyes. "Your father was one of those people everyone loved. He was almost six feet tall, the color of milk chocolate. He had a pleasant voice and magnetic smile. He could wrap anyone around his little finger, including me. He always came back to me ... until he made a huge mistake in judgment."

The boys heard the word "huge mistake" and gathered around, eager to learn what the misfortune was.

"OK, children. Imagine it was about eight years ago, 1940ish. Your Daddy registered for the draft for World War II. But a couple of weeks before Thanksgiving, Art showed up in a shiny 1937 Model Ford sedan. He said he borrowed it from a friend so he could search for a job. I was thrilled he was looking for work, instead of always living off me. But ... he never came home that night. Several days later, I learned he was arrested for "unlawfully and purposefully taking, driving and operating an automobile without the owner's permission.""

"Isn't that called stealing?" smarty pants George said.

I nodded. "A year later, your mother filed for divorce and asked for monetary support for you children. After a couple of months in jail, Arthur was moved to the Ohio State Penitentiary in Columbus. I believe he's still there." Art's fatherless children looked crestfallen. Perhaps that's why I've always had a special place in my heart for them. I'm all they've got on their Dad's side. Enough sadness. It's time to lift their spirits.

"Mary, you asked for an *uplifting* story, didn't you?" Mary nods. "I probably shouldn't tell you kids this—I look around to make sure no neighbors are listening—"but your mother has a HUGE surprise for you!"

"What is it, Grammie? Tell us, tell us, pleeeease!" They all clamber around me, begging me to tell. Hope replaces their abject sadness about their absent father.

"Oh my, I've already said too much already, kids, but you'll find out *real* soon. I promise!"

Little did the children know, but the Wayman AME Church owned a couple of inexpensive "parsonage" properties in town, one on Jefferson and the other on West Walnut Street. (Figure 92). As a reward for her service to the church, the Wayman Church Board just approved Pearl to be the next renter of the two-story house on 101 West Walnut Street. She should be able to afford the $7 per month rent. The kids will love the spacious indoor bathroom with a clawfoot tub, and three bedrooms upstairs. I can hardly wait to see the looks on their faces!

Figure 92: Carter home at 101 W. Walnut St., MV, OH, 1949-1988.

Decades later, my Mother Mary wrote in her memoir journal that: "When I was fifteen, our second house had a living room about 15-feet by 12-feet. It had a gas stove in the middle of the room that heated the old house which had a lot of "cold air coming in" spaces. We owned a TV, a desk, dining table with four chairs, a closet, and a long sofa (I always sat on the left side to do my art). It was very sparse, but it was enough."[95]

What's the Secret of Grammie's Wealth?

The reserved Ella Roy Carter never spoke about her early life in DC and Virginia. That left her family to wonder all sorts of horrible things about her earliest years. It didn't help that my research indicated Grammie Ella's first years *may* have been spent in the creepy old Alexandria Slave Pen while she and her mother, Agnes, cleaned Sheriff Millan's property. Or maybe Grammie was passed from one family to the next while her mother farmed somewhere in Manassas, then died in 1874. Grammie never spoke about her past, so we don't know the truth.

Grammie Carter's life story was not all sad violins, though. She was certainly lucky that her Uncle Albert Roy took her in as his own daughter, watching over her until his last breath in 1931. And she showed a large measure of pluck to keep her family together for fifty years after her husband died. She was a respected member of the Wayman AME church and participated in many events in Mount Vernon. Some of her children led very successful lives and had families that functioned well in America.

Young Ella may have learned to read and write in the Colored School in Manassas in the 1870s, since Uncle Albert was a Trustee for that school. Cousin Kenora said she heard Grammie helped educate others during her lifetime.

Grammie may have gotten a break while living in the Delano's mansion during her early years. Her family resided in the spacious third floor to use as they pleased.[96]

Our Roys were exposed to fine food, famous visitors, honest work, and a measure of personal agency they likely would not have had in Virginia. And it's likely that Ella furthered her education with the Delano grandchildren living at the Lakehome mansion.

From the Delanos' job, then working for bridge builder and real estate mogul, John Sellers Braddock, Uncle Albert made significant inroads with the rich folk in Mount Vernon. His reputation was legendary, being one of the few Blacks mentioned in local history books. And Albert seemed to share his good fortune with Grammie and her children.

But everything was not rosy for our heroine. Grammie Ella Roy Carter birthed 11 children from about 1885 to 1908, but only six survived their childhood years. She muddled through life after husband Robert Carter died in 1909, receiving government financial assistance for one year. She worked in Uncle Albert's restaurant, sometimes worked as a domestic, and took in ironing at her home. Yes, for a time, Grammie may have relied on Uncle Albert and Aunt Alice, and her church tribe, to help sustain her family.

But make no mistake. Grammie Carter was not a helpless waif. By accounts from my mother, Mary Carter, Uncle Dale Carter, and cousins Kenora and JoAnn, Grammie had a well-appointed house at West Vine and Cherry Streets. Her mortgage-free property featured a fairy-tale house with a vibrant front garden, backyard with vegetables, fruit trees and a chicken coop. The interior was smartly decorated with carpets, an ornate dining table, a Victrola, and fancy Tiffany lamps. My Mom and living cousins fondly recall visits to her elegant home. But were those *really* Tiffany lamps?

For instance, Grammie's mortgage-free house was appraised at $3,000 in 1930—equivalent to roughly $55,000 in 2025 dollars. Many Mount Vernon houses originally built in the early 1900s were torn down and rebuilt, or have since been updated with vinyl siding, enhanced electrical service and other modern amenities. Grammie's neighborhood now bears little resemblance to what my family saw during visits in 1967, 1983, 2003, and 2009. In today's market, $55,000 would be considered limited purchasing power. Still, the house Mom, I, and Cousins Kenora and JoAnn remember, *was* enchanting from our perspective.

Did wealthy politician/banker/sheepherder Columbus Delano give Ella Roy, a former servant, those so-called riches? After much deliberation, I doubt my Roys worked for Delano long enough to receive such expensive gifts from him before he died in 1896. I saw nothing to that effect in his probate records and his daughter Elizabeth received most of his estate. However, it is *possible* that Columbus Delano rewarded Uncle Albert.

What about real estate mogul John Sellers Braddock whose daughter Katherine's diary described regular shopping trips to Tiffany? The Braddocks kept Albert Roy as their personal servant for ten years, holding him in the highest regard, according to that diary. And specific accolades in *Politics and Peril, Mount Vernon, OH in the Nineteenth Century* confirmed that Albert had a stellar reputation among local Blacks and Whites. When the rich Braddocks moved to Arkansas in 1892, did they let Albert choose, or purchase, some of their fine furnishings? Maybe Albert gave some of those treasures to Ella. That's my best guess, but I found no documents that confirmed or refuted my theory. Based on the revelations presented in this book, which theories do you think are true?

Grammie's Last Years

When Ella was in her nineties, she was frail and perhaps a bit depressed. The treasures in her house were disappearing one by one. Some family members believe that my grandfather, Arthur, and his older brother Roy were selling off

Grammie's lovely things. MomBessie invited her mother to move in next door during Grammie's last five years, from about 1957 to 1962.

Surrounded by family and friends, Ella Roy "Grammie" Carter died at 96 years of age. People remembered Grammie as a faithful member of the Wayman Chapel AME Church. (Figure 93) She was a proud charter member of the Ben Carter Post 349 American Legion Auxiliary, named after her oldest child who died a hero in World War I. Ella was also a beloved Gold Star Mother and Auxiliary Chaplain. Her life was long and full of mystery, pathos, resilience, and joy. Ten grandchildren, 18 great-grandchildren, and two great-great-grandchildren survived Grammie Carter, as of 1962.

Figure 93: Wayman AME Church, MV, OH. Is Grammie Sitting Here?

I wonder if Grammie Carter is one of the seated women in Figure 93.

During the 2020-2023 Covid pandemic years, when most people were stuck in their homes to avoid contagion, my cousin Kenora mailed me an envelope of amazing photographs of Grammie Carter. Figure 94 shows Grammie in different stages of her life. I never saw any pictures of her with her mouth open, so I don't know whether she had misshapen or missing teeth, or just preferred to sow off her pleasant smile.

Figure 94: Different Phases of Grammie Ella Roy Carter

EPILOGUE

Sleuthing the enigma of Grammie Ella Roy Carter (Figure 94) has been like managing a three-ring circus. There were so many people with the same names in various locations. I found a plethora of Freedman's Bureau (FB) records, Census records, City Directories, a smattering of newspaper clippings, references in local books, deeds, and wills. But which records were for "my" Roys and Carters? Growing up in California, 2,500 miles away from Mom's hometown meant I rarely heard stories about *any* of my ancestors born before 1900. So, I put on my Black Ancestor Detective hat and established several major goals for this family investigation:

1) To discover my Great-grandmother Ella Roy's parents and their enslaver(s).
2) To uncover my Great-grandfather Robert Carter's parents and enslavers.
3) To investigate what happened to my Grandfather Arthur Carter.
4) To determine how Grammie Carter afforded her reported luxuries.

With transcription and digitization making original source documents more accessible, I looked for fact-based answers to my questions. When I began this book in March 2023, online Freedmen's Bureau records about Albert Roy popped onto my computer screen. What? He stole two horses from someone named Birkett? Then he and a friend escaped as "contrabands of war"[97] to Fort Monroe where the first Angolans arrived in 1619?[98] I felt so connected to my family's controversial role in American history when visiting that hallowed spot in May 2024.

Freedmen's Bureau records referenced an Albert Roy who lived in Yorktown, Jamestown, and Williamsburg—the cradle of English-speaking America. His enslavers carried the names of Spessard or Menard. Precise answers to my questions kept tumbling forth. This ancestor detective project was so easy that I expected to meet my write-one-book-per-year mandate on time.

But twenty months after a deep dive into writing a historical saga involving Black contraband, politician Columbus Delano, and Native American buffalo hunters, I only found credible evidence about Grammie's mother. That thrilling information about Albert riding to freedom and the enslaver hints were transcription errors. Not my Albert at all. So, I started over in 2025.

Did I accomplish my goals? Partially. Specific support documents are presented in the chapters and appendixes, but here's a summary of my theories and the findings.

1) Who were Ella Roy's parents and their enslavers?

Ella's Mother: Ella Roy's mother was Agnes Roy, born about 1847 in Virginia and died a farmer in 1874, in Manassas, Prince William County, VA. According to the 1865 Alexandria Census, Agnes was under 20, mulatto, enslaved prior to 1863 in Alexandria, and not working in 1865. Several Freedmen's Bureau hospital and transportation records indicated Agnes and Ella were both living in the East Capitol Hill Barracks in Washington, DC in 1866-1867. Walker Reid Millan signed a Work Contract with "Agnes Roy and child" in December 1866, introducing a suspicion that he was Agnes' former enslaver and perhaps Ella's father.

Ella's Grandparents: Peter Roy and Agnis Chew also lived in the East Capitol Hill Barracks. Three City Directories, one Freedman's Bureau Bank Record and the 1870 Census found Peter and Agnis living in DC with children named Lucy, Ella (not mine), Jesse and Louisa Roy. A Freedmen's Bureau Marriage document indicates Peter and Agnis were married in Spotsylvania County, VA, in 1827. The uncommon name of Agnes appeared in generations of records.

Ella's Father: I am confident that a Jackson was involved in Ella's paternity. Agnes Roy became pregnant with Ella in March 1866, probably in Alexandria, VA. I found a dozen DNA matches to people who had Roy ancestors living in Alexandria, Manassas, Spotsylvania, and Caroline Counties in Virginia. Their common ancestor with my family was William Henry Jackson (1849-1925). In 1874, the same year my 2xGGM Agnes Roy died, he married Mary Jane Roy––who was likely Agnes' cousin according to DNA match information for Mary Jane's father, William E Roy.

Or, Ella's Dad could have been William Henry Jackson's father, US Colored Troop's Henry Jackson (1823-1888). A land record proves he was in Alexandria just before Ella's birth.

Ella's mother's enslaver: I think my 2xGGM Agnes Roy's enslaver was future Fairfax County Sheriff, Walker Reid Millan's slave/servant, working at the infamous Slave Pen property in Alexandria before 1863.[99] That same year, Millan joined the Black Horse Cavalry in support of the Confederacy. That's when I think Agnes began her life of freedom, and why I think Millan so readily entered into a Work Contract with her in Dec 1866. But I never found evidence that Agnes actually fulfilled that contract with Millan. It seems she lived life on her own terms after Ella's birth.

2) Who Were Robert Carter's Parents and Enslavers?

I never imagined how difficult it would be to achieve this goal. My great-grandfather, Robert Carter, arguably had the most common name in all of Virginia. Thanks to enslaver Robert Carter III, who freed over 400 of his family's enslaved people in 1791—his Gift of Emancipation—many kept the Carter surname, perhaps as an homage to their benefactor. In fact, 35 percent of people named Carter are Black.[100] So … did I find unequivocal answers to the following questions? No, but I found genealogical records that suggest possible truths.

Robert Carter's Father: The 1870 Manassas Census found a 53-year-old William Carter and 13-year-old Robert Carter living together, fairly close to Ella Roy's Uncle Albert Roy in Manassas. They were living with a woman named Lucy Jett and her five children surnamed Jett. By 1880, formerly surnamed-Jett children Richard, Randolph, and Georgiann carried the surname Carter, and Lucy was classified as a widow. I theorized that William Carter married Lucy Jett sometime after 1870, giving his last name to three of her children, then dying before 1880. *Or, perhaps Lucy chose to say she was a widow because William left her to migrate with son Robert to Springfield, OH, before 1880.* My future great-grandfather Robert Carter made his way to Mount Vernon, marrying 18-year-old Ella Roy there in 1884, then moving to Springfield about 1885 until 1905/06.

Robert Carter's Mother: It is often difficult to identify historical details about women of any race. One generally must look for women associated with the documented men in their lives. Since I could not be sure which William Carter was my 2xGGF, it was difficult to determine Robert's mother's name. I do not think Lucy Jett was Robert Carter's mother; the order in which Robert Carter and the Jett children were listed on the 1870 Census leaves one to believe that Lucy Jett was not Robert Carter's mother.

Robert Carter's Enslavers: After searching an armload of documents, trying to isolate which Robert and William Carters were my kin, I developed the belief that Robert Carter was born *free* in 1859 in DC, and that his father, William Carter, may also have been born *free*. Further research might determine whether my Carter family benefitted from enslaver Robert Carter III's magnanimous Gift of Emancipation.[101] Future research may result in a definitive answer.

3) What Happened to Arthur Carter?

My mother, Mary Ellen Carter Marshall, only remembered seeing her father once in 1939 when he gave her a nickel on her fifth birthday. After that, he disappeared from memory. During her last years, Mom had a desperate need to locate her errant dad who made seven (living) babies with his wife but forced his family to survive on their own. I took up the mantle in this ancestor detective project and learned a few things about my grandfather, Arthur Taft Carter (1908-1995).

Studying Census records, City Directories, military documents, divorce decrees (plural), thirty pages of incarceration records, and a Death Certificate, painted a picture of a hedonistic, fun-loving, attractive person who may have used his looks and charm to float through life. Arthur had jobs as a newspaper carrier and car washer, but often he was unemployed, living off his mother, Ella Roy Carter, and other family when he wasn't in Dayton, Toledo (1950?), or Cleveland, OH for short stints.

Born 2 May 1908 in Mount Vernon, Grandpa Arthur dropped out of school after the seventh grade to work as a newspaper delivery boy, then had various low-level jobs in car shops. On 7 Mar 1929, he married Pearl Lavata Williams in Dayton, OH. The first of their eight children, Norma Carter, was born two months later on 5 May 1929. The threesome lived for six months with Ella, then with Pearl Williams's family in 1930, but Arthur soon moved back to his mother's house, visiting Pearl often enough to make eight babies in eight years from 1929 to 1938. One child died at birth.

Grandpa registered for the draft in 1940, but around Thanksgiving, he "borrowed" a car without the owner's consent and ended up in the Knox County jail. Grandma Pearl was granted a divorce on 24 Nov 1941, then Arthur was sent to the Ohio State Penitentiary. I found a note that said Uncle Sonny reported to my mother that their dad wasn't released until 1956.

Arthur obtained a Social Security Card by 1951, which listed his last residence as Pittsburg, Pennsylvania. Between those dates, Arthur remarried in Columbus, OH. I chuckled after finding a 1971 divorce decree from Martha A. Carter because the reason she filed was his Gross Neglect of duty!

Grandpa Arthur Carter died 15 Mar 1995, in Pittsburgh, PA. Right before publishing this book, I noticed an unfamiliar person copying some of my images of Arthur Carter onto her Ancestry.com tree. She has family living in Pittsburgh ... Hmm, I think it's time for me to make friends with a possible new cousin!

4) How Did Grammie Carter Afford Those Luxuries?

My mother and cousins said "Grammie" Ella Roy Carter rarely, if ever, spoke about her present emotions or her future dreams, and she kept her past private.

Petite and reserved, Grammie bore eleven children—six of whom survived beyond eight years of age. Her husband of 25 years, Robert Carter, died in 1909. Supported by her guardians, Uncle Albert and Aunt Alice Roy, Grammie provided for her family as best she could in Mount Vernon.

Somehow, some way, Ella and her sons Roy, Arthur, and Richard were living in a mortgage-free house on 1300 West Vine Street by 1930. Her living descendants remember a lovely "gingerbread house" at the corner of West Vine and Cherry Street. Colorful camellias, geraniums and a manicured lawn welcomed visitors. The inside decor was beyond what most would assume an elderly Black woman would have amassed: handsome carpets, an ornate dining table, a Victrola, and several expensive-looking Tiffany lamps topped the list of special furnishings.

My mother and her cousins loved visiting Grammie's lap-of-luxury home. Were their perceptions accurate? Consider that my mother lived her first 15 years in a cramped bedroom with six other kids, forbidden from entering any other part of her Williams grandparents' house, except a small kitchenette where their mother slept and cooked. A chicken coop might have seemed spacious to my mother.

Second, when you are poor and barely have a "pot to pee in" as my mother often reminisced, they might overestimate the value of items they did not possess. For example, Grammie's house was valued at $3,000 in 1930, but it sold for $190,000 in 2019.

Back in the day, many less affluent people kept their "good" furniture covered under white sheets that were only removed for company. That's how they kept their prized possessions in pristine condition. Cousins Kenora and PattyAnn dusted Grammie's furniture every weekend for Sunday after-church dinner parties. After company left, the prized furnishings were covered up again during the week, over and over, keeping the cherished furnishings in pristine condition.

Did Columbus Delano's family bequeath Ella those lovely furnishings when he died in 1896? I found no written evidence of that. After all, even "if" Delano did bring my Roy family to Mount Vernon around 1875, it didn't seem that Albert and Ella worked for him long enough to expect such niceties from him. Although ... Albert did buy his first property right after Delano's death, and Albert was running a profitable restaurant by 1900 ...

My best guess? Real estate mogul John Sellers Braddock's daughter, Katherine, wrote in a revealing unpublished memoir that her family regularly shopped at Tiffany in New York. According to her, Albert worked for the

Braddocks for ten years, during the 1880s, and they held him in the highest regard. When the Braddocks moved to Arkansas in 1892, I think it *is* possible they let Albert choose, or purchase, some of their upscale pieces of furniture. Maybe they did not want to take a chance that those fragile lamps would be damaged during a lengthy move across country. Sure. Why not give or sell them to Albert, who had been such a devoted servant for ten years? Maybe Albert gave or sold some of those gifted items to Ella after his second wife died in 1919. That's my best guess of how Ella obtained such nice furnishings. And she took great care of them so they did not lose their appeal over the decades.

Future Ancestor Detective Investigations

My intention for every family heritage book has been to collect as many genealogy facts as possible in a nine-month period, composing the book as I do the research, then transforming the dry data facts into engaging stories that everyone can read and enjoy. Try as I might, I could only touch the surface of some of my goals for this book, even though this book project is more data-laden than most of my other book projects.

My mandate since 2016 has been to publish at least one book per year about a different family line. It has always been my intention to update each book project in a few years when more data becomes available.

For *Finding Grammie's Secrets*, I plan to seek the services of a DNA expert to help me nab the truth about Ella's blood daddy.

I've already started writing my last family heritage book. I saved the story our Myers family in Maryland for last. Why? Because DNA don't lie. It proclaims that my maternal ancestors' B4a1a1b haplogroup[102] indicates they were born in Madagascar in the 1700s. I must find two more generations on my mother's line in order to learn which of eldest of my ancestral queens came from Madagascar. I'm already planning the next genealogy trip! Stay tuned.

ABOUT THE AUTHOR

Figure 95: Author Kathy Lynne (& Kanika) Marshall

Kathy Lynne "Kanika" Marshall isn't just a family historian; she's a Black Genealogist Detective, giving voice to the forgotten. Through meticulous research and a touch of creative empathy, she unearths the stories of women, African Americans, and other unsung heroes who also shaped America.

Imagine experiencing history through the eyes of those who lived it—that's the power of Kathy's "speculative nonfiction." But she doesn't stop there. Kathy empowers others to reclaim their heritage, leading workshops and sharing her successful research and self-publishing secrets so anyone can find their own ancestors and author their own family story.

Kathy has been featured in *Sacramento Magazine*, *The Sacramento Bee*, *The Sacramento Observer*, *Sacramento News & Review*, and the *Elk Grove Citizen*. She has been interviewed on CBS-TV, Fox40-TV for the annual Genealogy Seminar in Sacramento, as well as on several podcasts. She has delighted audiences at local and national genealogy and writing conferences, including as a keynote speaker in 2024. She also served as a consultant to West Virginia's Beverly Heritage Center.

Nine book awards grace Kathy's bookshelves from the Next Generation Indie Book Awards, Northern California Publishers and Authors (NCPA), Afro-American Historical and Genealogical Society (AAHGS), and Sons and Daughters of the US Middle Passage (SDUSMP). She is a member of the California Writers Club, NCPA, Elk Grove Writers Guild, Black Women Write, AAHGS, and SDUSMP.

As the multi-award winning *artist* known as Kanika, her Afrocentric welded steel and ceramic sculptures were featured on *American Spark-TV*, at the California State Capitol, and in many galleries. Kathy Lynne and Kanika Marshall's books are available on Amazon and the *African American Literature Book Club*, her website KathyLynneMarshall.com, and libraries where her family lived.

Let my books help you find your family's secrets. Feel free to leave a book review on *Amazon*. I would love your feedback, especially if my books encouraged you to begin your family research journey.

Figure 96: Sample of Kathy Lynne Marshall's Books on Amazon

ACKNOWLEDGMENTS

This book project was a daunting, two decades-long task. Many thanks to the many people who helped me find evidence of my Carter and Roy family lineage, including:

- Our family historian Myrtle Lavata Williams, whose early genealogy work in 1982 resulted in a 22-page booklet of the Williams, Booker, Myers, and Roy/Carter family who migrated to Mount Vernon. Other family members who patiently answered my never-ending questions and freely provided ancestral documents or stories were, in alphabetical order: Joe Booker, Suzanne Booker, Dale Carter, Karen Cross, JoAnn Fields, Alaunda Gates, Kenora Hogan Davis, Robbin Ingram, Carrie Marshall, Greg Marshall, Joyce Myers, Julie Sanders, and Susan Walker.

- Former Archivist Walter Baughman gave me an A+ day-long tour of Columbus Delano's house where my Roys lived in 1880. The Mount Vernon Nazarene University now encompasses part of Columbus Delano's former sheep ranch, with their Administration Building in the former manor house. Mr. Baughman toured me around the Delano's house and the University Campus and introduced me to the Director of the Library, Professor Timothy Radcliffe, who granted us admittance to their Archives. I marveled at the photographs, memorabilia, and a research report which described a tour of the manor house in 1871. Diana Tocheff, a longtime staffer, proudly showed me their incredible chapel, and other impressive school buildings. Everyone I encountered was welcoming and helpful. Oh, and we found an unexpected fact: my Great-granduncle George Booker was listed as staff in one of their publications—none of our family knew about that.

- Kenyon College: Professor emeritus and author of *We Got By*, Ric Sheffield, and Professor Howard Sacks, encouraged their graduate students to research every bit of Black history documented in Mount Vernon. The "Community Within" traveling exhibit, as well as Digital Kenyon online photographs and references are available to everyone, providing invaluable, lasting insights into Black life in Mount Vernon. Karen Greever and Jenna Nolt helped me research Kenyon files and accepted a couple of my books for Kenyon's library.

- Knox County Historical Society Museum: Jim Gibson and Susan Ramser provided so much insight into the history of Mount Vernon. They let me hold my two-times great-grandfather, Joseph Booker's Masonic sword, and allowed me to read an unpublished diary that mentioned my great-granduncle Albert Roy. Genealogist Courtney Cannon Scott helped connect me to this museum and shared her advice.

- Ohio History Center staff gathered all the research materials I requested for my 2023 visit, the most interesting of which was reading 400 personal letters between Columbus Delano and his fellow politicians and constituents.

- Thanks to fellow genealogists who lent their knowledge and support:

    - DNA cousin Linneall Naylor, who visited me in Alexandria, VA, and has been a knowledgeable sounding board in helping me nail down my Roy family connection to Manassas, Virginia, and our Weir enslavers. Chrystal Gaskins shared her family tree to help me locate possible Millan relatives.

    - Podcast host, instructor, and author of *Tracing Their Steps* and *Black Homesteaders of the South*, Bernice Bennett—my mentor—who graciously traveled from her Maryland home to give me a tour of the Daughters of the American Revolution research library where I made a major breakthrough.

    - Char McCargo Bah, Black history activist and author of *Alexandria's Freedmen's Cemetery: A Legacy of Freedom and African Americans of Alexandria, VA: Beacons of Light in the Twentieth Century*. I appreciate the historical background she provided me about my great-grandmother Ella Roy's birthplace.

    - Renate Yarborough Sanders drove me around York, Jamestown, Hampton and Fort Monroe in May 2024 to learn about the history of the first Angolans who arrived in 1619 and early history of America.

    - Pat Smith Jenkins, Afro-American Genealogy Society of Northern California, has been such a stalwart ally, trying to find our common Roy/Carter ancestors from Virginia.

- Rachel Goldberg, Programs and Education Coordinator at The Manassas Museum, Parks, Culture and Recreation. Showed me around the Liberia plantation house and provided me with a copy of Some Slaves of Prince William County, Virginia, and Prince William Reliquary RELICs about the

Descendants of Nellie Naylor and an Account of William Weir During the American Civil War.

- Elk Grove Senior Center Writers Critique Group, and author/editor Penelope Clark are always willing to give helpful feedback to make my writing more interesting to the average reader.

- ML Hamilton, author of over 80 books, whose 18-week writer's workshop and other support helped me start two books on this topic. And thanks to ML's critique group, including authors Marcia Ehringer and Ida Jones and who provided important feedback to early versions of this book.

- And many thanks to my editor, Jean Cooper, for her thoughtful suggestions on how to make this book better.

APPENDIX A: Guide to Research *Your* Ancestry

These tried and true suggestions can help you find your ancestors by focusing and structuring your research efforts.

Start Your Research by Focusing on One Ancestor

The first step is to determine which ancestor(s) you want to learn about. It's hard to be a successful genealogist if you are trying to research all of your ancestors at once. So, focus on one person initially.

- **WHO** among your ancestors would you like to investigate *first*? A great-grandparent? An unknown biological parent? A formerly enslaved relative? A slaveholder? An immigrant ancestor? Print the name of your WHO on paper or type it into your computer. It's helpful to spell out your intentions.

- **WHY** did you choose that WHO person to investigate? For example, if I wanted to learn about my Marshall ancestors back to slavery times, I had to first learn about Grandpa Austin Henry Marshall's life story before going further back.

- What three things do you already **KNOW** about your WHO? For example, My Grandpa was born in Columbus, GA, was a Pullman Porter, and smoked cigars.

- **WHERE** did your WHO person live? List all the known places.

- **WHAT** do you want to find out about your WHO person?

    These are your goals. I always want to know: 1) The parents of my WHO person; 2) Their descendants up to the present day; 3) The names of their enslaver(s); 4) Whether DNA can help me find more relatives with family trees; and 5) Descendants to the present.

Plan to Document Your Findings

1. Adopt an **ATTITUDE THAT YOU MUST WRITE DOWN YOUR FINDINGS**, before all else. Otherwise, any mundane activity will divert you from your goal to leave a written legacy for your future generations. This does **not** mean you must publish a book for sale. No, you could type your findings in a family newsletter, a blog, your social media pages, or a

photobook. Most people can't decipher what a binder of documents means, so jotting down your theories of family relations for others is the main idea.

2. **FOCUS ON ONE** specific family line, or one person, or one specific aspect of the family, for example, a specific enslaved ancestor from one of your family lines.

3. Determine the **SCOPE** (extent) of your research. I wanted to find my grandfather's parents and grandparents, write about their lives, then write up your findings. What, specifically, do you want YOUR research efforts to be about?

4. Develop a **LIST OF QUESTIONS** you want to answer (e.g., who were my third great-grandparents, what jobs did they do, where did they live, who were their slave masters?).

5. Understand that you may not answer all your questions but accept that it is OK. Write about the **steps you took to find your family history** and present what you *found* and *did not* find.

6. Decide on the **AUDIENCE** (e.g., children, family, genealogists, the public) and use words for that audience.

7. (If desired) Include **Appendixes**, lists of tables, maps, etc.

8. Add a **Bibliography** listing which sources you used to develop your ideas in the book.

9. Include **End Notes** with complete citations, using this basic format: Author, *Title*, (Publisher State, Publisher, Year), page number.

10. **Refine the book layout** after about fifty or so pages have been typed. Print a draft to motivate you to finish the manuscript and print the final copy.

Gather More Information

11. **INTERVIEW YOUR ELDERS** and other family members. Videotape the interview and take pictures of their house and documents. Type their stories into the manuscript.

12. Do **DNA TESTING NOW** for yourself, your **elders**, and other family members. The major DNA companies are ancestry.com, FamilyTreeDNA.com, and My Heritage.

13. Gather **FAMILY PHOTOGRAPHS**, using your camera or smartphone to take high-resolution photos. Copy the photos to a folder on your computer; add them to the manuscript.

14. Analyze/add **PROBATE, CENSUS, and LAND RECORDS** pertinent to your research.

15. Visit family **HOME SITES** and **CEMETERIES** (search Findagrave.com), take photographs and type your findings, and **FEELINGS,** about visiting these places in your manuscript.

16. **PRINT DOCUMENTS** for each family line and organize into **GENEALOGY BINDERS**.

17. Start an **ONLINE FAMILY TREE** (e.g., **ancestry.com** or **familysearch.org**) with names, dates, locations, etc., and **KEEP IT PUBLIC** so others may connect with you.

18. Keep **FAMILY TREE DATA ON YOUR COMPUTER** (e.g., Family Tree Maker).

19. Use **ONLINE GENEALOGY SITES** (e.g., ancestry.com, familysearch.org, WikiTree.com, newspapers.com, fold3.com, and Genetic Genealogy Tips and Techniques.)

20. Become a member of **GENEALOGY FACEBOOK PAGES** and other web pages (e.g., Our Black Ancestry, Our Black Legacy, Genealogy Adventures).

21. Watch free **GENEALOGY HOW-TO VIDEOS** from ancestry.com or youtube.com.

22. Take **GENEALOGY COURSES**, enroll in genealogy conventions to learn the best genealogy practices. Conduct an exhaustive search. Document accurate citations. Analyze information. Resolve conflicting evidence. Develop a reasoned conclusion.

23. Discuss your book ideas and theories with other authors, editors, and family, and **ASK THEM TO GIVE FEEDBACK** on your work in progress.

Alternatives to Printing Paperbacks and E-Books

24. Photo Book (Figure 97): Instead of a narrative, self-published book as described in the previous steps, you could create hardcover, photo album-style books. Simply upload your high-resolution (300 dpi or more) .jpg family photos, charts, graphs, or maps to shutterfly.com or costco.com or photo.walgreens.com. Get on their mailing lists to get periodic discounts. This is an easy way to commemorate your ancestors' lives, and/or to write poetry or short story books of any kind. Twenty-page photo books are particularly useful for documenting a genealogy or travel trip, writing about individual ancestors, writing a first-five years book for each grandchild, etc.

Figure 97: *Examples of Kathy's genealogy-based photo books*

25. Hire a Ghostwriter to Write, Print, and/or Publish Your Book: Ghostwriters are professionals who are contracted to write for others and do not receive public credit for their work. They are typically compensated before completing the project. Fees often begin at approximately $6 per page or $60 per hour, with total costs potentially amounting to several thousand dollars. It is advisable to sign a work proposal that outlines costs and payment schedules for each phase of the work. Seek recommendations for a "Ghostwriter" on Google, Facebook.com, and "LinkedIn.com" websites.

26. Use a Local Commercial Printer: Your manuscript must be in a digital format, so you can print it on your home printer from a computer or emailed to a professional print business in your town.

27. Find a Traditional Publisher: Truly, it can be difficult to get a traditional publisher. Find a literary agent, sign a contract, and hope your book gets published within a year, and that you earn more than $2 per book sold. A winning idea is to join the Northern California Publishers and Authors group and author a short story to include in one of their anthologies to become a published author. You could also contract with one of the NCPA editors or publishers. (https://www.norcalpa.org)

28. Try These Other Methods for Leaving a Written Legacy:

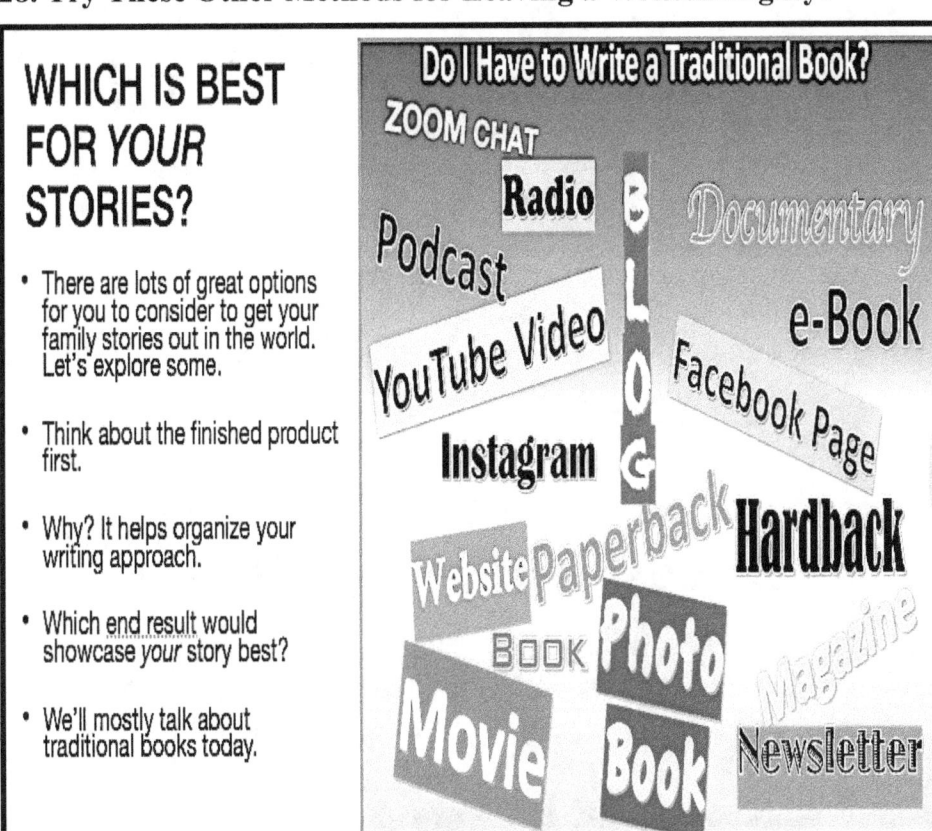

Figure 98: Different Methods for Leaving a Written Legacy

Always Remember

Be so passionate about commemorating your ancestor's stories that you have an overwhelming need to publish your book. Be focused on writing about a specific person or family line. Create a book template and begin typing what you already know about your ancestors into it and type all your new findings into it. Include source citations as you enter information. These important actions will cause the quick development of a manuscript that looks like a ready-for-printing **proper book**.

I hope the tips provided in this book will help you research your own family stories. Remember, when the ancestors call, we must listen.

The Ancestors Are Smiling!

APPENDIX B: Can DNA Find Ella's Dad?

I manage DNA test results for 19 family members with all the major testing companies. I chose seven of them to provide DNA data for this book project. DNA testing helps identify people who have the same ancestors as my family. They may have genealogy documents that can prove my lineage. Entering DNA match family data into my family tree helps the DNA tools work their magic to help find blood ancestors. I usually use Ancestry.com's matching, clustering, and ThruLines tools to find my relatives. I look at their trees to find common names and places where both of our families lived. Then, I contact those DNA relatives to discover more relatives in common. For example, I searched for the Jackson surname in Virginia.

Figure 99 shows ten descendants of a fellow named William Henry Jackson who share DNA with me (KM), my siblings (CM and GM), a first cousin (JC), an Uncle (DC) and two second cousins. My family super-testers are shown in the lower left square. We can trace our lineage up the left column to 1xGGM Ella and 2xGGM Agnes Roy.

Our DNA cousins at the bottom of the remaining columns share between 9 and 58 centimorgans (cMs) with my family. Looking at their ThruLines trees, it's easy to see that all of them have a William Henry Jackson as our potential most recent common ancestor.

It's important to determine whether those shared cMs are statistically significant. Grammie Carter's father would be my two-times great-grandfather (2xGGF). According to the cM chart in Figure 100, my super-testers should share an average 73 cMs with our matches, or a range of 0 to 234 cMs. Our actual matches are only 9 to 41cMs.

What does all of that mean? Our cM results are not good. Even though my family's super-testers found 10 people who are blood related to us, and they all have William Henry Jackson in their trees, it is unlikely that William Henry Jackson is Ella Roy's Daddy, as discussed on the next page.

Figure 101 shows a summary of results from the "Shared cM Project" chart, developed by Blaine Bettinger. It shows the expected average number of cMs, and the range of cM differences between people who share a common ancestor.[103]

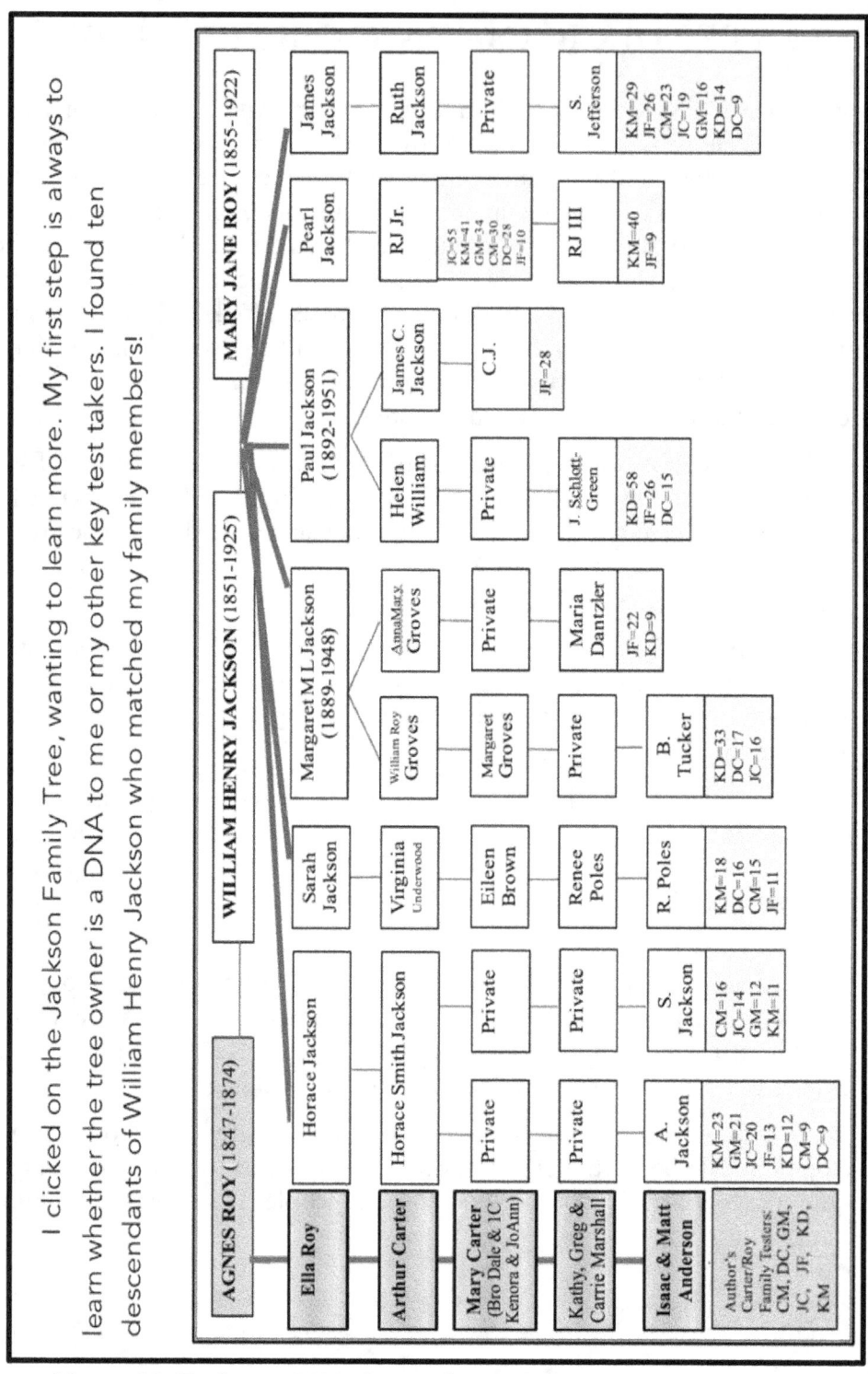

***Figure** 99: Exploring DNA cM matches with Jacksons in Their Trees.*

For example, my family found 9 to 58 cMs of relationship with our 10 DNA matches. There's a 29% probability that we have enough cMs to be a Half third cousin (Half 3C) or third cousin once removed (3C1R), etc. For my results, I am looking for a probability for a great-great-grandparent, but it does not appear in this list of probabilities. Cousin Kenora (KD) had the highest cMs; she is one generation closer to Ella's father.

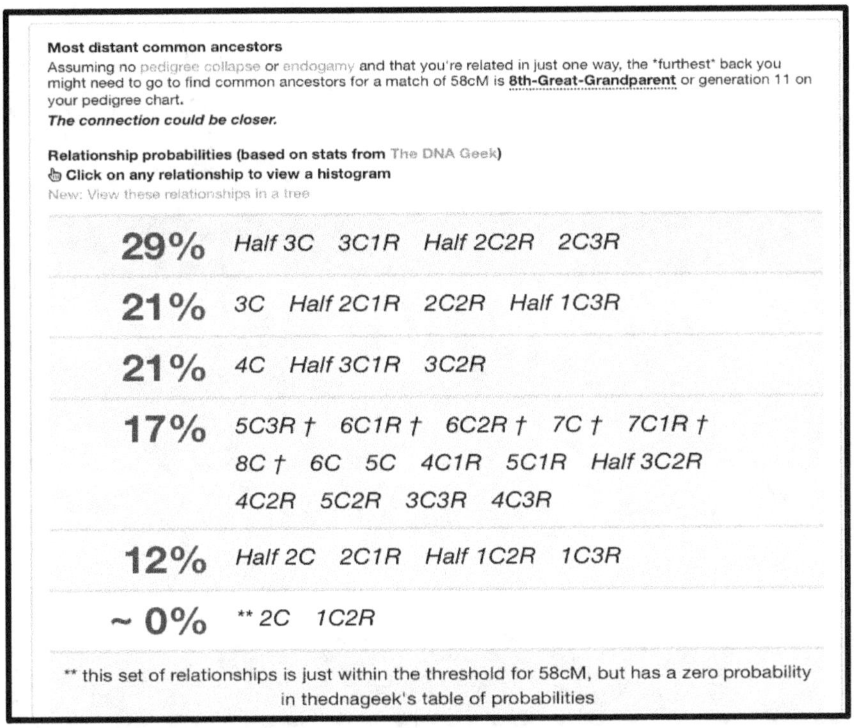

Most distant common ancestors
Assuming no pedigree collapse or endogamy and that you're related in just one way, the "furthest" back you might need to go to find common ancestors for a match of 58cM is **8th-Great-Grandparent** or generation 11 on your pedigree chart.
The connection could be closer.

Relationship probabilities (based on stats from The DNA Geek)
Click on any relationship to view a histogram
New: View these relationships in a tree

29%	Half 3C 3C1R Half 2C2R 2C3R
21%	3C Half 2C1R 2C2R Half 1C3R
21%	4C Half 3C1R 3C2R
17%	5C3R † 6C1R † 6C2R † 7C † 7C1R †
	8C † 6C 5C 4C1R 5C1R Half 3C2R
	4C2R 5C2R 3C3R 4C3R
12%	Half 2C 2C1R Half 1C2R 1C3R
~ 0%	** 2C 1C2R

** this set of relationships is just within the threshold for 58cM, but has a zero probability in thednageek's table of probabilities

Figure 100: Blaine Bettinger's Shared cM Project Chart.

It can be complicated to determine these cMs using the full chart. I decided to use DNApainter.com relationship probability tool in to do our dirty work. We simply type in the total number of cMs for our match, and the program will show us the possible relationships that could fit our data. Figure 98 reveals that my family super-testers had 9 to 58 cMs to our DNA matches. I entered 58 cMs into the equation. Here's the automated verdict: the grayed out squares mean the desired relationship is unlikely. What does that mean for me? One the top row, Great-great-grandparent is grayed out (see circled area); thus, our 9 cM to 58 cM Jackson results are not likely good candidates to be Ella's father.

Great-great-grandparent is grayed out. Our DNA match centimorgans (9-58 cMs) are probably too low for William H. Jackson to be Kathy's great-grandfather.

							Great-Great-Grandparent	GGG Aunt / Uncle
						Great-Grandparent	Great-Great Aunt/Uncle	1C3R 117 25–238
					Grandparent	Great-Aunt / Uncle	1C2R 221 33–471	2C2R 71 0–244
				Parent	Aunt / Uncle	1C1R	2C1R 122 14–353	3C1R 48 0–192
	Half Sibling	Sibling	SELF	1C	2C 229 41–592	3C 73 0–234	4C 35 0–139
	Half Niece / Nephew	Niece / Nephew	Child	1C1R	2C1R 122 14–353	3C1R 48 0–192	4C1R 28 0–126
	Half Great-Niece / Nephew	Great-Niece / Nephew	Grandchild	1C2R 221 33–471	2C2R 71 0–244	3C2R 36 0–166	4C2R 22 0–93
	Half GG-Niece / Nephew	Great-Great-Niece / Nephew	Great-Grandchild	1C3R 117 25–238	2C3R 51 0–154	3C3R 27 0–98	4C3R 19 0–60

Figure 101: DNAPainter.com Table with DNA Matches.

There are many more tests that I tried, but the bottom line is that I have not found DNA matches whose common ancestors with my family are not strong enough to prove our genetic connection. So, even though we do have over a dozen Jackson matches, Roy and Carter matches, I cannot yet claim victory over the "find our ancestor" puzzle game. I shall keep plugging along, attending DNA seminars, cleaning up my theoretical online tree, and organizing my record files. As more data become available from transcribing handwritten documents, as more people seek their ancestry, and as genealogy tools become even more sophisticated, I'll be ready to pounce. I shall update all of my family heritage projects. My main goal during my last 30 years is to leave a written legacy of genealogy results for my family and the world.

APPENDIX C: Neighborhood Analyses

Seeing Albert Ray, Alice Ray, and Delcenia Burrows on the 1870 Census in Manassas caused my heart to flutter (Figure 50). They had the same names as family members who lived with my Ella Roy at Columbus Delano's Mount Vernon home in 1880 (Figure 9). Could these people be my kin? I like to copy the transcribed view of Census reports and put them into a spreadsheet so I can sort the data however I wish.

How did your family compare to others in their neighborhood? Table 12 shows a partial page from the 1870 Census in Manassas, VA.

TIP: Notice how close Ray (our Roy) family is to the Enslaver Weir Family on lines 20-23. They were the largest enslavers in Prince William County. Notice which residents have valued ($$) estates, and where Blacks are living near Whites. Sometimes, that indicates the former enslaved and their enslavers.

Could I find my Agnes and Ella living near those Roys in Manassas? After all, Agnes' entry in the Death Register said she died a farmer in Manassas in 1874. I explored the entire Manassas community, copying 42 Census pages of 1,653 residents into a spreadsheet, then sorted and color-coded the data to aggregate the statistics by gender, race, and occupation. the town had around 1,650 total residents; 14 percent were Black, 20 percent were mixed-race Mulatto, and 66 percent were White. Half the population was female.

In summary, there were 322 Mulattos, 233 Blacks, and 1074 Whites living in Manassas in 1870. Persons of color (POC) were surnamed Brown, Burrows, **Carter**, Field, Gaskins, **Jackson**, **Jett**, King, Lewis, Lomax, Monroe, **Naylor**, Page, Paynes, Pinn, Randle, **Ray/Roy**, Robinson, Spittle, Stafford, Stokes, Thomas, Washington, and William.

After the Civil War, schools opened their doors to all children, though they were still segregated by race. **Albert Roy** was a Trustee for the colored school. In Manassas, 10 percent of the students were Black (12), while 37 percent were mixed-race Mulatto (44), and the remaining 53 percent were White (62).

Job opportunities for POCs were quite limited in PWC. There were only 10 Black individuals in skilled trades positions like blacksmith, carpenter, plasterer, stonemason, joiner, tinsmith, bricklayer, cooper, and hostler. For the Black population, common jobs included farm laboring, with 47 people in that role, housekeeping (43), farming (9), and 12 children attending school.

Mulattos had similar job distributions: 58 were farm laborers, housekeepers/domestics (57), farmers (10), and 44 children went to school.

Surname	Given Name	Age	Birth Year	Gender	Race	Occupation	Real Estate Value
Hornbaker	John R	35	1835	Male	White	Miller	16000
Hornbaker	Elizabeth	28	1842	Female	White	Keeping House	
Hornbaker	Edwin	11	1859	Male	White	At School	
Merritt	Oliver P	24	1846	Male	White	At School	
Hornbaker	Levi J	23	1847	Male	White	At School	
Hagon	Annie	19	1851	Female	White	Domestic Servant	
Sheilds	William	23	1847	Male	Black	Farm Laborer	
Ray	**Albert**	**30**	**1840**	**Male**	**Mulatto**	**Farm Laborer**	
Ray	**Alice**	**23**	**1847**	**Female**	**Black**	**Keeping House**	
Ray	Frank	16	1854	Female	Mulatto	At Home	
William	Roughton			Male	Black	Farm Laborer	
Burrows	Jacob	69	1801	Male	Black	Farm Laborer	
Burrows/ Burris	Delcenia	70	1800	Female	Black	Keeping House	
Diggs	Randolph	59	1811	Male	Black	Blacksmith	
Diggs	Mary	33	1837	Female	Black	Keeping House	
Diggs	Andrew	4	1866	Male	Black		
Wacuber	Mary	14	1856	Female	Black		
Cawthon	Edward	27	1843	Male	White	Farmer	1500
Cawthon	Frederick	25	1845	Male	White	Farmer	1500
Charleton	Susan	73	1797	Female	White	Keeping House	
Gaskin	Oliver	40	1830	Male	Black	Farm Laborer	
Gaskin	Maria	36	1834	Female	Mulatto	Keeping House	
Gaskin	Thomas	11	1859	Male	Mulatto		
Gaskin	Charles	2	1868	Male	Mulatto		
Gaskin	Sophia	19	1851	Female	Mulatto		
Robinson	Frances F	69	1801	Male	White	Farmer	
Howard	John R	50	1820	Male	Black	Farm Laborer	
Howard	Jane	51	1819	Female	Black	Keeping House	
Howard	Margaret	2	1868	Female	Black		
Monroe	Harriett	12	1858	Female	Mulatto		

Table 12: 1870 Manassas, VA, 1870 Census Community Analysis

However, wealth distribution was far from equal. Out of the 231 Black residents, only 21 had any real net worth, totaling $16,482. This amount included $11,817 in real estate and $4,665 in personal wealth. If you divided this wealth among all Black residents, the average Black person earned about $71. The wealthiest individual was farm laborer John Randolph ($7,275). (Surprisingly, he is the ancestor of my author friend, Lisa Randolph). Farmer Archie Hobbs had $2,150, and shoemaker William Lomax had $1,500.

When it comes to the 323 mixed-race Mulattos, only 24 had measurable wealth, totaling $33,081. If the total wealth was shared equally, each mulatto would have approximately $101. The wealthiest among them was miller John Cangyher, boasting $6,300. He was followed by farmers James Robinson ($3,800), Houson Pinn ($3,480), and Charles Donohoe ($3,316).

Now, let's compare this to the 1,096 White residents, who had a collective wealth of $843,684. On average, each White person had about $769. The wealthiest White individual was farm laborer Benjamin Johnson, with an impressive $22,675. Farmer James Raley ($21,133), farmer John Hooe ($19,050), and miller John Hornbaker ($18,280) follow.

After the Civil War, educational opportunities opened up for all children, though schools were segregated by race. Among the students, 10 percent were Black (12 children), 37 percent were Mulatto (44 children), and 53 percent were White (62 children).

Occupational opportunities were constrained for nonWhites. Only five Black individuals held skilled trades, such as blacksmith, carpenter, plasterer, stonemason, tinsmith, and bricklayer. In comparison, there was one Mulatto and seven White individuals in those trades. The more common jobs for Blacks included farm laborer (47), housekeeping (43), farming (9), and attending school (12). Mulattos were mostly farm laborers (58), housekeepers/domestics (57), farmers (10), and students (44).

The White residents had a wider range of job opportunities. Many were housekeepers (185), farmers (120), farm laborers (43), domestics/servants (12), and those affiliated with the railroad (10). There were also teachers (7) and store-related employees (7). Other occupations held by Whites, but in smaller numbers, included clergy, constables, gardeners, real estate sales, lawyers, postmasters, publishers, innkeepers, milliner/tailors, wagon/carriage makers, shoemakers, restaurateurs, butchers, and physicians.

So what? Who cares about all those statistics? I believe it's helpful to perform a community (also called cluster) analysis like this to see how our ancestors compared and might be related to others in the same city and county. Maybe they migrated together. This analysis might give a clearer perspective on how progressive or restrictive the community was, how fortunate or poor our ancestors were, and who might share DNA with my supertesters.

Comparing community analyses over the years can indicate the relative progress (or the opposite) of our ancestors. Table 13 shows part of the 1880 Census from Knox County, OH, where all of my mother's family lines eventually came together in Mount Vernon. Many of these people lived in Belmont County, OH, for one or two generations before landing in Mount Vernon.

Contrasting the 1880 and 1870 Censuses helped me analyze when my Roys landed in Mount Vernon, how they connected to other Blacks and Mulattos, where they were living, besides their occupations and birthplaces. I color-coded the information by race, gender, and birthplace after copying the information to a spreadsheet. This made it easy to compare residence information for our FAN Club from 1870 to 1880.

My primary aim was to determine which families migrated from Virginia, Maryland or DC to Mount Vernon, OH. Did some of those families travel together and intermarry with my family? Examining their and their parents' birthplaces, marriage documents, and DNA information might help me get a handle on their connections.

My Roys were in Mount Vernon by 1880, but my Bookers, Williams and Carters were not yet present in Mount Vernon. Joseph Booker and his wife Sara Elizabeth Myers (1858-1906) arrived in 1881 from Barnesville, Belmont, OH, bringing my great-grandmother, Myrtle. Records for my Carters surfaced as of 1883. For example, I noted that Albert Roy's second wife, Maggie Hackley, was in Mount Vernon as of 1870, but her family came from Virginia before that. I did an intensive DNA analysis on Hackleys (shaded in yellow on the 1880 Census) and found they were all living on Norton Street. That's near where my mother lived in her grandparents row house that was owned by Cooper's Foundry. It's all about family connections.

The FAN Club clusters become complicated as these Black families migrated from Virginia, West Virginia, and Maryland into Belmont County for a generation or two. Many of them then traveled to Mount Vernon, Knox County, OH, and intermarrying with more of the families shown in Table 13.

Let's take the Newsome family. While searching the Freedmen's Bureau in 2023 at the beginning of this book project, I found an astonishing record which stated Ella's adopted father, Albert Roy, and his friend, Henry Newsome, stole two horses from man named Birchette. They ended up in Fort Monroe. I pictured a heroic 169-mile ride from enslavement in Manassas, VA, to *contraband* status in Fort Monroe. But that lead might have been typo, so I lost interest in pursuing that thrilling story, until ... I noticed in Table 13 that there were Newsomes who married Simmons who married my Bookers. And cousin JoAnn is a DNA match to Sharon Newsom: they both have Thomas T. Jackson in common.

1880 Knox County, OH, Blacks & Mulattos

Race	Name	Birth	Birth State	Father	Mother	Father Birth	Mother Birth	Resid 1880	Dwell# 1880	Street 1880	Occupation	Cannot Read	School?
B	Albert Rolls	1858	VA			VA	VA	MV	99	Main Street	Servant		
B	Albert Roy	1838	VA	Peter Roy?	Matilda?	VA	VA	Clinton	800	Martinsburg	Servant (Delano)		
B	Albert Williams		OH	James Williams	Rilla Williams	TN	OH	MV	87	Front Street			
B	Alice Roy	1843-45	VA	Jacob Burrows	Delcenia Burrows	VA	VA	Clinton	800	Martinsburg	Servant (Delano)		
B	Allen Keys	1855	KY						146		Laborer	y	
B	Alonzo Baler	1861	OH	?	E. M. Baler	OH	SC?	Clinton	134				
B	Andrew Hackley	1867	OH	James Hackley	Maggie	VA	VA	MV	34	Norton Street			Y
B	Anna Burk	1810	VA			VA	VA	Monroe	84		KeepingH	y	y
B	Anna Burk	1868	VA	John A. Burk	Anna Burk	VA	VA	Monroe	84		AtHome	y	y
B	Anna McGruder	1840	VA					Liberty	92		HouseK	y	
M	Bessie Cross	1874	PA	Thomas Cross	Elizabeth			Fredericktov	13	Pleasant	AtHome		y
B	Bud. Burk	1860	VA	John A. Burk	Anna Burk	VA	VA	Monroe	84				
B	C. T. Berry	1810	VA			VA	VA	MV	65	W. Gambier			
B	Caroline White	1841	OH			OH	OH	MV	1	Vine Street	KeepingH		
B	Charles McGruder	1872	VA	Joseph McGrude	Anna			Liberty	92				
B	Charles White	1845	VA			VA	VA	MV	1	Vine Street	Laborer		
B	Delcenia Burrows	1800?	VA	?	?	VA?	VA?	Clinton	800	Martinsburg	?		
B	Delilah Lewis	1852	OH			MD	MD	MV	175	Coshotcton A	KeepingH		
B	E. M. Baler	1837	VA?			VA	VA	Clinton	134		KeepingH		
B	Ed Rudisill	1835	NC						146			y	
B	Edith Davis	1878	OH	James Davis	Hattie Davis	MS	OH	MV	57	High Street	Laborer		
B	Eliza Hill	1872	OH	John Hill	Ellen Hill	Carolina	Eng	MV	87	Front Street			
B	Ella Roy	1866	VA	?	Agnes Roy	VA?	VA?	Clinton	800	Martinsburg	Servant (Delano)		
B	Ellen Hill	1851	Eng	John Hill	Ellen Hill	Carolina	France	MV	87	Front Street	KeepingH		
B	Emma Williams		OH	James Williams	Rilla Williams	TN	OH	MV	87	Front Street			
B	Fannie N. Wright	1868	OH	J. W. Wright	S. A.	TN	TN	MV	26	Norton Street			
B	Flem Jackson	1820	VA			VA	VA	Clinton	142		Farmer		
B	Francis Jackson	1862	OH	Flem Jackson	?	VA	VA	Clinton	142		KeepingH		
B	George Baler	1876	OH	W. M. Baler	E. M. Baler	OH	VA	Clinton	134				
B	Grace Lewis			John Lewis	Delilah Lewis	VA	OH	MV	175	Coshotcton Avenue			
B	Grant Hackley	1871	OH	James Hackley	Maggie	VA	VA	MV	34	Norton Street			Y
M	Hattie Davis	1853	OH			OH	OH	MV	57	High Street	Laborer		
B	Henry Hill	1871	OH	John Hill	Ellen Hill	Carolina	Eng	MV	87	Front Street			
M	Ida May Cross	1879	OH	Thomas Cross	Elizabeth			Fredericktov	13	Pleasant	AtHome		
B	Idella Bright	1850	WV			WV	WV	MV	104	Norte St	KeepingH		
B	J. W. Wright	1853	TN			TN	TN	MV	26	Norton Street	DayLaborer		
B	James Davis	1849	MS			NC	TN	MV	57	High Street	Laborer		
B	James Jackson	1871	OH	Flem Jackson	?	VA	VA	Clinton	142				
B	James Moyce	1863	St Helena			Malay	Malay	Clinton	800	Martinsburg	Servant (Delano)		
B	James Rolls Ralls	1840	VA			VA	VA	MV	115	Chestnut Stre	Laborer		
B	James W. Hackley	1839	VA			VA	VA	MV	34	Norton Street	Laborer		

Table 13: 1880 Knox County, OH, Blacks and Mulattos Analysis, page 1 Orange (dark shading) indicates live-in workers for Columbus Delano.

1880 Knox County, OH, Blacks & Mulattos

Race	Name	Birth	Birth State	Father	Mother	Father Birth	Mother Birth	Resid 1880	Dwell# 1880	Street1880	Occupation	Cannot Read	School?
B	John Baler	1868	OH	W. M. Baler	E. M. Baler	OH	VA	Clinton	134		FarmLaborer		
B	John Green	1844	VA			VA	VA	MV	5	W. Vine	Laborer		
B	John Hill	1844	Carolina			C	C	MV	87	Front Street	Laborer		
B	John Lewis	1852	VA			VA	VA	MV	175	Coshotcton A	Drayman		
B	John Rolls	1825	VA			VA	VA	MV	115	Chestnut Street			
B	John White	1873	OH	Charles White	Caroline	VA	OH	MV	1	Vine Street	AtSchool		Y
B	Jonathan Jackson	1866	OH	Flem Jackson	?	VA	VA	Clinton	142		FarmLaborer		
B	Joseph Lewis	1870	OH	John Lewis	Delilah Lewis	VA	OH	MV	175	Coshotcton A	At School		
B	Joseph McGruder	1825	VA					Liberty	92		Farming	y	
B	Joseph McGruder	1859	VA	Joseph McGrude	Anna			Liberty	92		Farmer		
B	Kate Green	1856	VA			VA	VA	MV	5	W. Vine	KeepingH		
B	L. J. Rolls	1823	VA			VA	VA	MV	115	Chestnut Stre	KeepingH		
B	Lorenzo Martin	1856	VA			VA	VA	MV	5	W. Vine	Laborer		
B	Losson Burk	1861	VA	John A. Burk	Anna Burk	VA	VA	Monroe	84		FarmLaborer		
B	Louis Davis	1879	OH	James Davis	Hattie Davis	MS	OH	MV	57	High Street	Laborer		
B	Lucy Man	1835	VA			VA		MV	103	Norte St			
B	Lydia A. Hackley	1879	OH	James Hackley	Maggie	VA	VA	MV	34	Norton Street			
B	M. W. Baler	1879	OH	W. M. Baler	E. M. Baler	OH	VA	Clinton	134				
B	Maggie Hackley	1846	VA			VA	VA	MV	34	Norton Street	Washing		
B	Maggy McGruder	1870	VA	Joseph McGrude	Anna			Liberty	92				
B	Major Wade	1844	MO			MO	MO	MV	116	W. High Street			
B	Malveney Hill	1874	OH	John Hill	Ellen Hill	Carolina	Eng	MV	87	Front Street			
B	Mark Durbin	1844	OH					MV	2	W. Vine	Laborer		
B	Martha Hackley	1877	OH	James Hackley	Maggie	VA	VA	MV	34	Norton Street			
B	Mary C. Hackley	1874	OH	James Hackley	Maggie	VA	VA	MV	34	Norton Street			
B	Mary Martin	1860	VA			VA	VA	MV	5	W. Vine	KeepingH		
M	Mary Rolls	1856	VA			VA	VA	MV	115	Chestnut Street			
B	Mary Wright	1867	OH	J. W. Wright	S. A.	TN	TN	MV	26	Norton Street			
B	Matta Bright	1876	OH	William Bright		WV	WV	MV	104	Norte St			
B	Maud Davis	1876	OH	James Davis	Hattie Davis	MS	OH	MV	57	High Street	Laborer		
B	Maud Williams		OH	James Williams	Rilla Williams	TN	OH	MV	87	Front Street			
B	Minnie Davis	1875	OH	James Davis	Hattie Davis	MS	OH	MV	57	High Street	Laborer		
B	Monroe King	1861	OH			VA	VA	MV	99	Main Street	Servant		
B	Nellie Baler	1875	OH	W. M. Baler	E. M. Baler	OH	VA	Clinton	134				
B	Nimrod McGruder	1861	VA	Joseph McGrude	Anna			Liberty	92		Farmer		
B	Oliver Williams	1872	OH	James Williams	Rilla Williams	TN	OH	MV	87	Front Street			
B	Ralph Green	1879	OH			VA	VA	MV	5	W. Vine			
B	Ralph Martin	1879	OH	Lorenzo Martin	Mary Martin	VA	VA	MV	5	W. Vine			
B	Rebecca Rolls	1861	VA			VA	VA	MV	115	Chestnut Street			
B	Rilla Williams	1856	OH			OH	OH	MV	87	Front Street	KeepingH		
B	Robba Hill	1875	OH	John Hill	Ellen Hill	Carolina	Eng	MV	87	Front Street			
B	Romeo Baler	1869	OH	W. M. Baler	E. M. Baler	OH	VA	Clinton	134				
B	S. A. Wright	1850	OH			TN	TN	MV	26	Norton Street	Washing		
B	Sally McGruder	1864	VA	Joseph McGrude	Anna			Liberty	92				

1880 Knox County, OH, Blacks and Mulattos Community Analysis, page 2

Wait! There are Jacksons in the 1880 Mount Vernon Census. I did a deep dive into "Flem Jackson" who was born in Virignia in 1824 and living in Warren, Belmont County, OH in 1850—where my Bookers lived in 1870. I built Flemming's family tree, excited to learn he had a daughter named Mary Jane Jackson! Was she Agnes Roy's sister or cousin? No, she is not the same Mary Jane that William Henry Jackson married in 1874. This Mary Jane married Walker Goins, and that's a surname I've been trying to connect to Mount Vernon, OH.

Flem (Flemming) Jackson had a son named William Henry Jackson! Was he Grammie's daddy? No, he was born in Belmont County in 1856, ten years before Grammie was born.

And there is potentially more DNA magic to examine. I looked at how many people born in Mount Vernon, OH, were matches to some of our super-testers, as well as what surnames they had in common:

- Seventeen matches to Uncle Dale Carter (from 1396 cMs to 6 cMs, with common surnames Myers, Booker, Jackson, Carter, Roy, Crewett)
- Eighteen matches to Kathy Marshall (707 to 9 cMs, with Ruth Carter)
- Six to Kenora (999 cMs to 16 cMs, with Mason and Payne)
- Seventeen to JoAnn (1760 cMs to 8 cMs, with Jacksons)

I did a similar search in DNA matches' tree for people born in DC and various places in Virginia, with similar results as above.

The Bottom Line

There are lots of possible leads via Census, DNA, and other factors to find more connections to my family. However, I found little that could stand up to scrutiny by a Genealogical Proof Standard panel of experts. Therefore, I shall revisit this book project in the future to see if I can solidify my theories of who Grammie Ella Roy Carter and Robert Carter's fathers were.

APPENDIX D: Roy Deeds in Mount Vernon, OH

On May 24, 1912, Albert Roy and wife Alice Roy, executed a mortgage deed for property to secure a $2,300 loan with 6 percent interest (about $20,000 today). The Roys agreed to pay $23 monthly ($750 in 2025 dollars), with the entire balance due if they missed two consecutive payments. A year later, on 22 May 1913, an "Estate Settlement" record indicated Albert and Alice Roy had two $600 mortgage notes and a total of $44.40 in interest payments. Did Albert pay those mortgages off or did they lose the property? Was one mortgage for his adopted daughter, Ella Roy Carter? Or did someone else—like maybe a former employer named Delano or Braddock—pay off those notes on Albert's behalf? Unlikely, since both of them were out of the Mount Vernon picture before 1900.

Sadly, I am not an expert at legalese, so I did my best to pore through these, and many other deed records involving the Black folk in Mount Vernon. It was a clear sign that the African Americans fully participated in their agency to manage their finances as they wished, even though segregation was alive and well in Mount Vernon, OH.

Chapter 9 took a deep dive into the Mount Vernon, Black community. Initially, the emphasis was on Albert Roy and the part he may have played in supporting Grammie Carter. What follows is a cursory look at Albert's deed portfolio. Table 14 and Figure 102 provide specific deeds involving Albert Roy.

Sample of Deeds for Albert and Alice Roy in Knox County, Mount Vernon, OH

Index Date	Grantor to (from)	Grantee (to)	Book	Page	#Lot Streets	Describe transaction
1883	L P Rosa	Albert Roy	80	529-30		Albert Roy to pay $1200 to the Rosas. Five acres in Walkers Addition, all estate and title.
1892	Albert & Alice	Jennie Waxler	123	591	#219: Gambier & Mechanic	East half of lot 219. 20' off the east end of lot where brick building now stands.
1892	Albert Roy	Caroline Clark	96	188	#265: Gambier & Sandusky	Caroline Clark paid Albert and Alice Roy $1,200. (Walker's Addition, near MV)
1897	Alice M. Elliott	Albert Roy and wife			#219: Gambier & Mechanic	Alice M. Elliott to Albert Roy and wife, part lot 219 in Mount Vernon, old plat, $900
1908	ROY, Albert & Maggie H. Roy	Max Myers	132	354	#219: Gambier & Mechanic	East half of lot #219 in Mount Vernon, except for part deeded to Jennie Waxler in 1908.
1914	ROY, Alice	Sarah and James Sites	131	325	#219: Gambier & Mechanic	Part lot 219 in Mount Vernon.
1916	ROY, Albert	Maggie Roy	134 121	169 335	213 & 214: 104 W. Front (or W. Ohio Av.)	James Schaffer, Adm of deceased Maggie Roy's estate orders the sale of real estate which Albert paid $500: 33 feet off the east halves of lots 213 and 214
1916	ROY, Albert	A. H. Simmons	N/A	N/A		Albert appointed appraiser for A. H. Simmons property inventory.
1916, Sep	ROY, Albert	Rose A. Turner	135	414		Rose paid Albert $550.
	ROY, Alice (deceased)	Albert Roy	130	528	#37: at Gay St. at Ohio Ave.	

Table 14: Albert Roy's Properties in Mount Vernon, OH

Mount Vernon, OH, Properties Albert Roy Purchased or Sold, 1883-1931, Mapped

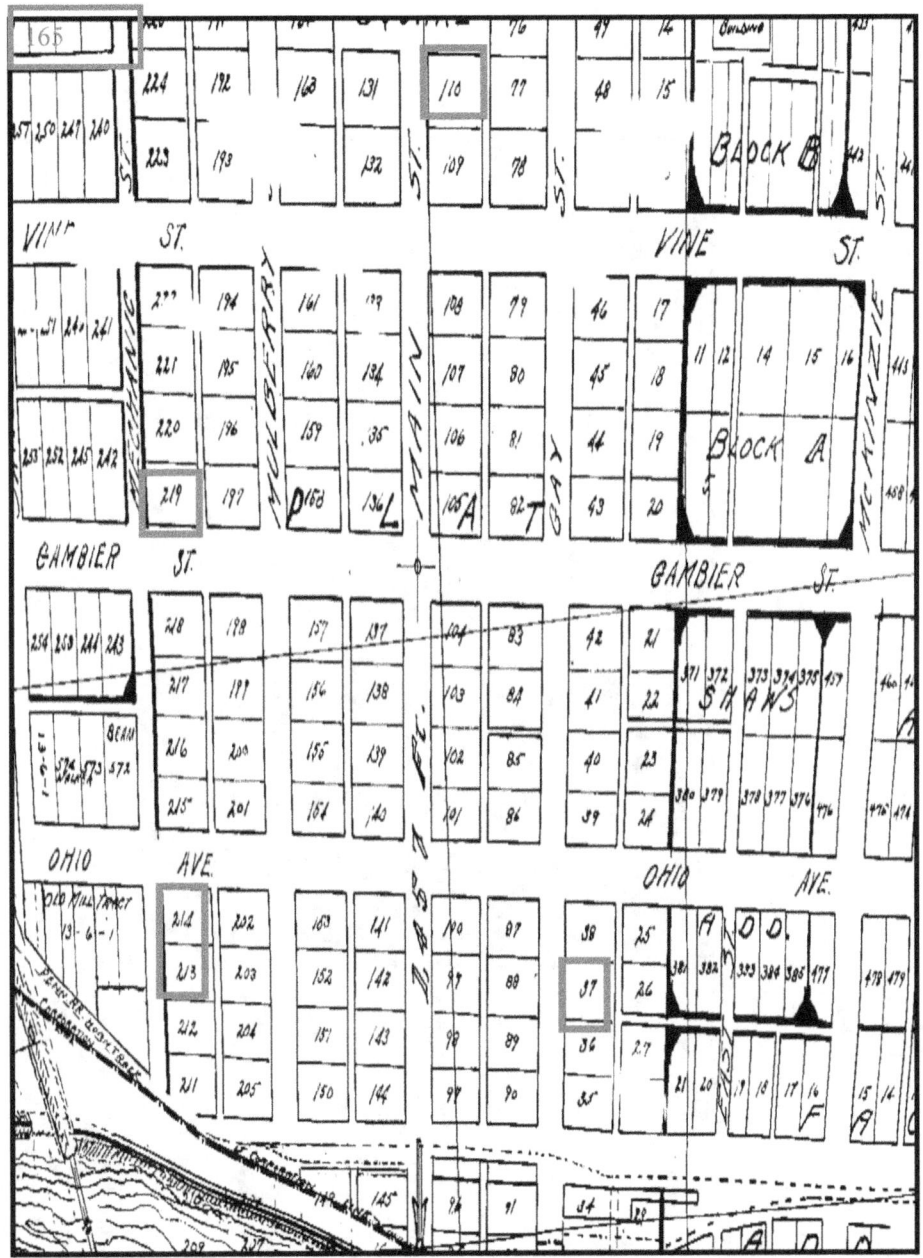

Figure 102: Map--Albert Roy's Properties in Mount Vernon, OH

BIBLIOGRAPHY

1871 Guide to Washington with a description of public buildings, works of art, etc. Library of Congress Online Catalog.

A Look Back at Springfield and Clark County, OH's Black History - Program Record, 2021.

Barlau, Sandra (compiled by), *Some Slaves of Prince William County, Virginia, Partial Will Books 1734-1872*, Heritage Books, 2019.

Blight, David W., *A Slave No More: Two Men Who Escaped to Freedom*, First Mariner Books, New York, 2009.

Boyd, Donald Edgar, *Images of America Mount Vernon*, Arcadia Publishing, 2004.

Boyd's Directory of Washington, Georgetown and Alexandria, 1871.

Butts, Heather, *African American Medicine in Washington, D.C. Healing the Capital During the Civil War Era*, The History Press, Charleston, SC, 2014.

Cain, Charlotte, *Divided Loyalties: An Account of the Family of William J. Weir During the American Civil War*, Prince William County Reliquary, 2004.

Digital Kenyon, *The Community Within: Knox County Black History Archives*, American Studies Senior Seminar at Kenyon College, 1993.

Dobak, William A., *Freedom by the Sword: U.S. Colored Troops, 1862–1867*, Army Historical Series, I. Title. E492.9.D63 2011.

Eby, Jerrilyn, *They Called Stafford Home: The Development of Stafford County, Virginia, from 1600 until 1865*. 1997.

Fitzgerald, Ruth Coder, *A Different Story: A Black History of Fredericksburg, Stafford, and Spotsylvania*, 1979.

Fling, Sarah, *Slavery in the President's Neighborhood: Washington, DC's Contraband Camps*, 2022.

Georgetown and the City of Washington: the capital of the United States of America, 1871. History of Alexandria's African American Community.

Harrell, Gavin, Dr., *The Freedmen's Village Life After Slavery, The Lives of Newly Freed Slaves in Arlington, Virginia and the Rural South from 1850-1900s*, Book 1, Sankofa Legacy Press, Atlanta Georgia, 2024.

Lorey, Frederick, N., *History of Knox County, Ohio, 1876-1976*, Publication of the Knox County Historical Society, Mount Vernon, OH, 1976.

Manning, Chandra, *Troubled Refuge Struggling for Freedom in the Civil War*, Alfred A. Knopf, Vintage Books, New York, 2016.

Marshall, Kathy Lynne, *Finding Daisy: From the Deep South to the Promised Land,* Kanika African Sculptures and Books, 2017.

Marshall, Kathy Lynne, *Finding Marshalls: A Genealogy Trip with a Black and White Twist,* Kanika African Sculptures and Books, 2017.

Marshall, Kathy Lynne, *Finding Otho: The Search for Our Enslaved Williams Ancestors*, Kanika Marshall Art and Books Publishing, 2018.

Marshall, Kathy Lynne, *The Ancestors Are Smiling!* Kanika African Sculptures and Books, 2017.

Meyers, David and Elise Meyers Walker, *Historic Black Settlements of Ohio*, The History Press, Charleston, SC, 2020.

Mills, Andrew L., *Haunted Prince William County,* Haunted America A Division of The History Press, Charleston, SC, 2020.

"Mount Vernon Democratic Banner March 26, 1891" (1891). *Mount Vernon Banner Historic Newspaper* 1891.

One Hundred Seventy-five Years of Struggle: a History of Black People in Springfield, Ohio, Clark County Public Library Digital Archives, 1976.

Parry, Dave, *A Day at the Delano's Lake home Mansion*, Knox County Historical Research Project, 1975.

Peters, Joan W., *A Source Book for African-American Family History, Research, Part 1, Albemarle Research,* Slave & Free Negro Records from the

Prince William County Court Minute & Order Books: 1752-1763; 1766-1769; 1804-1806; 1812-1814; 1833-1865.

Prince William County Slave Index, Index to People Records of PWC, Virginia Compiled by Greg Mason, RELIC Volunteer Bull Run Regional Library, Manassas, VA, 2024.

Porter, Lorle, *Politics and Peril: Mount Vernon, Ohio, in the Nineteenth Century*, New Concord Press, Zanesville, OH, 2005.

Rothman, Joshua D., *The Ledger and the Chain How Domestic Slave Traders Shaped America*, Basic Books, New York, 2021.

Sacks, Howard and Judith Rose, *Way Up North in Dixie: A Black Family's Claim to the Confederate Anthem*, Smithsonian Institution Press, Washington and London, 1993, pages 16, 19, 68, 73.

Sheffield, Ric S., *We Got By: A Black Family's Journey in the Heartland*, Trilliam, an Imprint of the Ohio State University Press, Columbus, 2022.

Sperry, Kip, *Genealogical Research in Ohio*, Third Edition, Genealogical Publishing Company Inc., Baltimore, Maryland, 2023

Steward, Austin, *Twenty-Two Years a Slave and Forty Years a Free Man*. Austin Steward (1793 – 1869) was an African-American abolitionist and author. He was born a slave and escaped from Virginia at about age 21, settling in Rochester, New York, and then Canada, 2002.

Sullivan, Pat, *Voting with their feet: "This day ran away from my premises, servants..."* Spotsylvania Memory, 2016.

The History of Alexandria: Discovering the Decades. [website] https://www.alexandriava.gov/historic-alexandria/the-history-of-alexandria-discovering-the-decades, 2025. This includes an excellent timeline chronicling the presence of African Americans in the neighborhood around the United States Capitol

Washington, John, *A Slave No More*. 2007.

Wilson, Etta, with Rita Colbert, Linneall Naylor, Rondia Prescott, Jenee Lindner, *Black Communities of Fairfax A History*, The History Press, Charleston, SC, 2024.

END NOTES

1. The surreal story of the Ella's dress came from Ella's great-granddaughter, Alaunda Gates.

2. Grammie's great-granddaughter, Kenora Davis, wrote a description about our Carter family to Kathy Marshall: "We, are a rainbow from the lightest to the darkest. Grammie's sons, the one's I knew, were uncle Richard and Uncle Roy Carter. Richard was a medium light brown very similar to Dale Carter, and Uncle Roy was a very dark brown. The photo I had of Grammie's husband, Robert Carter, was very dark brown. The photo of Benjamin was medium light brown. I remember as a kid seeing Art Carter (Kathy's grandfather) but I cannot remember him being dark."

3. America's Bicentennial was a series of observances, celebrations, and commemorations leading up to the 200th anniversary of the adoption of the Declaration of Independence on Sunday, 4 July 1976.

4. Grammie Carter's great-granddaughter, Author Kathy Marshall worked as a researcher, analyst and technical writer for the California Highway Patrol in Sacramento, CA, from 1976 to 2012. 1976 photograph courtesy of Kathy Lynne Marshall.

5. Alex Haley authored a seminal book that would change American history forever. His *Roots: An American Family* hit the presses in 1976 and became a worldwide hit as the first TV miniseries in 1977. Kunta Kinte was a teenage African boy stolen from his home in Africa and eventually sold to the Waller plantation owners in Spotsylvania County, VA. The series continually describes how Kunta keeps passes down the stories from his African ancestors to his descendants, and they to their progeny, to Alex Haley. Chapter 8 describes the potential Waller nexus to Kathy Marshall's family.

6. Ella Roy's Death Certificate. Ohio Deaths, 1908-1932, 1938-1944, and 1958-2002, Certificate: 60019; Volume: 16999.

7. Map from Alexandria to Mount Vernon, OH, enhanced by the author from Google maps.

8. Dial-up Internet access was an early form of Internet access that uses the facilities of the public switched telephone network (PSTN) to establish a connection to an Internet service provider (ISP) by dialing a telephone number on a conventional telephone line. Wikipedia: https://en.wikipedia.org/wiki/Dial-up_Internet_access. Last access 31 Aug 2025.

9. A precursor to the Internet, a Bulletin Board System is a computer server running software that allows users to connect to the system using a terminal program. Wikipedia, https://en.wikipedia.org › wiki › Bulletin_board_system. Last accessed 31 Aug 2025.

10. FamilySearch.org is a free genealogical service that provides access to one of the world's largest collections of historical records and a collaborative, single, public family tree.

[11] Mary Ellen Carter Marshall's Social Security Death Index, Birth date: 1 Apr 1934 Birth place: Death date: 27 Jan 2007 Death place: Sacramento, Sacramento, California, United States of America.

[12] Sister Sara wet the bed: from Mary's *Reflections from a Mother's Heart* Memoir Journal, p 15.

[13] Mary yearned to have her own home: *Reflections from a Mother's Heart* Memoir Journal, p _.

[14] Grammie looked like a little Dutch lady: *Reflections from a Mother's Heart* Memoir Journal, page 23.

[15] Pearl Lavata Williams graduated from Mount Vernon High School in 1926.

[16] Pearl served tasty food: *Reflections from a Mother's Heart* Memoir Journal, page 19

[17] *Reflections from a Mother's Heart* Memoir Journal, page 19.

[18] Mary's intentions: *Reflections from a Mother's Heart* Memoir Journal, pages 86 and 88.

[19] Mary Carter and Thomas Marshall marriage: 1956-1957, Volume 27, page 92, Cuyahoga County, Ohio, U.S., Marriage Records and Indexes, 1810-1973

[20] Thomas Marshall graduated from Ohio State University College of Medicine 13 June 1958.

[21] Thomas Marshall became a lieutenant in 1958 as part of the Commissioned and Warrant Officer of the U.S. Naval and Reserve: U.S., Select Military Registers, 1862-1985.

[22] Redlining is the historical and illegal discriminatory practice of denying financial services, such as loans and mortgages, to residents of specific neighborhoods, primarily those with a high concentration of racial or ethnic minorities. Originating from color-coded maps used by the federal government in the 1930s to mark "risky" areas for investment, redlining has resulted in significant racial wealth and housing gaps, with provisions in the Fair Housing Act of 1968 outlawing the practice.

[23] Myrtle earning $312 as a laundress in 1940; Census Place: Mount Vernon, Knox, Ohio; Roll: T627_3093; Page: 3A; Enumeration District: 42-14

[24] Columbus Delano was appointed Commissioner of Internal Revenue from March 11, 1869, to October 31, 1870. https://en.wikipedia.org/wiki/Columbus_Delano. Accessed 18 Sep 2025.

[25] Columbus Delano became President Ulysses S. Grant's Secretary of the Interior 1870-1875. https://en.wikipedia.org/wiki/Columbus_Delano. Accessed 18 Sep 2025.

[26] Columbus Delano argued that the most humane Indian policy was to force tribes onto small reservations in the Indian Territory, ceding their land to the United States, and assimilating them into white culture. https://en.wikipedia.org/wiki/Columbus_Delano. Accessed 18 Sep 2025.

[27] Roys living with Columbus Delano in 1880: Year: 1880; Census Place: Clinton, Knox, Ohio; Roll: 1038; Family History Film: 1255038; Page: 91D; Enumeration District: 145; Image: 0185

[28] Delano second the motion to select Abraham Lincoln to be the Republican candidate during the 1860 Presidential election. https://www.loc.gov/item/2017895072/. Accessed 18 Sep 2025.

[29] The National Parks Service provides an excellent description of *Living Contraband - Former Slaves in the Nation's Capital During the Civil War:* https://www.nps.gov/articles/living-contraband-former-slaves-in-the-nation-s-capital-during-the-civil-war.htm#:~:text=At%20Fort%20Monroe%20in%20Hampton,they%20were%20classified%20as%20property, accessed 1 Sep 2025.

[30] AmTrak California Zephyr cross country Train Schedule: https://content.amtrak.com/content/timetable/California%20Zephyr.pdf Accessed 18 Aug 2025.

[31] Mom talked about the endless cornfields in Ohio: *Reflections from a Mother's Heart* Memoir Journal, page 22.

[32] Did Cooper-Bessemer shorten my ancestor's lives?: *Reflections from a Mother's Heart*, page 35.

[33] Kathy Lynne Marshall's *Finding Otho: The Search for Our Enslaved Williams Ancestors*, https://www.amazon.com/stores/Kathy-Lynne-Marshall/author/B07PNLWJRY. Accessed 18 Sep 2025.

[34] *The Mystery of Margaret Booker: One Woman's Triumph Over Slavery*, https://www.amazon.com/stores/Kathy-Lynne-Marshall/author/B07PNLWJRY. Accessed 18 Sep 2025.

[35] Knox County Historical Society Museum. https://visitknoxohio.org/places/knox-county-historical-society-museum. Accessed 18 Sep 2025.

[36] Professor Emeritus Howard Sacks at Kenyon College, Gambier, OH, https://www.kenyon.edu/directory/howard-sacks/ was one of the two founders of The Community Within digital and traveling display of African American history information.

[37] "*The Community Within*" and Digital Kenyon African American database. https://digital.kenyon.edu/thecommunitywithin/ Accessed 18 Sep 2025.

[38] Professor Ric Sheffield (https://www.kenyon.edu/directory/ric-sheffield/) and Professor Howard Sacks (https://www.kenyon.edu/directory/howard-sacks/). Accessed 18 Sep 2025.

[39] *Politics and Peril in Mount Vernon, OH, in the Nineteenth Century*, by Lorle Porter. Page 201 describes a typical morning for Albert Roy.

[40] Wayman Chapel of the African Methodist Episcopal Chapel built in 1874. History of Knox County, Ohio, 1876 to 1976, page 293. History of Knox County, Ohio 1876 to 1976. Editor Frederick and Lori. A publication of the Knox County historical Society, Mount Vernon, OH, 1976.

CHAPTER 3: No citations.

CHAPTER 4:

[41] "Life on a Sheep Ranch" was adapted from an unpublished typed research project, found in the Mount Vernon Nazarene University Archives, Knox County, OH, during Kathy Lynne Marshall's 2023 genealogy trip. The author was Dave Parry. Kathy Marshall combined the rooms and grounds that she photographed with historical information from Parry's text and told the story from Columbus Delano's and the servants point of view. The accompanying opening photograph of the house was taken by Kathy Marshall from a photo on the wall in the MVNU Archives.

[42] Columbus Delano: https://en.wikipedia.org/wiki/Columbus_Delano#Reconstruction_Era. Last accessed: 31 Aug 2025.

CHAPTER 5:

[44] Fort Monroe: The history of the Fort Monroe site spans nearly four centuries, dating back to the birth of America with the first settlers in 1609, to being a haven for slaves during the Civil War. Kathy Lynne Marshall toured the site in May 2024. https://www.nationalparks.org/explore/parks/fort-monroe-national-monument. Accessed 18 Sep 2025.

[44] Bureau of Refugees, Freedmen, and Abandoned Lands: http://www.archives.gov/files/research/microfilm/m1902.pdf

[45] National Archives: The official repository for the records of the U.S. federal government. https://www.archives.gov. Accessed 18 Sep 2025.

[46] Indexing records refers to the process of creating a structured list of data, making it easier to search and retrieve information quickly. For genealogy, indexing can allow genealogists to search for a specific name, place of birth, state, type of record, etc. Source: Quora.

[47] Smithsonian Museum's Freedmen's Bureau Portal URL to easily access digitized Freedmen's Bureau records. https://nmaahc.si.edu/explore/freedmens-bureau. Accessed 18 Sep 2025.

[48] 31 Dec 1866 Freedmen's Bureau Hospital record for infant Ella Roy treated for sickness in the East Capitol Hill Barracks. URL to record. Accessed 18 Sep 2025.

[49] Location of East Capitol Barracks from Wikipedia "Barracks Row". Image: https://en.wikipedia.org/wiki/Barracks_Row#History, accessed 1 Sep 2025.

[50] *Mapping the Freedmen's Bureau.* The purpose is to help researchers find documents involving formerly enslaved people. This site points out the many places that affected newly freed survivors of slavery.

[51] Lucretia Mott and Women's Radical Reconstruction Movement: https://dokumen.pub/womens-radical-reconstruction-the-freedmens-aid-movement-9780812203912.html

[52] This 27 April 1867 Freedmen's Bureau "Received from the Bureau" document for Agnes and Ella Ray/Roy is the only document that shows Agnes and Ella Roy, by name, together. This, among several other documents, cinched the theory that Agnes and Ella were mother and daughter.
https://www.ancestry.com/search/collections/62309/records/1635506?tid=&pid=&queryid=bbbae064-c3f6-4902-8b19-952d699b7351&_phsrc=Ocx1532&_phstart=successSource. Accessed 18 Sep 2025.

CHAPTER 6:

[53] African American Neighborhoods in Alexandria: https://www.alexandriava.gov/historic-alexandria/history-of-alexandrias-african-american-community

[54] The City of Alexandria Contrabands and Freedmen Cemetery Memorial, https://www.alexandriava.gov/FreedmenMemorial#:~:text=The%20Contrabands%20and%20Freedmen%20Cemetery%20Memorial%20in%20Alexandria%2C%20Virginia%2C%20is,immediately%20following%20the%20Civil%20War.

[55] Partial/Unburnt 1865 Colored Alexandria Census: (http://www.freedmenscemetery.org/resources/census1865/census.shtml). Accessed 18 Sep 2025.

[56] 1865 Alexandria district boundaries are described in this pivotal document; http://www.freedmenscemetery.org/resources/census1865/census.shtml.

[57] Armfield and Ballard were among the most notorious Slave Traders, profiled in *The Ledger and the Chain*: https://www.amazon.com/Ledger-Chain-Domestic-Traders-America/dp/1541616618. Their place of business at 1315 Duke Street, District 6, in Alexandria was called the Slave pen. The same place used as a jail by Sheriff Walker Reid Millan in the late 1850s and probably mid-1860s. It is entirely possible, and maybe probable, that Agnes Roy worked/lived there too, before the Civil War and after leaving the Freedmen's Bureau (then, somehow, Agnes ended her days as a farmer in Manassas).

[58] The phrase "sold down South" is an expression that referred to the tragic practice of selling enslaved people from the Upper South (like Virginia or Kentucky) to the Deep South (like Georgia, Florida, or Louisiana). The Deep South, with its intensive cotton and sugar cane plantations, was known for more brutal conditions, harsher labor, and a higher mortality rate for enslaved individuals compared to the Upper South.

[59] https://encyclopediavirginia.org/primary-documents/negro-womens-children-to-serve-according-to-the-condition-of-the-mother-1662/

[60] Letter from Assistant Commissioner about Agnes stealing clothing. Field Offices_District Of Columbia (M1902), Offices of Staff Officers Assistant Inspector G, Roll 001, Letters Sent, 21 Mar 1866-7 Sep 1868,

https://www.ancestry.com/search/collections/62309/records/1633287?tid=&pid=&queryid=0e94be6a-902f-4952-b042-742570f9b66c&_phsrc=tbw14&_phstart=successSource

CHAPTER 7:

[61] "Book" for the Field Offices, DC (M1902), Local Sup. for Washington and Georgetown, Roll 019, Target 10, Volume 38.,page 139, image 36 of 53. NARA 939. Image: https://www.ancestry.com/imageviewer/collections/62309/images/005681791_01010?pId=1733172, accessed 1 Sept 2025.

[62] 1870 Census for Peter Roy, Agnis Chew and children Lucy, Ella, Jesse and Lousa, Washington Ward 6, Washington, District of Columbia, USA

[63] In June 1871, the Secretary of the Interior [Columbus Delano] was directed to execute the provisions of House bill H.R. 7247 to increase the pension of Mary A. Gibson from $30 to $50 per month. This is significant because Lucy Roy worked for Mary A. Gibson and she was likely the sister of the author's two-times great-grandmother, Agnes Roy. Thus, it is possible that Lucy Roy came into contact with Columbus Delano. Her sister Agnes was living/working near Columbus Delano's office in 1871, according to Figure 35.

[64] The US Department of the Interior was located in Ward 6 in the District of Columbia, and that's where the author's Roy family lived: https://planning.dc.gov/sites/default/files/dc/sites/op/publication/attachments/Ward%206%20Heritage%20Guide%20Final.pdf

[65] 1840 Spotsylvania County Free Negro, Slave Papers, Bills of Sale, Deeds and Mortgages. Elizabeth Taylor to John Pratt, https://crhc.pastperfectonline.com/archive/7307C3DF-2696-4110-9CBC-511476935303,1802-1840, accessed 19 Oct 2025.

[66] *Spotsylvania Memory Blog* by Pat Sullivan describes numerous important historical events that happened in Spotsylvania, VA, where Freedmen's Bureau records indicate my ancestors came from before migrating to DC, Prince William County and Mount Vernon, Ohio. http://spotsylvaniamemory.blogspot.com

[67] Voting with Their Feet: "This day ran away from my premises, servants…" posted by lunchcountersitin. on 6 Apr 2016 in the Jubilo! The Emancipation Century: African Americans in the 19th Century: Slavery, Resistance, Abolition, the Civil War, Emancipation, Reconstruction, and the Nadir. This article lists Nancy Rowe's enslaved property who voted with their feet (ran away) in 1862. Several of those freedom seekers had Kathy Marshall's ancestor's names. https://jubiloemancipationcentury.wordpress.com/2016/04/06/voting-with-their-feet-this-day-ran-away-from-my-premises-servants/

[68] Prices for enslaved men and girls in Stafford, VA: from *They Called Stafford Home: The Development of Stafford County Virginia from 1600 until 1865*, by Jerrilyn Eby

[69] A trove of facts and the daily lives of Black and White people who lived in Fredericksburg, Stafford and Spotsylvania, by Fitzgerald, Ruth Coder, *A Different Story: A Black History of Fredericksburg, Stafford, and Spotsylvania*, 1979.

[70] Trail to freedom: Located halfway between Richmond, Virginia and Washington, DC, The Trail to Freedom retraces the routes of these freedom-seeking men, women, and children through the City of Fredericksburg, Virginia and the County of Stafford, Virginia. https://trailtofreedomva.com

CHAPTER 9:

[71] *RootsWeb's WorldConnect Project: Knox County, OH webpage* about Albert Roy. Last changed 2010.

[72] Albert Roy bought Alice M. Elliott's home in Coshocton, Knox County, OH.

[73] Front Street was shown on the *1871 Knox County, OH Atlas*, Reprinted 1971, by Mayhill Publications, Knightstown, IN, page 16

[74] 1866 "Census Returns of the Black Population of Montgomery, Grayson, Smyth, Giles, Roanoke, Craig, and Floyd Counties, Volume (497), NARA Publication M1913, Roll 198.

[75] James Campbell Roy, 1807-1864 had enslaved 20 persons by 1840. Some people indicate his housekeeper "wife" was Mary Ellen Roy (1842-1916), who is sometimes defined as white and sometimes as mulatto. There are records that show Mary Ellen Roy's husband as William E Roy (1830-1885). All I know is that Kathy Marshall's family has as many DNA matches with people who descend from the William E and Mary Ellen Roy ancestral couple. 1850 Slave Schedule: https://www.ancestry.com/family-tree/person/tree/171401245/person/132401501919/facts.

[76] Spessard Enslaver: https://nmaahc.si.edu/freedmens-bureau/record/fbs-1662423774659-1662424252583-0?destination=%2Fexplore%2Ffreedmens-bureau%2Fsearch%3Fedan_fq%255B0%255D%3Dp.nmaahc_fb.pr_name_surn%253Aspessard%26page%3D0

[77] Linneall Naylor, educator, genealogist, and author of *Black Communities of Fairfax*.

[78] A Freedmen's Bureau letter indicated Albert Roy was a Trustee of a Colored School in Manassas. https://www.ancestry.com/discoveryui-content/view/461573:62309?tid=&pid=&queryId=efe45ebe-6f68-4ce8-9f32-7dba34e84d72&,phsrc=Cog11&,phstart=successSource

[79] Loyalty Oath signed by Albert Roy. https://www.ancestry.com/discoveryui-content/view/92724:1218?tid=&pid=&queryId=eaad3aa5-a73a-498a-8ce7-a7295b94fd1f&,phsrc=Ocx925&,phstart=successSource

[80] "Who was Redmond Foster?" *Prince William Reliquary* Vol. 4, No. 4 (October 2005), https://www.pwcva.gov/assets/2021-07/PWR_4-2005.pdf

CHAPTER 11:

[82] A description of Manassas plantation work: https://patch.com/virginia/manassas/the-life-of-a-slave-on-historic-manassas-plantation#

[82] Gerard Mason: Prince William County Genealogy, https://pwcogenealogy.blogspot.com/2013/10/friend-of-friends-friday-gerard-mason.html

[83] Some stories indicated slave Agness killed her enslaver, Gerard Mason, becuase he held her child over a vat of boiling oil: https://www.historicprincewilliam.org/pwcvirginia/documents/AGNES.pdf

[84] Slave Agness was hanged at the Brenstville jail in Prince William County, VA, in 1850 because she killed her terrible enslaver: https://www.historicprincewilliam.org/pwcvirginia/documents/AGNES.pdf .

[85] Future Fairfax County, VA, Sheriff Walker Millan was involved with the Mason family: https://www.newspapers.com/article/alexandria-gazette-walker-r-millan-she/114404043/. Kathy Marshall wondered if Gerard's enslaved woman, Agness, was perhaps her three-times great-grandmother.

[86] Editor Jean Cooper offered this intriguing interpretation of what Walker Reid Millan's 1860 Fairfax Census entry means. It gives voice to his business as a slave trader/leaser.

CHAPTER 12:

[87] Kinky hair: Kinky hair refers to a hair texture with a very tight, dense spiral or zigzag pattern, most often seen in people of African descent. This texture is characterized by its extreme curliness, tendency for significant shrinkage, and a coarse or fragile feel because natural scalp oils struggle to travel down the hair shaft.

[88] A "Golden Ticket" a way or chance to obtain something valuable or desirable that is often hard to get. The expression was made popular in the Roald Dahl story entitled, *Willy Wonka and the Chocolate Factory*.

[89] Haplogroup B is essentially a sub-Saharan clade. An exception is represented by haplogroup **B-M109**, which is present in central, eastern, and southern Africa. https://journals.plos.org/plosone/article?id=10.1371/journal.pone.0049170. Accessed 18 Sep 2025.

[90] The Shared cM Project (ScP) is a collaborative data collection and analysis project created to understand the ranges of shared cM associated with various known relationships .https://dnapainter.com/tools/sharedcmv4/23

[91] Info about Springfield's history as a manufacturing magnet: https://en.wikipedia.org/wiki/Springfield,_Ohio#:~:text=Springfield%20became%20known%20as%20%22The,into%20International%20Harvester%20in%201902.

[92] Ohio, Springfield City Directory, 1890, page 88 said Robt. Carter was a laborer at res 98 Central Av.

[93] Lynchings became a problem in Springfield, OH, 1904-1906. *Race, Sex and Riot: The Springfield, Ohio Race Riots of 1904 and 1906 and the Sources of Anti-Black Violence in the Lower Midwest*, by Jack S. Blocker, Jr. https://filsonhistorical.org/archive/ovhpdfs/OVH_V6N1_Blocker.pdf. Accessed 18 Sep 2025.

CHAPTER 15: No citations.

CHAPTER 16: No citations.

CHAPTER 17:

95 Mary Carter Marshall describes their house at 101 W. Walnut Street: *Reflections from a Mother's Heart*, page 20.

96 In November 2023, Walter Baughman, former alumnus, gave Kathy Marshall a tour of the Mount Vernon Nazarene University Administration Building, which was Columbus Delano's former house. Walter mused that the servants were allowed to use the entire third floor as they saw fit.

CHAPTER 18: No citations.

CHAPTER 19: No citations.

EPILOGUE:

97 Black contrabands of war: https://savingplaces.org/stories/the-forgotten-the-contraband-of-america-and-the-road-to-freedom#:~:text=By%20war's%20end%2C%20approximately%20half,issue%20of%20the%20Civil%20War.

98 First African Angolans arrived in 1619

99 Slave Pen property in Alexandria was located at 1315 Duke Street in Alexandria, VA.

100 35% of Carters are Black, according to the 2010 US Census, via 23andme.com: https://discover.23andme.com/last-name/Carter

101 Robert Carter III's Gift of Emancipation

101 B4a1a1b haplogroup indicates Kathy Marshall's maternals lines originally came from Madagascar: https://discover.familytreedna.com/mtdna/B4a1a1b/story

Please feel free to leave your comments about this book by scanning this QR code:

www.ingramcontent.com/pod-product-compliance
Lightning Source LLC
Chambersburg PA
CBHW081354070526
44583CB00020B/2551